The Paites

A Study of the Changing Faces of the Community

The Paites

A Study of the Changing Faces of the Community

Dr. Th. Siamkhum

notionpress.com

Notion Press

5 Muthu Kalathy Street, Triplicane,

Chennai - 600 005

First Published by Notion Press 2013

Copyright © Th. Siamkhum 2013

All Right Reserved.

ISBN: 978-93-83416-22-6

Dedicated to

My loving and caring father, (L) Th. Thangsiam
who left his near and dear ones for his heavenly eternity on
17th April, 2005.

PAITE TRIBE COUNCIL
General Headquarters: Hiangtam Lamka
P.O. Churachandpur, Manipur. PIN- 795 128.

E-mail ID : ptc_hq_manipur@yahoo.in
ptcghq@gmail.com

Website :

Foreword

HiangtamLamka, the 3rdSeptember, 2013.

No.1/PTC-GHQ/EC-3/2010: It is learnt that a well-known writer and Philosopher,Dr. Th. Siamkhum, Associate Professor, Department of Political Science, Churachandpur Government College is producing a bulky book entitled "The Paites : A Study of the Changing Faces of the Tribe" and I have gone through all the contents of the book that which entirely satisfied me.

In his research and study book, he touches all corners of the Paitesbehaviours like its origin, migration till its present situations; their primitive religious beliefs and the emergence of Christianity and educations; their social and political institutions; political movements as well as political participations including voting behaviour; their economic development from ancient times; their administration and judiciary systems; and then, their traditions and customs. Besides, his bibliography shows that how the Paite-Zomis are rich in publications.

While representing the President and his Executive Members of the Paite Tribe Council: General Headquarters (the apex body of all the Paites), I heartily appreciated the Dr. Th. Siamkhum's authored book called,"The Paites : A Study of the Changing Faces of the Tribe". Let his sincere endeavour be a great boon to all who read this book and I really hope that this valuable book will enlighten the younger generation to the world of reality.

(K. Chinkhansuan)
General Secretary,
PAITE TRIBE COUNCIL
General Headquarters: HiangtamLamka.

Preface

THE PAITES are one of the Zo ethnic tribes who migrated to Manipur and Mizoram from Myanmar in the late 19th Century. Though the mass migration of Paites took place during the later part of the 19th Century, some of them had already settled in Manipur and Mizoram much earlier. The present work, entitled "The Changing Faces of Paite Community is an attempt to present all the aspects and facts of the Paite Society. An attempt had been made to study the changes that took place in the Paite society as a result of their contact with the British, the western Christian missionaries and with the dawn of Indian Political Independence.

In the first chapter, the geographical distribution and growth of the population, origin and migration of the tribe from China to Chin Hills, Manipur and Mizoram have been discussed in detail. The chapter also presents the relation of Paites with other Chin-Mizo-Kuki tribes. It also gives a brief account of the British annexation of Lushai Hills and Chin Hills.

The second chapter deals with the traditional aspect of the society like traditional type of house, dress, weapons, festivals and dance, ceremony of birth and death, slavery, and marriage and divorce.

The third chapter is devoted to the study of the religious belief of the Paites, both past and present. In the first part of the chapter, a study has been made on the traditional religion which is animisam. A study has also been made on the concept of life after death, different kinds of ritual ceremony, ancestor worship, etc. An attempt has been made to study how and when the people were converted into Christianity, and its impact on the Paite society, in their material outlook, fashion, way of living.

The fourth chapter, entitled 'The Social Institution' deals with the kinship, the clans and sub-clans, the dormitory system, etc.

The later part of the chapter deals with the social institutions of the Paites in the present day like the Siamsinpawlpi (Students Union) and the Young Paite Association (a Charitable and Philantrophic Organization), etc.

The fifth chapter deals with the economic life of the people; like how the Paites had self-sufficient village economy, the method of cultivation, merits and demerits of shifting cultivation; problems face by the Paites to change their method of cultivation and suggestions for removal of shifting cultivation. A study has also been made of the small scale industries, emergence of neo-economic elite, and the existence of private money landers in the urban Paite society.

The sixth chapter deals with the administration of village, i.e. chieftainship. A study has been made on the origin, powers and functions of village chief; also of the declining powers of the chiefs as a consequence of the enactment of Village Authority (in the Hill Area) Act, 1956.

The seventh chapter is devoted to the study of the administrative development in hill areas of Manipur since the annexation of Manipur by the British. A study has since been made of the enactment of Manipur Hill Areas (Autonomous District Council Act, 1971).The chapter deals with the Paite National Council, its various political demands and its relation with the Mizo National Front (MNF).

The Eight chapter is the study of the level of political participation and political socialization of the Paites from 1947 onwards.

The last chapter, entitled 'Conclusion' is a comprehensive account of social change as a result of the operation of several factors upon the Paite Society and an appraisal of the preceding chapters.

The present work on the tribe, therefore, is the product of investigation, collection of data, interview with elders, field visits and a study of available literature on the life and people of different region, particularly the North east of India for supplementing the scientific inquiry of the tribe under study.

Contents

CHAPTER I

Introducing the People

The Paites are one of the most prominent Zo tribes living in the trans-Indo-Myanmar border areas. They are Mongoloid by race and speak Paite, which belongs to Tibeto-Burman goup of languages. Originally, like any other hill tribes of North-East India, they were animists, worshippers of ancestor and evil spirit. However, with the coming of Western Christian missionaries in 1910, they started embracing Christianity, and now 99%, of them are Christians.

The Paites live in the Indo-Myanmar border areas of both sides. In Myanmar, they indentified themselves and called themselves as Zomi, and in Mizoram, majority of the Paites, identified themselves as Mizos. In Manipur, it is one of the major recognized tribes, and they identified and called themselves as Paite. However, in whatever name they might have called themselves in Myanmar, Mizoram or Manipur in India, the people are the same Paite people, speaking the same language and sharing the same customary and traditional practices.

1. THE PAITES IN MANIPUR:

In Manipur, the Paites live in the southern part of the state bordering Mizoram in the south, and Chin Hills of Myanmar, in the east. Though the largest concentration of Paite-Speaking community is in Churachandpur District, a good number of Paites are also found in Jiribam Sub-Division and the Imphal Municipality areas of Central District. According to the 1971 census, the total population of Paites in Manipur was 21,206. But according to the report of the *Tribal Bench Mark Survey of Manipur South (Churachandpur) District* in 1982, the total population of Paite –speaking community in Manipur South alone was 30,004. From this, it is obvious that, there is a sharp increase in the population of Paites in Manipur between 1971 and 1982. The following table shows the tribe wise population growth in Churachandpur District between 1971 and 1982.

Table 1:1   Tribewise Population Growth in Manipur South (Churachandpur) District

Sl.no.	Tribe	Tribal population as per		Rise in Population	Growth rate Percentage
		1971 Census	TBMS 1982		
1	2	3	4	5	6
	Paite	21,206	30,004	8,798	41.5
	Hmar	20,387	26,353	5,966	29.3
	Vaiphei	8,392	11,211	2,819	32.6
	Other Tribes	41,999	60,376	18,377	43.6

Source: Tribal Bench Mark Survey of Manipur South (Churachandpur) District 1982. page. 14.

The above table shows that there was a significant rise in the tribal population of Churachandpur District, specially in the case of Paites. The figure indicates an increase of 41.5% as against the rise of 39.1% in the total Paite population.

The second largest concentration of Paite population is in Thanlon Sub-division with a population of 9,478 which is 31% of the total population of the Sub-division.

The following table shows the population of the various tribal communities in Churachandpur District:

Table 1:2 Distribution of Households of population by Tribes

Sl. no.	Tribe/Caste Others	No. of Households	Percentage to the toal	Population	Percentage to the total
1	2	3	4	5	6
1.	Paite	4.619	19.4	30.004	21.7
2.	Hmar	4.281	18.0	26.353	19.1
3.	Vaiphei	1.948	8.2	11.211	8.1
4.	Gangte	1.011	4.2	5.796	4.2
5.	Thadou	1.036	4.3	5.562	4.0
6.	Lushai	246	1.0	1,269	1.0
7.	Simte	918	3.9	5.480	4.0
8.	Zou	1.733	7.3	10.251	7.4
9.	Kuki	2.036	8.5	11.414	8.3
10.	Thangkhal	73	0.3	393	0.3
11.	Tedim Chin	126	0.5	825	0.6
12.	Teijang	19	0.1	127	0.1
13.	Haokip	1.269	5.3	7.000	5.0

Sl. no.	Tribe/Caste Others	No. of Households	Percentage to the toal	Population	Percentage to the total
14.	Sukte	30	0.1	250	0.1
15.	Ngaihte	3	0.0	16	0.0
16.	Rongmei	257	1.1	1,748	1.3
17.	Kabui	119	0.5	78	0.5
18.	Singson	25	0.1	206	0.1
19.	Mizo	658	2.8	4,188	3.0
20.	Chongloi	10	0.0	62	0.1
21.	Sitlhou	1	0.0	4	0.1
22.	Chiru	86	0.4	438	0.3
23.	Neihsel	9	0.0	55	0.0
24.	Kipgen	11	0.0	64	0.1
25.	Hangsing	2	0.0	13	0.0
26.	Khongjai	30	0.1	157	0.1
27.	Maring	12	0.1	47	0.0
28.	Kom	690	2.8	3,549	206

Sl. no.	Tribe/Caste Others	No. of Households	Percentage to the toal	Population	Percentage to the total
29.	Maram	1	–	8	0.0
30.	Tangkhul	12	0.1	37	0.0
31.	Chothe	36	0.2	220	0.2
32.	Aimol	44	0.2	260	0.2
33.	Anal	50	0.2	304	0.2
34.	Scheduled Caste	127	0.5	706	0.5
35.	Others	2,296	9.7	9,335	6.8
		23,824			

Source: Tribal Bench Mark Survey of Manipur South (Churachandpur) District 1982,.page. 23.

As seen in the table above the Paite tribe constitutes 21.7% of the total population of Churachandpur District, and it is the largest single community in the District. The bulk of the population of Paite tribe is to be found in Churachandpur Sub-Division, Thanlon Sub-Division and Singngat Sub-Division. The population of the Paite in Henglep and Tipaimukh Sub-Division is negligible as only 1.139 and 1.356 Paites were there respectively. The following table shows Sub-Division wise population of Paite community in Churachandpur District.

Table 1:3 Sub-division wise population of Paite Community in Churachndpur District.

Sub-division	No.of House-hold.	Percentage to the total	Population	Percentage to the total
Churachandpur	1,660	14.5	10,968	19.8
Singngat	1,031	47.4	6,563	50.4
Thanlon	1,452	51.9	9,478	54.5
Henglep	188	6.0	1,139	6.4
Tipaimukh	288	8.1	1,156	8.6
Total	4,619	19,4	30,004	21.7

Source: Tribal Bench Mark Survey of Manipur South (Churachandpur) District 1982, p.24

As seen above, the largest number of Paite population is concentrated in Churachandpur Sun-division with a population of 10,968. This is followed by Thanlon Sub-division with a population of 9,478. The population of Paites is thinest in Henglep Sub-division which is only 1.139.

The population of Manipur, according to 2001 General Census was 21,66,788. Out of this, 741,141 were Scheduled Tribes (ST) which constitutes 34.2 percent of the total population of the state. There are a total of 29 recognised/notified schedule tribes in the state, the population of which together constitutes 34.2 percent of the total population of the state.

Among the Scheduled Tribes in Manipur, as per 2001 Census, the Thadous constitute the largest with 1.8 lakh which is some 24.6% of the total state population followed by Tangkhul

(19.7%), Kabui (11.1%), Paite (6.6%), Hmar (5.8%), Kacha Naga (5.7%) and Vaiphei (5.2%). Among othe major tribes, Maring, Anal, Zou, Any Mizo (Lushai) tribes, Kom and Simte, are having percentages between 3.1 and 1.5 and the rest of the Scheduled Tribes are comparatively small in number having less than 10,000 population each.

Table 1:4   Population of major STs in Manipur, 2001 Census Report:

Name of the Scheduled Tribe	Total Population	Proportion to the total ST Population
All Scheduled Tribes	741,141	100%
Thadou	182,594	24.6
Tangkhul	146,075	19.7
Kabui	82,356	11.1
Paite	49,271	6.6
Hmar	42,933	5.8
Kacha Naga	42,013	5.7
Vaiphei	38,267	5.2
Maring	23,238	3.1
Anal	21,242	2.9
Zou	20,567	2.8
Any Mizo (Lushai) Tribes	15,164	2.0
Kom	14,602	2.0
Simte	11,065	1.5

Source: Data Highlights: The Scheduled Tribe Census, 2001.

As seen in the above Census Table, *The Paites* constitute the fourth largest tribal groups in Manipur. Though they are found living in other districts of Manipur, they found heavily concentrated in Churachandpur District. The PTC conducted its own census in 2010 according to which the Paite speaking population figure is a little over 50, 000. The distribution of the Paites in different districts of Manipur could be seen in the following table:

Table 1:5

District	Paite Population
Imphal - East	1317
Ukhrul	11
Chandel	354
Imphal - West	1,814
Bishnupur	19
Thoubal	71
Senapati	19
Tamenglong	147
Churachandpur	45,549

Source: The Scheduled Tribe Census of India, 2001

According to the above given table, the total population of Paite tribe is 49,301 out of which 45,549 live in Churachandpur District. In other words, 92.3% of the total Paite speaking tribals live in Churachandpur District. Even in Churachandpur District, they are mainly concentrated in three sub-divisions – Churachandpur sub-division, Thanlon sub-division and Churachandpur Sub-division. The presence of Paite speaking people in other sub – divisions – Tipaimukh sub-division and Henglep-sub-division is negligible. In other words, more than 80% of the Paite population live in Churachandpur, Singngat and Thanlon Sub-divisions.

2. PAITES IN MIZORAM:

In Mizoram, the Paites are found living in a compact geographical area of Sialkal Tlang (Sialkal Range) of Champhai District bordering Manipur in the North and Chin State of Myanmar in the East. They are also found in large number in other parts of Mizoram, living together with other Mizo tribes. While the Paites of Sialkal Range still retain their identity as Paite, those Paites living in other parts of the state are, in one way or the other, almost completely assimilated and integrated to the dominant Duhlian speaking Mizos. They speak Duhlian Mizo, live as Duhlian/Lusei Mizos, think as Duhlian Mizos, and are infact, Duhlian Mizos for all intents and purposes. They are as much Mizos as the Duhlian speaking Mizos are.

Regarding the population of Paites in Mizoram, there had not been official regular Census prior to 1901. In 1901, there was the Assam State General Census according to which, there were 2,870 Paites living in Mizoram (Lushai Hills) Twenty Years after 1901 Census, there was again, the Lushai Hills District Census in 1921. According to this Lushai Hills District Census of 1921, there were as many as 10,460 Paites living in Mizoram (Lushai Hills) showing an unprecedented growth of the population. However, as per the record of the Lushai Hills District Council Language Table in 1951, 1961 and 1971, the number of Paite speaking population in Mizoram (Lushai Hills) are 3368, 1658.

The following table shows the irregular growth rate of the Paite population in Mizoram.

Table 1:6

Year of Census	Total Paite Population	Increase	Decline	Total Population of Mizoram	Percentage to the Total Population
1901	2, 870	x	x	82, 434	3.48
1921	10, 460	7590		98, 406	10.62
1951	3, 368	x	7,092	1, 96, 202	1.71
1961	1, 659	x	1,709	2, 66, 063	0.62
1971	3, 220	1561	x	3, 32, 390	0.96
1981	1764	x	1,456	4, 93, 757	0.35
1991	1797	33	x	6, 89, 756	0.26
2001	14, 367	12,570	x	8, 88, 573	1.61

Source: The Assam State General Census 1901, the Lushai Hills District Census, 1921, the Lushai Hill District Language Table, 1951, 1961, and 1971.

As per in the above table, there was a sharp and unprecedented rise in the Paite population of Mizoram between 1901 and 1911 which could be attributed to largescale migration from Chin Hills of Myanmar (Burma) to Mizoram (Lushai Hills). It is believed that, such largescale migration of the Paites from their original home at Chimnuai Geltui in Chin Hills was necessitated by inter-tribal war and the search for a better and a more fertile cultivable land. But, there was a sharp decline in the population between 1921 and 1951. This marked decline in the population of Paites in Mizoram during this period could be collectively attributed to the following factors:

1. There was a mass-assimilation of the Paites to the comparatively larger Duhlian speaking Mizo Community.

2. There was mass-migration of the Paites from Mizoram (Lushai Hills) to Manipur led by Kamzamang, The then Guite Chief of Mimbung Village.

3. Since the Paite tribe was not recognized as a separate Scheduled Tribe of Mizoram, there was no separate census for the Paites as such.

From 1951 to 1961, there was comparatively a low decline in the population of Paites in Mizoram. From 1961 to 1971, the table shows relatively a more stable growth, though not entirely in conformity with the natural growth of human population. However, as per 2001 General Census, the total population of the Paites in the state was 14,367 showing a record growth of the population by 12, 570 which is certainly an abnormal growth rate of human population.

In 2003 the Paite tribe has been accorded a constitutionally recognized scheduled tribe status in Mizoram. However, the Census report of 2011 General census in respect of tribe-wise figure has not yet been released till date.

The following villages in Sialkal Range of Champhai District and its adjacent areas are entirely Paite villages (more than 80% of the villagers are Paite speaking Mizos)

1. Mimbung	2. Hiangmun
3. Teikhang	4. Kawlbem
5. Selam	6. Vaikhawtlang
7. Khawkawn	8. North-East Tlangnuam
9. Leisenzo	10. Daido
11. Nausel	

The following villages could not entirely be called Paite villages, but a sizeable Paite speaking people live along with other Mizo tribes.

1. North-East Khodungsei   2. Vanbawng

3. Bukpui

In Aizawl, the capital city of Mizoram, though minority, a good number of Paites are found living in the following localities

1. Sihphir   2. Dinthar
3. Durtlang   4. Chaltlang
5. Ramlhun Venglai, Vengthar,
    Ramlhun North and Ramlhun South
6. Ramthar   7. Zemabawk

A part from the above mentioned villages and localities, the Paites are also found scattered in almost all villages and towns of Mizoram.

3. PAITES IN ASSAM:

In Assam Paite is not a constitutionally recognised tribe (ST) and that a separate official Census could not be held. However, it is unofficially estimated that there are some 2, 260 Paites living in Karbi-Anglong District of Assam. They are found living together with the Kukis in the following villages:

1. Khawnuam village   2. Zawllian village
3. Phaiphengzawl village   4. S.Muallian village
5. Khiangzang village   6. Suangsang village
7. Basamili village   8. Khawlian village
9. Hidipi village   10. Zoar village

Apart from the above mentioned villages, Paites are also found living in some packets of Diphu town.

4. PAITES IN MYANMAR:

In Myanmar, the entire Northern Chin State is occupied by Zomis who speak the same language as Paites. The Zomis of Myanmar and the Paites of Manipur and Mizoram in India share common culture and tradition, and are in fact the same people of different name. They belong not only to the same racial stock, but are in fact the same people. In Myanmar, they called themselves as Chin or Zomi; when a Chin or Zomi comes to India, he automatically becomes a Paite.

From the above discussion on the distribution of the Paite-speaking community in India and Myanmar, we come to know that the Paites are scattered in almost the entire Indo-Myanmar border areas. Right from the Khuga valley of the Manipur South in the north, down to the Champhai District of Mizoram in the south, the Paites are found living together with other a like tribes like the Lushais, the Hmars, the Pawis, etc.

5. ORIGIN AND MIGRATION:

The name 'Paite' is a very old name indeed, though some people tend to say blindly that it is a new name. It is said that the Lushais are the descendants of a Paite. The ancestor of a Lushai, Thangura, was said to be the son of a Paite and Myanmarese woman. In the light of the above theory, the term 'Paite' had been in existence before the term 'Lushai' emerged. Col. J. Shakespear mentioned that the Lushais decended from Bawklua, and Bawklua was said to be the illegitimate son of a Paite chief, Ngeknguk. K.Zawla puts Sailo clan of the Lushai tribe to be the descendants of a Paite. Regarding the meaning of the term 'Paite', '*Pai*' means to go or move and '*te*' is the plural form of '*pai*'; Thus, Paite means those who are moving, In the whole of history, the Paites as a race have been moving from place to place and region to region in search of food, shelter and secured place.

The origin of the Paite is believed to be *Chimnuai Geltui*. There are different opinions among the people regarding the location of Chimnuai Geltui. Some people hold the view that *Chimnuai Geltui* was situated in the present Shan state of Burma. The chief of Khampat, Sou Rum Khum, was defeated by Soohongpha. After their defeat the people left Khampat for Chimnuai Geltui. In the lilght of the above statement it is unlikely that the location of Chimnuai Geltui could be in Shan state. It is widely accepted by the Paites that Chimnuai Geltui is situated in the present Chin State of Myanmar. Though the exact location of Chimnuai

Geltui is yet to be traced, all the Paite-speaking community of the Chin-Mizo-Kuki group strongly believed that their original homeland is Chimnuai Geltui. In Chimnuai Geltui, people were prosperous as there were fertile lands for cultivation. They built a strong kingdom at Chimnuai Geltui. However, most probably due to internal dispute, some people left Chimnuai Geltui and went westward to the present Tedim areas of Chin Hills. When they left Chimnuai Geltui, those people remaining in Chimnuai Geltui called them 'Paite'. There is another view according to which those people who migrated from Chin Hills to Manipur and Mizoram in a particular period of time were called Paite by those who remained in Chin Hills.

In 1870 a large group of Paites left Chin Hills. They were moving by two routes; the first group moves to the north and settled at and around Mualpi village which was an old Thadou village; and the second group migrated to Lushai Hills and settled at Selam under the Lushai chief Poiboi. The first group entered Manipur under the Guite chief, Goukhothang who was treacherously seized by the Manipuris in the course of expedition in 1871-72. When the Manipur troops were returning after the conclusion of the expedition, they fell in with a party of Kamhau (Goukhothang), who were carrying away 957 captives from the two Lushai villages. The Kamhaus (the people of Kamhau, chief of Sukte) came into the camp of Manipur contingent apparently not expecting to be treated as enemies, but were all made prisoners by the contingent and taken to Manipur and put them in the jail. The 957 captives were also taken but not as prisoners. They were settled in the valley. General Boucher stigmatized this act of treachery on the part of the contingent, though it had been admitted a raid on Manipur village in 1871. Goukhothang, died in the jail in 1872. After the death of Goukhothang, Sumkam, his eldest son occupied the chiefship of Mualpi. Sumkam led his people from Mualpi to Tonglon tract, which after the demarcation of Chin-Manipur boundary in 1872 falls under Manipur territory. It is, therefore, evedent that Manipur boundary with Chin Hills was drawn primarily to meet the administrative needs of the British without the approval of the people of the areas. Sumkam, chief of Mualpi village and his people spread in the whole of the

Chin-Manipur border areas, the principal villages of which were Lousau and Songtal. In this way, the Paites under the Guite chief entered the present Guite Kual (Guite area) in the south District of Manipur.

As mentioned earlier, the other group of Paites migrated to Lushai Hills and settled among the Lushai under Lushai chief of Selam, Poiboi. Lt. Col. J. Shakespeare in his book, 'The Lushai-Kuki Clan' mentioned the existence of eleven Paite villages numbering 877 houses in the southwest corner of Manipur, and two villages in the adjoining portion of Lushai Hills. He also mentioned that many of the Paites were living in spices of slavery in the village of important Sailo chiefs. In 1881 Col. E.B. Elley, Assistant Quarter Master General in his book, 'Military Report on the Chin Lushai Hills' mentioned that in 1881 some 3, 000 Paites who had been much oppressed by the Lushai moved off into Manipur territory. However, all the Paites did not leave Lushai Hills. Many of the Paites are still living in Lushai Hills. They are now found in the Sialkal Range in Aizawl District and among the Lushais in the Lushai dominated villages.

In the beginning of the 20th century, a group of Paites left Manipur. This group of Paites moved westward into the Cachar District and settled there for some time after which in 1933 they left for North Cachar Hills. Here they set up new village called Zawllian village which was about 20 kilometers from Haflong. But life in North Cachar Hills was difficult as there was scarcity of fertile land. They move northwards and entered the then Mikier Hills District in the early 50s and set up new villages.

Besides, a group of Paites entered the present Karbi-Anglong District of Assam between 1968-1971 following the out break of violence in Mizoram. Following the declaration of Independence by MNF, the India army adopted repressive measure near to contain the MNF uprising which caused immense hardship as a result of which many Paites, left Mizoram and the author of this book himself was among the group leaving Mizoram for Zawllian village in Karbi Anglong District in January, 1970.

6. TRIBES OF ZO ETHNIC GROUP:

According to T.Gougin the population of the Mizo/Zomi - ethnic group was roughly 2 millions comprising of about 44 distinct tribes. The following are some of the major tribes of the Zo ethnic group:

1. Thadous	2. Paites	3. Lushais
4. Suktes	5. Siyins	6. Hmars
7. Zos	8. Simtes	9. Gangtes
10. Raltes	11. Pawis	12. Lakhers
13. Hrangkhawls	14. Tashons	15. Biahtes
16. Anals	17. Koms	18. Bangolis
19. Paukhu	20. Aliams	21. Langrongs
22. Aimols	23. Chirus	24. Jirois
25. Lamgangs	26. Kolrens	27. Purums
28. Chinmes	29. Welaung	30. Chimbohs
31. Yindus	32. Chibus	33. Shos
34. Khamis	35. Raltes	

In 1931, the total population of Zo ethnic tribes in India and the elsewhere, East-Pakistan (now Bangladesh) was estimated to be roughly 34, 5000. In Mizoram, as per 1971 Census, over 6 lakhs Zo ethnic tribes were there constituting 95% of the total population of the state.

In North Cachar Hills, Nagaland and Karbi-Anglong, roughly25, 000 of these tribes are there. They settled in the Khunbamor pahar and Koilajan areas in Karbi-Anglong District and Haflong in North Cachar Hills. In Manipur, roughly $2^{1/2}$ lakhs of these tribes are there. Besides, over 25,000 of these various hill tribes are found in Chittagong Hill tract of Bangladesh and Tripura in India.

The different tribes of the Zo ethnic group speak a very closely related languages and that they can communicate using each of their languages. All of them claim to have been originated from Khul or Chhinlung. They share uniform social and religious tradition. They are all closely related to one another and have many common characteristic features which cannot really separate them from one another. Some of their common characteristic features can be seen as follows:

Belief in common Origin: All the Zo ethnic tribes have a common belief that they originally emerged out of a cave or hole in the earth. This mythological cave is known by different names like Khul, Khur, Khurpui, Khurtubijur, Sinlung, Chhinlung and so on. Having a common belief in the common origin is clear proof of their ethnic affinity.

Common Folktales: There are many folktales common and current among all the tribes of Mizo/Zomi family. For instance, there are folktales told in the Paite society such as the story of Penglam, the story of Khupching and Ngambawm, the story of Liandou and Thanghou, etc. The same stories had been told among the Thadou, Lushai, Hmar, etc. but there had been slight variation in the name of the stories. The possession of the same folktales means nothing, but the people are of the same folk having the same and similar social ritual norms and similar philosophy of life. The same folktales reflect the thought, ideas and social life including value system.

Agamous Marriage: Majority of the Mizo/Zomi tribes follow agamous system of marriage which means a man can marry any woman except his sister and mother within and outside his clan. The distinctiveness of the tribes and clans of the Zo ethnic group is its agamous marriage, and it is another indication of their close ethnic affinity.

Linguistic Affinity: The following language table is clear proof of the close ethnic and linguistic affinity among the various Zo tribes:

Table 1:7

Paite	Lushai	Thadou	Hmar	English
Bel	Bel	Bel	Bel	Pot
Meh	Chawhmeh	Me	Hme	Curry
Vok	Vawk	Vohcha	Vawk	Pig
Ak	Ar	Ahcha	Ar	Fowl
Ui	Ui	Uicha	Ui	Dog
Tui	Tui	Tui	Tui	Water
Mei	Mei	Mei	Mei	Fire
Miksi	Fanghmir		Phaivang	Ant
Tutna	Thutthleng	Sihmi	Thungna	Seat
Inn	In	Tongkham	In	House
Nou	No	In	No	Cup
		Khon		

Though there exists a close ethnic and linguistic affinity among the tribes of Zo ethnic group, the absence of a common nomenclature acceptable to all of them stands in the way to the total unification.

7. COMMON NOMENCLATURE:

The idea of having common nomenclature was first heralded by the Lushais from Lushai Hills. They advocated the term, 'Mizo' as the most acceptable nomenclature as they said is, the most natural word in unifying the people. On the 9th April, 1945 the Mizo Union, the first political party in Mizoram was formed. Since then, the Mizo Union played an important role in arousing the feeling of oneness under the indigenous word, 'Mizo'.

The movement for reunification of Zo people under 'Mizo' was countered by the Paites and Thadous of Manipur. They felt that the term, 'Mizo' was coined by the Lushai or Duhlian community for absorbing the whole Zo group to the Lushai community. Besides, the Thadous and Paites were apprehensive of the domination of the Lushai community. Therefore, they put forward the idea of Khul Union. Accordingly, the Khul Union was formed in the early 50s which, however, died down soon as a result of the breaking away of Paites and Hmars from the Union. It is said that the Paites and Hmars broke away from the Khul Union on the question of language. The Thadous claiming themselves to be the majority wanted the Thadou language to be the link language of the Union. Opposing this idea, the Hmars and Paites broke away from the Union in the late 1956.

On the 12th October, 1962 the President of Mizo National Front (The then Mizo National Famine Front) Laldenga visited Manipur and held a meeting with the leaders of the Zo Communities of Manipur on the question of common nomenclature. In the meeting, all the leaders accepted Chi-Ku-Mi as the common nomenclature for all the Zo ethnic groups. However, due to lack of follow-up action by the leaders of the so called Mizos/Zomis, the idea could not be materialised.

Therefore, the problem of common nomenclature acceptable to all the Zo ethnic groups remain illusive as ever. With regards to Mizoram, the people accepted Mizo as their undisputed common nomenclature. But the problem is still unsolved in Manipur. On the 21st January, 1972 the Zomi National Congress (ZNC) was formed at Daizang in Manipur South District under the Presidentship of T.Gougin, and S.K.Samte as General Secretary. As stated by Gougin, the founding father, the ultimate goal of this newly formed ZNC has been the unification of all the Zo Communities under the common Zomi nomenclature, The leaders of the newly formed ZNC wanted to unify all the Zo tribes of Manipur under 'Zomi' as they claimed that the word, 'Zomi' is an indigenous word which means Zo, hill and Mi, men, and Zo-Mi Means hill men. They also claimed that the Zo are all the descendants of Zo, and therefore, they called themselves, 'Zo or Zomi'

This newly formed ZNC wanted to create a sense of Zomi nationalism among the people. For this, it organized a political platforms from the village level strictly based on principles and discipline. In the early stage of its formation the party (unrecognized) was making progress in uniting the people under the Zomi. But, when this party suffered a crushing defeat in the 1984 Manipur Assembly Election in Thanlon Constituency, its popularity has gone down considerably. Therefore, people began to lose faith in the leadership of the party. The ZNC also demanded the creation of a Union Territory for the Zomis of Manipur. A memorandum demanding the creation of a Union Territory was submitted to the Prime Minister on the 4th December, 1984. It also tried to organize a mass movement for removing poverty, exploitation and narrow communal politics among the various 20 tribes. But it failed to get the support of the majority of the people as people lost faith in the leadership of the party.

Thus, inspite of efforts being made by the leaders of the ethnic Zo a commonly acceptable nomenclature could not be found as yet.

8. ORIGIN AND MIGRATION OF THE ZO PEOPLE:

Since the Paites are one of the sub-tribes of the Zo group of people, it is not possible to trace the historical origin of the Paites without tracing the historical origin of the Zo ethnic groups by explaining the different theories put forward by different people at different time. The following are some of the theories put forward by different people at different time regarding the historical origin of Zo people:

1.   The Blibical Theory
2.   The Khul or Chhinlung Theory
3.   The Chou or Jo Theory
4.   The Great wall Theory
5.   The Tibeto-Burman Theory

Biblical Theory:

Rev. Liangkhaia traced the historical origin of Zo people to the third son of Biblical Noah, Japhet. According to him, the descendants of Japhet once upon a time settled in Mongolis, and from there scattered in the whole South and Far East Asia. He is of the opinion that the entire population of Far East and South East Asia belong to the Mongolian race, and are descendants of

Biblical Japhet. Therefore, as the Zo people are of Mongolian race, they must also be the descendants of Biblical Japhet. This theory is put forward by Rev. Liangkhaia with the support of the Biblical proof.

The Khul/Chhinlung Theory:

There are differences of opinion among the scholars and writers regarding the Khul or Chhinlung Theory of the origin of Zo people of the Northeast India and Chin State of Myanmar. According to one version, *Khul and Chhinlung* was a stone cave or a pit in the earth situated either in Central China or in Tibet. This theory is supported by a legendary tale which goes-once upon a time, the world was in a complete darkness *(Khimzing)* followed by catastrophe. In the midst of such darkness all human beings were transformed into animals and beasts. But a new civilization was restarted when people came out of a pit in the earth called *Khul and Chhinlung*, in Paite and Lushai respectively. After all the people of the clans came out, two men of the Ralte clan started chattering. Therefore, god thought that too many men had come out and thus closed the door of the pit with a slab of stone. The supporters of this theory are inclined to believe that the Zo people are originated from a pit or a cave in the earth. However, this theory cannot be regarded as realistic one for the following reasons:

1. Those people who believe in this theory are themselves confused with the exact location or *Khul* or *Chhinlung*.

2. The theory that a new civilization was restarted when men came out of the dark pit in the earth contradicts the Biblical origin of man.

3. It is absolutely impossible and unbelieveable that man transformed into animals and beasts.

There is another version of *Khul* or *Chhinlung* theory according to which, once upon a time there was a king in China who had a son called 'Chhinlung'. But Chhinlung had a quarrel with his father and left his father with a large number of followers. They moved southward and settled for sometime in the foothill of a high mountain (probably this high mountain was Himalayan Mountain). After living in the foothill of a high mountain, they then moved south eastward in search of a secured place and fertile land for cultivation and settled in the present Shan State under the strong rule of Pong king. Ava by about 1445 A.D. However, the Governor of Khampat, Sou Rum Khum who belongs to the Zo community had a quarrel with Soohoongpha, the then king of Pong Dynasty over the payment of tax and over the payment of Dowry of the third daughter of Soonghoongpha, who was married to Sou Rou Khum. As a consequence of this quarrel, the followers of Sou Rum Khum left Khampat and followed the river courses of Chindwin and Irrawadi and settled in the present Chin State of Myanmar. However, as population increased, there was enmities among themselves as a result of which, some of them moved westward and settled in the present Mizoram, Manipur, Tripura and Assam.

The Great Wall Theory:

According to this theory, King Shih Huangti ruled over China in 228 B.C. During his reign, he started the construction of one of the Seven Wonders of the World, called 'The Great wall of China'. He employed almost the entire population, and did not spare even women and children. Therefore, people wanted to leave as they were forced to work day in and day out. But, just before finishing the construction of the Great Wall, the king died suddenly. Taking advantage of the death of the king, many people left China for fear of force labour. Those who believe in this theory hold the view that the Zos are originated from the Great Wall of China. They hold the view that their forefathers were once upon a time the subjects of Shih Huangti, the then king of China. They left China after the death of the king. This theory is put forward by K. Zawla, in his book, *'Mizo Pipute leh An Thlante Chanchin'*.

The Chow or Jo Theory:

According to this theory, by about 1027-256 B.C. there was a king in China whose name was Chow or Jo. He was very strong king and commanded sovereignty over a very large population. However, as the population was too big there was scarcity of land to support the population. As a result, a section of the population migrated to Tibet in search of food and shelter. After staying in Tibet for generations, they moved South East ward and entered the Shan State of Myanmar. They lived under the rule of Pong King, Ava and his prodecessors. During this period they were known by the Pong King as Zo (this fact can be seen in the chronicle of Pong King). However, by about 1445 A.D. they had a quarrel with the then Pong King. Soohoongpha over the payment of tax and the marriage of Sou Rum Khum, the chief of Khampat with the daughter of Soohoongpha. As a consequence of this quarrel the Zomis (Zos) had to move down to the south following the river courses of Chindwin and Irrawadi. They then settled down in the Chin State of Myanmar. As they were fighting among themselves some of them had to leave China State and entered Manipur, the present Mizoram, Assam and Tripura.

The Tibeto-Burma Theory:

This theory is the undisputed theory of the origin of Zo ethnic group. All the above discussed theory mentioned that the Zo ethnic group once upon a time settled in Tibet. This theory is further supported by the linguistic affinity of the tribes with the Tibetans. In fact, the Nagas, the Kachin, The Burmese, the Meiteis, etc. belong to Tibeto-Burman group. This fact is revealed in the following language table:

Table 1:8

English	Tibetan	Burmese	Meitei	Paite	Lushai
House	Khyim	Ein	Jum	Inn	In
Fire	Me	Mi	Mei	Mei	Mei
Eye	Mik	Myet	Mit	Mit	Mit
One	Ching	Tit	Ama	Khat	Pakhat
Two	Nyi	Hnit	Ani	Nih	Panih
Three	Sum	Thon	Ahum	Thum	Pathum
Four	Ski	Le	Mari	Li	Pali
Five	Nga	Nga	Mang	Nga	Panga

Six	Khuk	Chauk	Taruk	Guk	Paruk
Seven	Dun	Kunhit	Taret	Sagih	Pasarih
Eight	Gya	Shit	Nipan	Giat	Pariat
Nine	Gu	Ko	Mapan	Kua	Pakua
Ten	Chu	Tase	Tara	Sawm	Sawm

If we look at the language table above we can see that the Burmese, the Meitei, the Lushai and the Paite are all linguistically inter-related with one another, and this is clear indication of the fact that the Burmese, the Tibetans, the Meiteis, the Lushais, the Paites, etc. belong to Tibeto-Burman group of people. But the language of Paites and Lushais are closer to each other than the rest.

After having a close examination of these theories of the origin of the Zo ethnic group, we come to establish that all the theories reached a consensus on the point that once upon a time the Zo people live in China, Tibet and Shan State. The second version of Chhinlung theory and the Chow theory, though different regarding the remote origin of the tribes could come to a point when the tribe entered Shan State. Therefore, the two theories are regarded as realistic. But of these two theories, Chow theory, is more realistic as it is supported by the nomenclature by which they called themselves and they are called by the others.

The Pong King called them Jo. Dr. Vum Ko Hau, a Zomi scholar and the diplomat from Burma in his *Profile of a Burmese Frontier Man*, reaffirmed that we have called ourselves 'Zomi' from time immemorial. Therefore, we have come to establish that the most probable and most realistic theory of the historical origin of the so called Zo ethnic group is the Chou or Jo theory. As mentioned earlier, the Zo people are once upon a time the subject of the Chow King in about 80 A.D. to 1604 A.D. They moved down southward in search of food and shelter and settled in Tibet. From Tibet, they migrated to Shan State and as a result of a quarrel with Pong King, Soohoongpha, they then moved further south and settled in Chin state of Myanmar where a large group of them are still living now. As a result of internal dispute, some of them migrated to Lushai Hills (now Mizoram), Manipur, Assam and Tripura. At present the so called Zo people occupied a large territory in the Indo-Myanmar border areas. According to Mr. T.Gougin, the president of ZNC, the Zomis as a distinct people equipt with all identifications of a distinct nation occupied a vast area. In the east, upto Chindwin river in the west, upto Chittagong Hill Tract, in the south Kampetlet and in the north Haflong, The rough estimate of the entire Zogam (Zoland) is about20, 000 sq.ml. The Zomi inhabited areas comprises of the entire Lushai Hills (say 8,000 sq.mi) in Assam upto Haflong, 2, 000sq.ml. in Manipur 4,000 sq.ml. the entire Churachandpur District, Tengnoupal District and Sadar Hills in the north Manipur and the entire Chin Hills roughly 9,000 sq.ml. plus some portion in Chittagong Hill Tract and some portion in Myanmar Chindwin River.

9. ORIGIN AND MEANING OF THE WORDS CHIN, MIZO AND KUKI:

Since we have discussed as to who are the Zo people we shall now shift our discussion to the origin and meaning of the three words, 'Chin'-'Mizo'-'Kuki' and examine them as to whether they are acceptable to the people.

Origin of Chin: Messrs Carey and Tuck in their book, 'The Chin Hills' attempted to know something about the Chins. According to them, those of Kuki tribes which we designate as Chin do not recognised the name which is said to be corruption of Burmese word, 'Yen' (Meaning *Men*). The Northern Chins called themselves Zo, Tashon, Haka and more Southern tribes have been christened by name unknown to them. For instance, 'Naga' the meaning of which is 'Naked' and the Abors who called themselves Padam. Captain Yule, the once Secretary of the Envoy to the Court of Ava, the capital of Myanmar, described the Chins and the Lushais as, 'the Indo-Chinese kindred known as Kukis, Nagas, Khyams and by many more specific names, " Mr. Taw Sin Khan, a Burmese lecturer of Cambridge, in a pamphlet on the Chins and the Kachins bordering Myanmar wrote "ethnically those tribes belong to that vaguely defined and yet little understood stock, the Tutarian which includes among others, the Chinese, the Tibetans, the Manchus, the Javanese, the Anamese, the Burmese and the Turks". From the above discussion, we know that the word, 'Chin' is a Burmese word which means *men*. Those people who are known as "Chin In Burma have completely discarded the name 'Chin' as their nomenclature and accepted Zomi as their nomenclature", wrote T.Gougin, President of ZNC. Therefore, though the Burmese and the Britishers called them 'Chin' most of the scholars among the tribes do not agree with the word 'Chin' to be their nomenclature.

Origin of Mizo: The meaning of the word 'Mizo' is said to be highlanders or hill men, 'Mi' means *men* and 'Zo' means *hill* or high altitude. But all the people living in the high altitude are not called Mizo. The word is used with reference to a specific tribes living in Manipur, Tripura, Cachar, Mizoram and Chin Hills of Burma who are closely related to one another in languages, custom and way of living. There is another explanation of the word 'Mizo' according to which the people were called after the name of the habitation they built around1765. This area was called Zopui, twenty kilometres to the west of Tiau River. It is said that during their stay in Zopui, they were successful in raids on the enemy, and therefore, were proud to refer to themselves as people of Zopui (men of Zopui), so Mi-Zopui=Mizo. However, of these two interpretations of the word, 'Mizo'. Mizo scholars are moreinclined to accept the former which means hill men. There is yet another view on the meaning and origin of the term. According to this view, the people in question are the descendants of Zo and therefore, they called themselves Zomi/Mizo after the name of their ancestor. In the early stage of the emergence of the word, 'Mizo' the Mizo Union, the first regional political party in Mizoram formded on 9th April, 1946 played an important role in arousing the feeling of oneness under Mizo.

Origin of Kuki: The 'Kuki' is an Assamese or Bengalese term applied to The hill tribes such as the Lushais, Rangkhols, Thadous, etc. wrote Z.Z.Lien, in his book the U-NOW PEOPLE. This suggests that the word, 'Kuki' is an imposed name on the various hill tribes of Manipur, Assam, Mizoram and Chin Hills of Myanmar. In the Raj Mala, Siva is stated to have fallen in love with a Kuki woman, and the word, 'Kuki' is mentioned in connection with the Tiperah Raja Chachag who flourished about 1542 A.D. Z.Z. Lien, in his book The U-NOW PEOPLE mentioned that 'Khuki' or 'Kuki' is a Bengali word which means a pretty girl of tender age. However, the real origin of Kuki is yet to be traced.

10. BRITISH ANNEXATION OF ZOLAND:

It was in 1824 that the Ahom King with the help of the British pushed the invading Burmese out of Assam. Since then the Ahom Kingdom was under the protection of the British. During those period the different tribes of Zo ethnic group used to come down to the plain areas of Assam and attacked villages in the plain killing the inhabitants, taking their heads and plundering and burning their houses. In 1849 Col. Lister, the Commandant of the Syhlet infantry and agent for the Khasi Hills was sent to punish the tribes. This expedition however, was partially successful as the expenditure could not reach beyond a village of Mulla, which contained 800 houses. This village was, however, destroyed as all male inhabitants were absent.

In 1868-69 the Lushais burnt a tea garden in Cachar and attacked Monierkhal. As a result of this raid, the British sent an expedition under the command of Gen. Nuthal. But this expedition totally failed due to heavy rain. This time no tribe was punished and no captive were recovered. The next season, the Deputy Commissioner of Cachar, Mr. Edger tried his best to make friendship with the wild hillmen, but it was in vain as the hillmen once again started raiding the plain area in 1871. The first raid occurred in the Chittagong Hill Tract on the 31st December. This time the raiding forces were about 200men. On the 3rd December of 1871 Arnerkhal village on the extreme West of Cachar District was burnt, 25 people taken prisoners. On the same day, the tea garden of Alenxandrapura was destroyed and Mr. Winchester, the planter was killed and his six years old daughter, Mary was carried off.

Again, on the 8th January Monierkhal garden was attacked in which one sepoy was killed and one was wounded. Emboldened by their success, raiders penetrated as far as Nundigram, and on the 27th January 1872 they killed 11 persons and carried off

3 persons. On the 23rd February, Jhalnacherra tea garden was attacked in which seven coolies were killed.

Therefore, as raids on plain areas were frequent occurance, the Government of British India decided that an expedition should be sent ot the Lushai country during the ensuing cold weather of 1872. It is, therefore, decided by the Government that the forces should consist of two columns. Gen. Browblow had commanded the right column from Chittagong while Gen. Bourcher with Mr. Edger, the Deputy Commissioner of Cachar commanded the left column from Cachar. In addition to these columns, a contingent of Manipuris led by Gen. Nuthal, the Political Agent made co-operation with Gen. Bourchier. The commanders of this expedition were instructed that the object of the expedition was not puretaliation, but surrender of the British subjects held under captivity. They were also asked to make effort to establish friendship and understanding with the tribes.

This two-front expedition was successful as a result of which Assam could enjoy a comparatively peaceful atmosphere until 1888-1889. When the expedition was completed the invading forces put two posts in North Lushai Hills, one at Aizawl and the other at Changsil and a Political officer was appointed to administer the North Lushai Tract. In this way the entire Lushai Hills fall into the hands of the British.

Though Lushai Hills was at last conquered by the British, Chin Hills, Inhabitant by the Paites, The Pawis, the Lakher, etc. still remained independent. The British at first did not want to conquer Chin Hills occupied by the Paites, the Pawis, the Lakher, etc. as they knew that they had nothing to gain by conquering them. But the hill tribes many a time attacked and plundered the plain areas of Myanmar. In 1850, 1857 and 1859 there were raids on the plain areas of Manipur by the Chins (Suktes). In 1881 Kale and Kabaw Valley inhabited by Shans were raided by the Tashon. Because of the repeated raids by the Chins on the plain areas of Manipur and Myanmar, the British Government of India decided to conquer the Chin Hills. Therefore, for the protection of their subjects in the plain areas, the British Government of India sent many expeditions against the Chin between 1888 and 1890.

They were able to conquer the Northern Chin Hiills inhabited by the Suktes (Paites), Thadous, etc. but the Southern Chin Hills inhabited by the Pawis and Lakhers remained unconquered. The British then moved down to the South. They met stiff resistance from the Pawis and Lakhers. But the British with their superior weapons at last conquered the Southern Chin Hills in 1930. Thus the British took nearly 50 years to conquer the entire Zo inhabited areas form 1880-1930.

Thus, when in 1930 the British completed their mission to conquer the Zo land, they divided the land into three administrative divisions to meet their convenience and their policy of divide and rule. The Lushai Hills was administered by the Chief Commissioner of Assam through a superintendent, and the Southern Manipur, inhabited by the Hmars, Paites, Kukis, etc. was administered by Political Officers stationed at Teddim, Haka and Falam. When in 1947, India and Burma were given political freedom, the land inhabited by Zo ethnic group was divided into two separate political entities, viz., India and Myanmar. The eastern portion went to India. Therefore, though the so called Chins, Mizos, and Kukis belong to the same stock and share common culture and heritage they are now separated by an imaginary line of international Boundary, and are said to be the worst victim of British imperialism.

11. THE IMPACT OF BRITISH RULE OVER ETHNIC ZOS:

The British rules over the Zos have both negative and positive impact. In the first place, we will see its positive impacts as follows:

The Zos were all animists in the past, they worshipped natural objects, like river, mountain, rock etc. They believed that spirits are dwelling in those natural objects which could do harm to men if not pleased by men. Therefore, they worshipped those spirits out of fear. They however, believed in the existence of a creator or high God, with the coming of the British, the Christian missionaries from the west got the opportunity to enter the land inhabited by the Zos. They moved freely through length and breadth of the land and converted the people into Christianity; the people gave up many of their traditional practices. They had stopped making sacrifices for the appeasement of evil spirit. Instead, they had been the true believer of the true God, the Creator of Heaven and Earth. The first missionaries to land in the Zoland were Messrs Savidge and Lorrain, who reached Aizawl on the 11th January, 1894. Later on they were joined by other 20 missionaries, with regards to Manipur, the Gospel of Christ reached in 1920 through missionary Watkin Roberts on the 7th May, 1910 from Aizawl. The Christian missionaries' established educational institutions for the people, raised the standard of the people. Therefore, Mr.T.Gougin, rightly wrote, "The British Government had given them light into darkness, peace from chao and money from destitution". The missionaries dis not only helps in spreading education, but also help in giving medical aids by establishing dispensaries. Regarding Chin Hills, the Gospel of Christ reached through Mr. Judson and Rev. A.B.Carson.

Judging from the point of view of its positive impact the British rule over the Zomi can be said to be blessing in disguise. Had the British not annexed their land, these people might not have known western education, they might not have been converted into Christianity and they might still be in constant fear of evil spirits.

Though there are positive impacts there are also negative impact of the British rule. Politically, the Paites, the Lushais, the Pawis, the Thadous who are all included in the Zo group were politically and economically independent. Each village was ruled over by a village chief who was supreme and whose judgment was final. But after the coming of the British, each sovereign village state was no more sovereign village state as the British appointed political officers and political agents to administer the village. When the Government of India Act, 1985 was passed, the Zo land was divided between India and Myanmar. Half of it, the Chin Hills went to Myanmar and the other half went to India. As a result the Zo groups are said to be the worst victim of British imperialism.

In short, the impact of the British rule over the Zos can be summed up as:

1. Conversion into Christianity.

2. Spread of Education.

3. The lost of sovereignty by the Zo chiefs.

4. Division of their land between India and Myanmar.

Chapter II

Physical Appearance and
Way of Living

MESSRS CAREY AND TUCK in their book, 'The Chin Hills' describes the characteristics of Chin the following words.

"The Chins are serious in manner, revengeful, treacherous method of warfare, the virtue of hospitality, clannish feeling, arrogance in victory, speedy discouragement, panicky in defeat, and impatience under control are the common traits followed and obsecured throughout Chin Hills, of course, subject to slight difference to its practical adherence". The Paites being one of the tribes of Chin possess all the qualities and characteristics of Chin.

1. PHYSICAL APPEARANCE:

As the Paites belong to the Zo family, the physical appearance of the Paites is the same as the physical appearance of the other groups of Zo family. According to Col. J. Shakespeare, "All the Lushai-Kuki clans resemble each other very closely in appearance, and the Mongolian type of countenance prevails". Messrs Carey and Tuck in their book the Chin Hills wrote,

"The Chin is a fine man, taller and stouter than his neighbours in the plain on both north and east although he falls short of the build of the Pathan, his measurement compare more than favourable with those of the Gurkhas."

Lt.Stewart Wrote,

"The Kukis are a short, sturdy race of men with a goodly developed muscle; their legs are generally speaking short, in comparision with the length of their bodies and their arms long. The face is nearly as broad as it is long and is generally round or square, the cheek bones high, broad and prominent, eyes small and almost shaped, the nose short and flat, with wide nostrils. The women appear more squat than the men even, but are strong and lusty. As put in the handbook of the Anthropological Institute, the colour of the skin varies between dark, yellow-brown, dark olive. Bears and whiskers are almost absent. There are of course a few exceptional people with hairy faces. The measurement of the so called Zo group of people is uneven in that it is hard to come amenable to discipline. The average height of men is about 5 feet 6 inches though there are also some people of 5 feet 10 inches or 5 feet 11 inches. There are also a few men of below 5 feet. The average height of women varies from 4 feet to 5 feet 6 inches."

2. TRADITIONAL DRESS OF THE PAITES:

The traditional dress of a Paite men consisted of a single cloth of about 7 feet long and 5 feet wide. One corner of the cloth was grasped in the left shoulder behind the back under the arm across the left shoulder. During the cold weather a Paite man also wears one or more clothes, one over the other, and also a white coat reaching down the thigh. When a Paite man was at work in hot weather, he wraped his cloth round his waist letting one end hanged in front. The garments wore by a Paite man was made of locally made produced cotton made by women of the household.

A Paite man was very fond of wearing hat. Hats were used for the protection of rain and sun heat. They are made of strips of bamboo or cane plaited and leaves with smoke leaf. The original hats were also circular, but these had been discarded in favour of a very clever imitation of helmet and solar topis. A Paite man also used to carry a haversack (Kawlzalpi) made of cotton slung over his shoulder by a string of the same material, in this haversack, he kept his flint and steel and his tobacco. His smoking pipe (Zabel) was almost all the time in his mouth. While not smoking this smoking pipe was also kept in the haversack together with his *Tuibuk*, a small gourd to hold the water which has been impregnated with nicotine in the pipe of his wife or sweet-heart. This remained for 4 to 5 minutes in the mouth after which it is spitted out.

During wartime, the fighters wore a single cloth wrapped tightly protected by a bear or tiger skin guard over one shoulder, and a fighting dao or sword over the other and a gun in his hand.

The style of the traditional hair dressing of men among the Zo groups was divided into two distint fashions, the topknot on the top of the head and the chignon on the nape of the neck. The Tashons, Yahow (Zahau) and Hakas of the Southern Chin Hills practiced top-knot style of hair dressing. But the Saijang, the Suktes, the Guites (Paites), the Zous and the Thadous of the Northern Chin Hills and southern Manipur practiced the chignon style of hair dressing. Among the chignon wearers the Saijang made their hair in three plaits whereas the Suktes, the Guites (Paites) and the Zous had only one plait instead of three. The fat of pig was used as a posmutum both by men and women.

A Paite man was very fond of wearing ornaments... He puts a variety of articles in his hair knot like a pronged pin with a head shaped like G. One end of the pronged was shape and pointed and was about 8-9 in long. He also puts on skewers of ivory, bones and metal of about 6-8 in long. The metal skewers were used for scratching the head. The hair comb was also an ornamental article, and consisted of a piece of ivory or wood of about 3 inch long, half inches wide, into which were inserted very close together teeths of strips of bamboo of about 2 inches long.

Like the women, men also had their ears pierced and inserted either small wooden studs cornelians suspended by a piece of string. Both men and women were fond of necklaces. Of the various kinds of necklace, those necklaces made of amber are considered the best. Besides ambers, agate, cornelians and various sorts of beads necklace are wore. Tiger's teeth were also found hanging round the neck as an ornament and were also thought to have a magical power. The young dandies were fond of hanging round their necks trofts of white goat's hair bound together with thread.

The traditional dress of Paites women was very simple. She puts on a cotton cloth just long enough to go round the waist with a slight over lap, and held up by a girdle of brass wire or a string only to the knee. Other garment used by Paite women was a short jacket made of cotton cloth which was put in the same manner as man.

A Paite woman was also fond of ornaments. Ornaments wore by man and woman were the same. With regards to earing, it was quite distinct that in order to be able to put, much preparation was necessary. At the time when the girl was a small child she had her ear pierced and a small wooden stug was inserted. This was replaced by larger one which in turn gave place to still larger clay, the size of which was gradually increased till the real earing could be inserted which was usually made of ivory.

3. TRADITIONAL TYPE OF VILLAGE AND HOUSE:

Like any other tribe of Zo ethnic group, the Paites are very much selective about the place of their residence: and a lot of time and thought was given in selecting the site of the village. In selecting the proposed village site the following factors were taken into consideration:

i.   Good defence position,

ii.   Good water supply, and

iii. Shelter from the wind and availability of fertile cultivable land.

As war between village and village, and between clan and clan was frequent occurance, the Paites usually preferred to build their villages on the top of a mountain or hill. A village situated on a mountain or hill is expected to have a greater advantage of winning the war, because the enemy always found it difficult to attack a village situated on the top of a mountain as attacking from below had always been difficult. However, while selecting the site of a village, the Paites also take into consideration matter like good water supply, good shelter from storm and the availability of fertile cultivable land around the village. Therefor, a good defence position alone was not the only factor responsible for selection of village site. They were much careful about the selection of the site, of the village. Before the final selection of the site, the elders of the clan would sleep the night at the site, taking with them a cock. If the cock did not crow like a good lusty cock should one hour before dawn, it was taken as a bad site and the site was rejected.

The houses in a village were laid out close to each other with a sense of regularity, arranged usually in two lines the front of the houses all facing in towards each other, and separated by a space treated as a village street. Since most of the villages were built on the top of the hills, it was necessary to level the grounds for the compound. Each of the compound was surrounded with timber fence or a cactus hedge or both. As there was no scarcity of land for building houses, each house had a large compound for gardening.

The village fortification was public matter, and all the people of the village were engaged in building fortified village gates: and in digging the necessary trenches outside the village. The fortified gate was usually narrow and that only one person could enter at a time; so to reach this gate, a zigzag path, and often a tunnel had to be made. At both side of the path, there were stones, wooden aungars and stockadesover thrown with brains, cactus and thorny bushes, which made entrance in 'face of resistance impossible'. B.S. Carey and H.N. Tuck wrote 'In the Siyin Sokte, and specially in the Sukte-Gungal tract, large trenches are dug and roofed with heavy timber flush with the ground inside the village; these trenches are maintained as a refuge for the women and children in case of sudden attack. The entrance hole was blocked up and there are some dozen loop-holes through which the defender shoot down any one who approaches this underground block-house'.

Regarding the naming of the village, most of the Paite villages were named after the jungle or hill on which they were built. For instance, 'Mualpi', one of the oldest Paite villages was named after the hill on which it was built, *'Mual'* means a hill, and *'Pi'* means big. Thus 'Mualpi' means the village on the big hill.

Traditional of House:

The Paites built their houses off the ground on the slope of the hill as the ground could not be properly leveled, and pigs are kept underneath of the house. A Paite house consisted of the following parts; the front verandah called '*Summun*' approached by a rough platform, the main room and a small closet partitioned off at the far end; beyond which there will sometimes be a small bamboo platform. The verandah is called '*Summun*'. '**Sum**' means mortar in which paddy is grind manually and '**Mun**' means place. Thus, '*Summun*' means, the place where hand made grinding mill was kept. On one side of the Summun, house-wife kept a stock of firewood; and the front wall of the house is full of skull of animals and birds hunted by the householder. There are also a long bamboo basket in which the fowl laid their egg. The fowl spent the night in the basket. From the verandah, a small yet a very high door opens into the house. Beneath the door, there used to be special hole for dogs. Immediately on the right side of the house there usually are bamboo tubes by which the female members of the family fetched water from the stream nearby. Just opposite to the place where bamboo tubes are kept there is a circular bamboo containing the stock of paddy for the year. Next to this, there is a sleeping place known as '*Khum-ai*' in which the parents of the family along with the young children slept. Next to this is a fireplace called, '*Tap*'. Beyond this fireplace, there is another sleeping platform (*Khumpi*) for the grandparents and the grown-up children. Sometimes beyond '*Khumpi*', there used to be another sleeping bed where other members of the family sleep. The dining place is just opposite to fireplace or *Tap*. The rest of the floor is vacant. The modern furniture like bench, chair, sofa, etc. are totally absent. The only furniture is a stool made of cane and bamboo called, '*Vaitutphah*'. Most of the houses had a bamboo platform in front of the house called, '*Inkatau*' in which the women folk sit and loom their looms while the young men sat beside them. The houses of the chiefs were usually larger than the house of the commoners. Each of the house have garden at the back of the house where sugarcane, guavas, lemons, mangoes, etc. were grown.

4. BUILDING MATERIALS:

In the past, no brick or iron was used for constructing houses. The material used for the construction of house are timber for upright and bamboo for the framework of the floor, walls, and roof, split bamboos for the floor, walls and even cane leaves were used for roof. In place of nails, split canes were used to tie the whole framework.　　In fact, in the absence of cane building a house was impossible. The whole material used was completed with wood, canes and bamboos.

5. CEREMONY OF BIRTH AND DEATH:

The Paites did not have a significant birth ceremony. Immediately after the birth, the child is washed; and a fowl is killed and its feathers are wore round the neck of the mother and child. Mother of the child is allowed to go out of the house after the birth of the child, but for four days after the birth of the child, both parents abstained from all works. At the time of naming of the child, pigs are usually killed and all the relatives of the parents are invited and rice beer (Zu) is served to the invitees. If the child is the first child, the name is usually given after the name of the parents of the father side. But if the child is the second child, the parents of the mother be given the chance to name the child. While naming the child, usually the last part of the name of the one who named the child may be taken as the first part of the name of the child.

For instance

LAL THANG LIAN　　　　(first giver)

LIAN SIAM　　　　(second giver)

SIAMKHUM

The Paites in the past performed a lot of death ceremonies. When a person dies, the corpse is placed on a platform and fires are lit round it; and young men and maiden sleep near it. The skin is then hardened and preserved. The body is then washed, the hair dressed and the corpse clothed with best cloths available as if about to go for a raid; with gun and spear in hands, powder-flasks and haversack slung over the shoulders. During daytime the body is kept inside the house, but in the evening it is brought outside the house and seated infront of the house, and the villagers danced round it and drink rice beer and pouring it, also into the mouth of the corpse. This sort of ceremony goes on for even a month or more according to the social position of the deceased. The corpse of those who attained '*Thangsuah*' honour the corpses are kept for years in a special shed enclosed in a tree trunk. Before burial the corpse is carried round the village. In the case of a violent death, the corpse is placed in a forge and 'Siampu' (priest) sacrifices a fowl. Only after this, the usual ceremony is performed. The chief oa a village when he dies, is not buried in the common cemetery, but usually buried by the side of the road leading to village. Memorial stone are also erected and decorated with the picture of animals killed during his lifetime.

6. DRINKS AND SMOKE:

Zu (Rice Beer) is the most important drink of the Paite; without it there was practically no enjoyment. No feast could be thrown, no sacrifice could be made and no marriage arrangement could be made in the absence of *Zu*. Therefore, *Zu* played an important role in the past Paite society.

There are three kinds of *Zu* such as *Zuha*, *Zupi* and *Zukha*. Of these zukha is the strongest. It is a distilled alcohol from rice. *Zupi* is a mere rice beer. Regarding *Zuha*, it is made of sticky rice and milder than *Zukha* or *Zupi*.

There are two ways of drinking *zu*; the first is the normal way of drinking but not in a cup of glass, but in a horn of *Mithun*. The outer cover of the horn of mithun is used for drinking *Zu*. The second method is by sucking the *Zu* out of *Zubel* (elongated earthen jar) by means of a long bamboo reed which is passed from mouth to mouth.

Smoking: Both men and women are very fond of it. They called the material they smoke '*Dum*' or '*Zanah*' which is a kind of tobacco. The leaf of the *Dum* is rolled and then dried for consumption. Paite women smoke unceasingly even while working in the field. She is smoking not only for her own pleasure, but also for the supply of her husband with nicotine water *Tuibuk*. The pipe of the woman is called, '*Buk*' which is made up of a clay bowl, a bamboo or gourd water receptacle and impregnated the water in the bamboo or gourd with nicotine. This nicotine water or '*Tuibuk*' is taken by almost all men and women. It is not, however, drank like water, it is merely kept in the mouth for sometime and spilledout again.

A Paite man also smoke '*Zabel*' which is made of bamboo bowl, metal to prevent it from burning and a bamboo stem for the pipe. The material used for smoking is the same as that of the woman. Like women men also smoke all the time except while sleeping and eating.

In the present day, apart from the traditional smoking pipe, the Paites imitate the modern cigarettes or biri which they called '*Zozial*'. They used a plain paper or newspaper for the cover and the material inside being the same as in the past.

7. WEAPONS AND METHOD OF WARFARE:

Prior to the time when guns were imported to Chin Hills from Myanmar, the weapons of the Paites like other Zo tribes consisted of bows and arrows, spear and short daos. The warrior who took with him a shield was capable of resisting the force of these primitive weapons.

Spears used by Paites are about 5ft. long shod at the butt with a long four-sided spike and at the other end with the spear-head which was sharpened at the side as well as at the point; the weapon is very heavy as one half and often two-thirds of its length is iron. Regarding bows and arrows, they did not only serve as weapons for war but they also serve as weapons for shooting wild animals. The bows were 1 to 18inches in length and were iron-bared and feathered. They also sometimes used poisoned arrows for shooting big animals like elephants, tiger, etc. Regarding the shields, it was very tough and effectively could stop arrows, it was made out of the hide of the mithun in some $2^{1/2}$ by $1^{1/2}$ ft. It is purely meant for protecting the body from the attack of arrows. Regarding the dao, it was a very poor and unsophiscated being too short, badly shaped and made of inferior metal.

After the coming of guns from Myanmar, the above mentioned weapons were almost totally discarded. About 50years before the coming of the British, guns began to find their way into the Chinland, at first chiefly through Burma and later on through Lushai Hills. Since then, gun had been the most sophisticated weapons for wars and for shooting wild animals. Messars Carey and Tuck wrote, "The Chins, the Lushais and the Kukis are noted for the secrecy of their plans, the suddenness of their raids, and their extraordinary speed and treating to their fastness". Being included in the Zo ethnic family, the method of warfare of the Paites is practically the same as mentioned above.

In most cases, the raids were conducted with due care and consideration. The village to be attacked was chosen, the date for the attack fixed, the warriors to be involved in the raids selected, and spies sent out to see the fortification of the village proposed to be attacked. When all arrangements were finalized, animal was sacrificed, and its liver was examined to make it sure that the spirits were propitious. The raid could be abandoned even at this stage if the liver was diseased and the omen bad. Taking that the omen was good, the raiding party started forth, each carrying his weapons, his food and his blanket. The raiding party took with them slaves who were supposed to carry off the dead bodies and wounded, to drive off cattle and carry loads of plunders. After reaching the border of the village proposed to be attacked, the raiding party waited for the darkness of the night and cooked meals. The attack was only launched in the darkness of night.

After the village had been totally plundered the raiding party returned to their village driving the cattle before and dragging the captives along with them. The success of the raid was informed to the village at once; and the villagers prepared for the triumphant entry of the heroes who approached the village, firing their guns in honour of their glorious return. On the arrival at their village, the raiding party was met by the entire population.

8. TRADITIONAL FESTIVALS, FEAST AND DANCE:

The most important festival observed by Zo group is '*Kut*'. There are many version regarding the origin of the festival. Mostly the Paites observed the following different types of '*Kut*'.

Mim Kut: This '*Kut*', festival is usually observed in the month of September. It is the festival to appease those who are already dead. The origin of this festival is those who are already dead. The origin of this festival is connected with a Paite legendary love story which goes as:

Once upon a time, there was a boy, Ngambawm by name; and a girl, Khupching by name. The boy and girl loved each other very much. But, unfortunately Khupching met a premature death. As a result, the boy was so sad and wept so much that he died at last. When Ngambawm also died, he went to the abode of the death (*Misikhua*) and found Khupching too lean and thin. He asked Khupching; why she was so lean and thin. Khupching replied, she happened to be so as there was nothing to eat there in '*Misikhua*', and asked Ngambawm to go back and take vegetables for her. Accordingly, Ngambawm went back home and take vegetables from the filed, and told Khupching, "Dear Ching, I brought for you all kinds of vegetables from our field, have them as much as you like". He made a platform on the wall and kept there things to eats for Khupching. But his longing for his beloved was more and more. He again wept and at last died again. After his death, he found Khupching in a better condition. He found her active and happy, and asked her as to why she was fat. Khupching too replied that she was becoming fat as she took the vegetables brought for her by him.

Therefore, '*Mim Kut*' is specially meant for the deads. This festival is usually observed for about three days during which, aged people sang mourning song. Though, rice beer is served people do not usually dance. The main purpose of the '*Mim kut*' is to appease the spirit of the deads.

Pawl Kut: This festival is usually observed after the harvest. It is believed that this festival is originated from the time when the Paites were in Shan State. There was a great famine called '*Singpitam*' which caused many deaths. This famine continued for three years. But, in the fourth year, people were able to properly cultivate land and the year happened to be a prosperous one. Being overjoyed, the headman of the village asked the village crier to announce that all people must cook as much rice as they could, and that, all people should eat together. People are happy and full of joy. As people were overjoyed, this continued for days. Unlike '*Mim kut*', '*Pawl kut*' is meant for joy and happiness. People had *Zu* (rice beer) and dance.

Chapchar/Taptal Kut: This festival is usually observed in the month of March. It is observed for about seven days. People had advanced preparation for the festival. They search for wild animals to be killed during the festival. Rice beer is collected by the young boys and girls of the village. The exact origin of this festival is yet to be traced.

There is no fixed days to be observed for '*Kuts*'. But 7-10 days is usually observed. It is the time for making happy and merriments. It is the time for dancing, playing and singing during both days and nights.

Feast:

Sa-aih: This feast is thrown when a man is able to kill big wild animals like tiger, lion, elephant, etc. This feast could be arranged by a well –to-do family of the village. If the big wild animals are killed, they celebrated the hunted animals with joy. On such occasion, they killed mithuns, pigs, etc. and make a big feast. All the people of the village joined and feast, drink *Zu* and dance – young and old alike beating gongs, drums, etc. They fire gun and sing a song of pride (*han-la*).

Buh-aih: This feast is usually given by a well – to –do family who had an exceptionaly good harvest. This feast is offered by only those who are able to harvest a crop of more than 100 baskets. In such occasion, red cock and a pig are killed and much rice beer prepared. There is a special pot of rice beer in front of the house which are meant only for those who had performed '*Buh-aih*' ceremony. The meat of the animal killed is eaten by the guest. At night the boys and girls dance. However this feast could be given by only a well –to-do family of the village.

Gal-aih: This feast is given by the warrior who is successful in bringing the heads of the enemy. It is believed that if a warrior do not perform *gal-aih* the spirit of the slained enemy could take revenge; and the warrior would not be in a position to put the spirit of the slained enemy for his slave in the abode of the dead.

Thangsuah: Thangsuah feast is meant only for those who are successfully performing the above mentioned feasts such as *gal-aih, sa-aih* and *buh-aih*.

The above mentioned traditional feasts and festivals of the Paite had no place in the Christianized Paite society. In place of them, Paites today celebrate Christian festivals like Christmas Day, Missionary Day, Good Friday, Easter Sunday, etc. The Paite people have the conception that celebration of traditional feasts and festivals is against the value and belief of Christianity. In the past, no feast could be arranged without rice beer being served. Therefore, the traditional feasts and festival of the Paites required rice beer which is against Christian belief. As a result, they are practically irrelevant in the Christianized Paite society.

Traditional Dance:

Regarding the traditional dance of the Paites, the following may be worth mentioning;

Phit Lam: This is usually performed when the adventurous heroes returned from head-hunting and ferocious game hunting. The heroes returning with amputated heads of the carcass were welcome at the outskirt of the village. The piping of tunes began and unceasingly continued as the joyous group came toward the heroes' house. The songs were not sang, but strictly piped. The cut bamboos produced alternate tunes harmonously and to the charm of the dance.

Zangta Lam: It is believed that the fore-fathers of the Paites were successful in subjugating other clans and used them as slaves. To commemorate this successful adventure, people sing songs and dance and the unique pattern of dance had been called, *Zangta;* which literally means living man and dance. After the communal war of *Sak-le-khang* in 1100 A.D. 'Zangtalam' came to harbor most of the Paite customary festival dances like (1) *Sial Sawm*, (2) *Lawm Annek* (Last Thursday and Friday of September).

Liandou Lam alias Ton Lam: The grains produced were consecrated amidst thanks giving by erecting a proportioned stone on which they inscribed their esteemed possession. The stone stood by their dwellings; and above it a, 'Liandou Lam' shows its performance. This occasion is sort of remembrance of the by gone miseries of ill-fated incidents. Mr. Liandou lamented over the death of his wife. Liandou and his brother Thanghou were forsaken by their mother for remarrying. Blessed by a considerate old witch disguised as an old lady, Liandou became rich overnight. The dance is traditionally performed in a melancholic manner. They sing pathetically and the course of misfortune.

Among the above mentioned traditional dance of the Paites, '*Zangta Lam*' and '*Phit Lam*' are still performed by the boys and girls in occasion like Independence Day and Republic Day of India.

9. SLAVERY IN THE PAST PAITE SOCIETY:

Slavery in its various forms existed also among the Zo group of people. However, there is a distinctives the Zos group in the sense that only the chiefs and nobles are entitled to have slaves, whereas in other parts of the world like the U.S.A. in days of old, all those who had money to buy slave were entitled to have slave. In other words, among the Zos, the common men were not entitled to keep slaves while in other parts of the world, the common men were also entitled to keep slaves provided that they have the money to buy.

Like any other tribe Zos ethnic group, slavery has also existed in the Paite society of the past. There were three classes of slavery in the past Paite society which are :

1. *Innpisung suak* (those who live in the chief's house).

2. *Temsan suak* (red dao slave), and

3. *Tuklut suak* (enter by promising).

Innpisung suak : This class of slaves consisted mostly of all those who had been driven by want of food to take refuge in the chief's house, like widow, orphan, illegitimate child who were unable to support themselves, and had no relatives to support them formed a bulk of this class of slaves. This category of slaves were treated as members of the chief's household. They work all the works of the chief in return to the food and shelter given to them. The young men cultivate the chief's jhum and attend to his fish traps. The women and girls collected firewood and fetch water, clean the daily supply of rice, make cloth and weed the jhum, and of course look after the children. In return to their valuable services, they live in the chief's house, wore ornaments given by the chief and used the guns and weapons of the chief. Since all the chiefs belong to the same family clan, the slave of one chief could be transferred for the slave of another chief. If the chief ill-treated his slave, then the slave could go and see refuge under other powerful chief. As a result, the slaves were generally well-treated. When a male slave reached the marriageable age the chief made all arrangements for his marriage. He had to stay for three years in the house of the chief after which he sets up a house of his own; and starts a family of his own; and worked for himself. But even after having a separate house, he had certain duties to the chief. He is still supposed to give one front leg to the chief whenever he happens to kill any animal; and if he fails to give it, he is liable to a fine of one mithun or its equivalence. If the chief is in want of rice, he can call on his ex-slaves and if they are in want, they can look to the chief for assistance.

Regarding the female slaves, they were allowed to marry; and the chief received the price. Once the price had been paid the chief had no further claim on the women or her children during her husband's lifetime. But if the woman is left widowed she can re – enter the chief's house. But, as a rule, if she behaves decently, she is allowed to remain in her husband's house and look after her children who are never misconsidered as slaves. But if remarried, the chief can again claim whatever sum is paid as her marriage price.

Of all classes of slaves among the Paites, *Innpisung suak* are most well-treated by the chief's household. They became slaves in their own interest and safety. They were allowed to be free from slavery as and when they wanted to be free by paying one mithun to the chief.

Temsau suak : (Red dao slave): This category of slaves were drawn from criminals, debtors, thieves, etc. when any person commited murder in the village, he used to take refuge in the chief's house as the chief's house is the safest place for him from the avengers. Once the murderer entered the chief's house, nobody can take any action against him, how serious the crime might be.

Debtors who were unable to pay their debts sought the protection of the chief by promising to become a slave of the chief. Thieves and other vagabonds avoided punishment by entering the house of the chief to become his slaves. However, after the settlement of the case, the slaves were allowed to live in a separate house; but their children are considered as slaves to the same extent as their parents are. The chief was entitled to take the marriage price of the daughters of such slave.

Tuklut Suak (Entered by promising): The third category of slave existed among the Paite society was *Tuklut Suak.* This class of slaves come from battle field. The warriors who practically deserted the losing side, and embrace the victors with a solemn promise to live as slaves of the victors. This class of slave can get their freedom by giving a mithun to the chief and live in a separate house. *Sal* (captive)-persons who were captured in raids are *Sal.* The position of *Sal* was quite different from that of any class of slaves mentioned above. *Sals* were personal property of their captors. As a rule, if children and marriageable women were taken captives the latter were disposed off for marriage by taking marriage price. The children grew up in their captive house as their children, and as a rule they were so well treated that they seldom wanted to return to their houses.

10. MARRIAGE AND DIVORCE:

In the past, marriage was arranged by parents of the boys and girls. Though the boys were given the maximum time to make love with the girls of their own choice, they were not free to marry girls of their own choice. This in other words means that love marriage had no place in the past Paite society. A Paite girl was supposed to marry any boy whom her parents found suitable for her, This sort of rigidity on the part of the parents caused a lot of difficulties to the boys and girls. However, as time went by, the Paite society has been undergoing changes specially as a result of their conversion into Christianity. What was not possible in the past has become possible today. As a result, the man and woman enjoy more freedom as the parents understand their problems in matter of love and marriage. The agreement of the two marrying partners is now treated as basis for making marriage arrangement. Their consent is now the deciding factor in marriage. The boys and girls are now free up to some extent to find their own life partners. In selection his life partner, a Paite boy takes into consideration all qualities like physical appearance, behaviour, willingness and efficiency in all kinds of woman's works and by her skill in social dealing.

We have mentioned that in the past marriage arrangements were made by the parents without the consent of the two marrying partners. However, in the Christianized Paite society, the interest and willingness of the boy and girl is taken as the first step for marriage arrangement. There has been a change in the system due to the following reasons;

In the first place, marriage arranged by parents were many a time proved to be a failure as the couple lack love and understanding between them. This sometimes, led to separation even after having children.

In the second place, when the parents were making marriage arrangement, they did not take into consideration with whom their daughter or son has fallen in love. This led to forcible separation between the two lovers. This many a time caused the lovers to commit suicide. When the parents separated their son or daughter from his or her lover, he or she sometimes, preferred to die rather than to live without his or her sweet-heart.

In the third place, with the advent of Christianity the people began to realize that love between the two marrying partners is most important for marriage arrangement. As a result, the interest and willingness of the two marrying partners have been the sole factor for marriage arrangement.

Proposal for marriage is first made by the boy's side. Parties consisting of the boy's *Inndongta* (family council) are sent to make the marriage proposal. In the past, rice beer was brought to the house of the woman for making marriage proposal. But as drinking beer is against Christian belief, it has been replaced by tea. Now *Inndongta* of the boy served the tea and discussion on the topic will be started forth-with. If both the party agreed to the proposal for the marriage, arrangement for the marriage is made. During the discussion, matters like the price of the bride, date of marriage, etc. come up. Generally, a bride price is two mithuns, it is called a mithun and a calf mithun. In earlier days the value of a mithn was fixed at Rs. 40 and that of a calf was fixed at Rs. 20. The present value of a mithun and a calf is some 30 to 35 thousand and 10 to 15 thousand respectively. The bride price may be paid either in cash or kind at a time or by installment, whichever is convenient on the part of the bridegroom. If the wife dies before making full payment of the bride price by her husband, then the husband is required to make full payment of the bride price. *Thaman* (service price) is settled along with settlement of bride price but it is not a part of the bride price. Rs. 2 is paid as *Thaman*. This *Thaman* is not only service price, but it means much more than that. Though small, it speaks much. The husband in paying this Rs. 2 has the right to bury his wife in the event of her death before paying bride price in full. Hence, it is obligatory on the part of the husband to give this first before marriage has taken place.

Sialkhumsa: When the parents of the bride accepted the bride price from the bridegroom. It is required to kill a pig or a cow as *Sialkhumsa*. Even if *Sialkhumsa* is arranged, it is not necessary to make full payment of bride price by the bridegroom. On the day of making arrangement of *Sialkhumsa*, the household council of the bride and bridegroom shall eat together the feast as an introduction to one another. The parents of the bride shall give a portion of the animal killed to the bridegroom as a formal duty or way of sending in *Seng* (Basket) with cover. However, if the parents of the bride do not accept the bride price from the bridegroom, it is not required for them to arrange *Sialkhumsa*.

Ukan Man: When there are two or more daughters in the same family and if the younger daughter get married before her elder sister gets married, it is called *Ukan* (jumping over her elder sister); the bridegroom has to pay a sum of Rs. 100 or *Puandum* (traditional Paite shawl) to the elder sister of the bride as *Ukan Man*.

In case there is a difference of customs between the bridegroom and the bride, the bride was to follow the customs of the bridegroom; and she shall give up the custom of her parents from the date of marriage, whether the bride price is fully paid or not.

After all the arrangement is made for the marriage, a date is fixed for the marriage and feast is arranged by the parents of the boy in which both side of the family, relatives and friends are invited. In the past, as there was no ritual ceremony to be performed by the religious leader, the marriage was simple. The bride was simply brought to the house of the groom; and then both man and woman lived as husband and wife. However, after conversion into Christianity, the agreement for the marriage is made, it is the duty of the Pastor to make arrangement for the marriage. When the date of marriage arrives the man and woman have to take oath to God before the Pastor that they will never separate unless death separates them. After the oath, the Pastor declares the two as husband and wife. This is the final stage of marriage in Christianized Paite society. The celebration of the marriage is done in the house of the boy. A man and woman however need witness for the marriage. This is how marriage ceremony is done in Christianized Paite society today.

Elopement: This system of marriage is entirely the result of the agreement reached between the two loving partners, and the consent of the parents is not taken into consideration. In fact, about 90% of the cases of elopement are the result of the disagreement on the part of the parents on the question of their son's and daughter's marriage. However, in case of elopement the boy's side has to give Rs. 40 to Rs. 100 to the parents of the girl as a fine for elopement. Once a boy and a girl eloped, it is the duty of the parents to decide and settle the marriage question amicably. However, in certain cases the parents may be too strict and may not allow the marriage even after elopement. This sort of behavior on the part of the parents is not justified by the established norm of the society. If the parents of the boy refuse to accept the woman as their son's wife, they have to pay three mithuns to the parents of the woman.

Dowry (Thuam): When a Paite woman marries a man, she has to take with her a dowry and will be in possession of woman's customary possession like *puan* (cloth), *puanpi* (athick mattress made of rolled cotton), *seng* (basket made of bamboo and cane), *lelpi* (along basket with a cover on it usually made of cane), tu (hoe), *hei* (axe), siambu (weaving loom), a pot of hair oil and a khi (necklace). In modern time, a Paite woman of wealthy family may take with her, almirah, wooden box and many more. There is, however, an effort on the part of the society to make certain limitations on a woman's dowry. In fact, a booklet of *Paite Customary Law* is published so that there can be a uniform dowry system among all Paite-speaking community. It is thought that If the increasing dowry system is unchecked, there will be stratification of the society into two, the rich and poor. However, at this stage, comparing to the Hindu society, dowry system is not a danger to the equality and integrity of the society.

The dowry brought by the woman is the woman's property and is in the possession of the husband, only if, the couples fall on really hard days and the wife agrees to tis realization to keep body and soul together. If the price of the woman is not full paid, the relatives of the woman have the right to claim back the woman's dowry after the death of the woman. But if the price of the woman is full paid, nobody can claim back the dowry.

Divorce: The bond of matrimony amongst the Paite is highly rigid and that divorce between husband and wife is neither suctioned nor allowed by custom except on the following grounds:

Divorce due to unsoundness of body and mind: If one of the married partners is found to be unsound physically or mentally after marriage, and if there is no hope of recovery from the unsoundness of the partner, the sound partner may separate or divorce on payment of 2 mithuns as a relief and the unsound person shall be escorted to his/her parents.

Incapacity to have sexual intercourse: If a husband or wife is incapable to have sexual intercourse with the partner due to physical defects in the body, it is deemed to be cheating of the partner of the marriage, and such person is liable to pay a fine up to 2 mithuns. But if the couple are not expected to produce a child in the absence of physical defects in the body. Either the husband or wife makes negotiation for separation with the partner. In this case, the woman is allowed to retain all her dowry she brought to her husband's house. A woman also may divorce her husband by simply walking out of the house. In this case, the woman is said to be *sumsuah*, which means returning the price which was paid for her. When a woman divorce a man the parents of the woman who received her price either in part or in whole have to return in favour of the husband. The woman is, however, entitled to retain her dowry and actual property acquired before she joined her husband's household.

Adultery: Adultery is considered as the greatest sin between man and woman. The *Paite Customary Law* is highly rigid on the matter of adultery. It is considered as anti social act in the society and the guilty is even punishable by the chief and his council. A woman may commit adultery during the lifetime of her husband and also after the death of her husband. In case a woman commits adultery during the lifetime of her husband, she has to return all the price paid for her, and all her property become the property of her husband. She has no right to claim back her *thuam* (dowry). In case the husband dies earlier, the woman by custom has to remain in the house of her husband at least for three months; and if she happens to marry another man during these three months she is considered as committing adultery; and she is liable to punishment in the same way as committing during the lifetime of her husband.

But if it is the fault of her husband, the wife can take back all her properties which she has brought to her husband at the time of marriage; she need not return the bride price already paid by her husband; the husband has to make full payment if the bride price still lies unpaid.

Fine for Divorce:

If a husband divorces his wife:

a) He shall be liable to pay a fine of one mithun, *sasat* (killing of animal) and *zubel* (apot of rice beer). But instead of rice beer, a pot of tea is accepted today as taking of rice beer is against Christian belief.

   b) He shall return all the properties brought by his wife at the time of marriage which are still available at the time of separation.

   c) He shall not be entitled to receive back the bride price already paid to the parents of the wife.

If the wife separates her husband:

   a) She has to refund in cash or in kind all the bride price paid by her husband to her parents.

   b) She shall not be entitled to receive back any property brought to her husband at the time of marriage except her own wearing's.

   c) She shall not have any claim over her children.

Mutual Consent: If there is a separation between a husband and a wife on mutual agreement, it is called *kipha khen*.

Widow Remarriage: There is no established rule prohibiting the widow remarrying. But if the widow had already a son with her deceased husband, it is always considered proper on the part of the widow to remain unmarried and look after her son and his interest. However, no one can force her to remain unmarried; and it is entirely in her own interest that she remains unmarried. In case a widow remarried, her children are looked after by the nearest relatives of her deceased husband.

CHAPTER III

RELIGIOUS BELIEF OF THE PAITE: PAST AND PRESENT

1. THE CONCEPT OF ANIMISM:

In the Imperial Gazetteer of India 1907-09 Rinsley describes the idea of animism current at that time as follows:

"It conceive of man as passing through life surrounded by a ghostly company of power elements, tendencies, mostly impersonal in this character, shapeless phantosm of which no image can be made and no definite idea can be formed. Some of these have departments or spheres of influence of their own. One presides over cholera, another over smallpox, another over cattle disease, some dwell in rock, another haunt trees, another again are associated with rivers, whirlpools, waterfalls, or strange pools hidden in the depth of the hills. All of them acquired to be diligently propitiated by reasons of the ill which proceed from them, and usually the land of the village provides the means for their propitiation".

The traditional religion of the Paites is said to be 'animism'. They worshipped certain natural objects like rocks, rivers, trees, streams, springs, mountains, etc. They believed that different kinds of spirits are dwelling in these natural objects and could do harm to human being, if not propitiated by making sacrifices. The Paites, therefore, worshipped those spirits out of fear of their wrath. They attributed all kinds of illness to the act of these evil spirits. The Paites at the same time believe in the existence of a High God, the Creator of heaven and Earth, and believed that the High God is in heaven, and had left the evil spirits to take care of the people. Most of the religious sacrifices are directed towards the propitiation of the evil spirits who are supposed to be the cause of their fortune and misfortune. The religious sacrifice is performed only by the village priest who is supposed to know what type of sacrifice would be necessary for curing the patient. The village priest (*Siampu*) is expected to know what type of sacrifice would be essential by touching the pulse of the patient, by looking at the patient and asking the patient a few questions regarding how and when he got the illness.

When the priest could identify the exact cause of the illness, he demanded the animal to be sacrificed for appeasing the spirit. If a fowl is deemed sufficient for offering to the evil spirit causing the illness, the *Siampu* kills the fowl, roasts it and eats on the spot pointed out by the patient as the place where he was first taken ill, throw what he cannot eat as an offering to the jungle and goes home. If the animal selected for offering is big animal like a pig or a dog, the priest takes with him some helpers.

We have mentioned earlier that there are different kinds of spirits dwelling in wood, rock, spring, etc, of all the spirits, those spirits dwelling in deep woods, caves and salt spring are the most dangerous. They are attributed to all kinds of illnesses, epidemics and other natural calamities like hail-storm, etc. If a person is sick, the priest would take the patient to such a place and offer a sacrifice of fowl or goat or pig as may be deemed necessary by the priest. It is considered that it is unlucky to jhum the land nearby such spots, and if a man at all decided to cultivate the land nearby such a place, he must first offer sacrifice to the spirit supposed to be dwelling in the spot.

2. EXISTENCE OF DIFFERENT KINDS OF EVIL SPIRITS:

Besides evil spirits mentioned above, there are also other kinds of demons which they called *Gamhuai* and which they believed to be dwelling in a thick wood and could be seen with naked eyes. There are some people who had reported that they had seen demons while hunting, fishing, trapping, etc. The author himself was told by Mr.Hawlkhai Guite of Zawllian village, Karbi-Anglong district, that he had seen a huge demon while he was hunting for a bear. He said that a very huge demon with a hairy body had step over him while he was lying on the ground in the jungle waiting for the coming of the bear. He said that the demon he had seen was as tall as tree. Demons or what the Paites called *Gamhuai* are superhuman beings, living in the forest which can make their appearance in different forms. The demons are much feared by the people as they can even have physical confrontation with man.

The Paites also believed in the existence of fairy which they called dawi or Lasi, and which are not cruel like other evil spirits. It is said that Lasi are spirits which lived in the forest and rocky montain, and they can fall in love with human being. If a maiden fairy falls in love with a man, the man is blessed with all kinds of wealth. If the man is a sportsman, he would be blessed to kill any kinds of animal he wanted to kill. If he happened to be cultivator, then he would be blessed to have a good harvest. The fairies are not cruel like other spirit, but are the protector of the people. The Paites still believe in the existence of this kind of evil spirit. It is the belief of the people that the fairies can no more be seen due to the conversion of the people into Christianity.

As mentioned earlier, though the Paites believe in the existence of different kinds of evil spirits which always caused harm and illness to people, they also believe in the existence of a High God or supreme God, who is the Creator of all things. The High God is omnipotent and benevolent to the people. Next to the High God, there is another benevolent God called *Lungzai*. Both the High God and the *Lungzai* dwell in heaven. Both the High God and *Lungzai* are appeased and worshipped by making various sacrifices, evil spirits which are supposed to be dwelling in the stream, spring, rocky mountain, forest, etc. to take care of human being.

3. THE CONCEPT OF LIFE AFTER DEATH:

The Paites believed in the existence of life after death. But the nature and condition of life after death is not well defined. The condition and nature of life after death can be seen in the Paite folktales, dreams and some sort of revelation. The story of Ngambawm and Khupching revealed the nature of life after death. The story goes-once upon a time there was a boy called, Ngambawm.

He falls in love with a beautiful girl called, Khupching. They loved each other very much. But, as Ngambawm belonged to a very poor family, the parents of Khupching did not want Ngambawm to be the husband of their daughter and do everything they could to separate them. In the meantime, the girl Khupching became ill and consequently died. On hearing the news of the death of his beloved, he was sad, and so sad that being unable to bear the pain of his lonely heart, died. After his death he met Khupching, his beloved at the abode of the deads '*Misikhua*' and found her lean and thin. He asked his beloved, why was she so lean and thin. Khupching, his beloved replies, 'she was lean and thin because there was nothing to eat there at *Misikhua* (abode of the deads)'.

From above legendary tale, of the Paites, we are able to make an idea that there exists life after death, and the nature of life after death is not better than lilfe of the livings on the earth. Khupching told Ngambawm that she was so thin as there was nothing to eat there in the abode of the deads. The reply she has given to Ngambawm suggests that life in the abode of the deads is hard and difficult. Therefore, we come to establish that the Paites believe in the existence of life after death and the condition of life there, was not better than life on the abode of the livings.

The Paites believe that when a person dies, his soul has to go to the abode of the deads. They also believe that life after death is in the form of invisible spirits. People rejoin their clansmen in the abode of the deads if they know their clan songs. A man who had killed more number of wild animals, and a man who had slained a good number of enemies and thrown the feast called '*Thangsuah*' thereby, satisfying their ancestors, had easy access to the land of the deads. It is believed that the soul of man has to cross a river called '*Gusun*' then it goes through *Nahzang* (a flat place) where they will be waiting for one another and beyond, there is a high mountain called *Teutevum*.

Here, in *Teutevum*, *Sahnu* and *Pu Pawl* will be blocking the road to the abode of the deads. In order to escape from them, the spirit of the deads has to give them, the liver of the animal killed by his family at the time of his death. But if the man happened to kill big animals like tiger, elephant, bear, etc. during his lifetime, he would ride on the spirit of the animals killed and that *Sahnu* and *Pu Pawl* would not dare to block him. It is also believed that the spirit of the killed animals and enemies serve them and attend to their needs in the abode of the deads. Beyond the place where *Sahnu* and *Pu Pawl* take their position, there is a crystal clear water called *Luangzuan Damtui* flowing. The spirits of the deads drink the water and forget the longing for the living left behind. After drinking this water, the soul directly reaches the abode of the deads and join their ancestors. The story also suggested that even animals have spirits.

As mentioned earlier, the Paites did not have a clear picture of life after death. But it is believed that life after there could be in the form of invisible spirit, which sometimes appears in a visible physical form. This belief is supported by the story of Khupching and Ngambawm which revealed that life in the abode of the deads is not free from want as the spirit of Khupching was in want of things to eat.

4. ANCESTOR WORSHIP:

Ancestor worship is performed by every household among the Paites. The eldest male in the lineage officiates the rite of ancestor worship. Ancestor worship is done to appease spirit of the ancestors to get their blessings. It is a sacred function which is performed usually inside the house. The meat of the sacrificed animal is cooked in the inner side of the house on a specially made fireplace. A son-in-law and his wife are not allowed to cook the meat even if they are ritual cooks ordained by custom and tradition. Only members of the clan and the householders are supposed to cook the meat; women from other clan marrying the householders clan can book the ritual meat as they become a part and parcel of the clan. The married off daughters of the household to other clan cannot be introduced to the ancestors.

As mentioned earlier, the senior most male in the lineage officiates the ritual ceremony of the ancestor worship. He invoked the spirits of the ancestors who are in the land of the dead. He addresses the ancestors first from the remotes ancestor down to the nearest dead ancestor. He called them to see the scene of the ritual ceremony. He asked them to bless all the lineage to be as strong and healthy as the hardest tree called *sesing* (a kind of oak tree) and the hardest bamboo called *gawpi*. Rice beer pots are arranged in a line from the inner side of the house in order of the seniority of the member contributing them. In some cases, the ritual meat is taken on the bed of the parents of the household from one wooden plate by selected representatives of the clan. The household performing the rite is under ritual taboo for six days, and on the seventh day a cleansing rite is performed by the officiating lineage head by killing two fowls. The ritual meat is eaten inside the house. The members of the clan suspected to be possessing evil spirit are not allowed to eat the meat inside the house and ordinary people are given to eat outside the house. A dog is not allowed to enter the house where the ritual meat is being cooked and slices of meat are being offered to the ancestors.

5. KINDS OF RITUAL CEREMONY:

We have mentioned earlier that the Paites attributed all of sickness and natural calamites to the act of evil spirits dwelling in trees, streams, cave, rocks, etc. Therefore, when a person suffers from any kind of illness, the *Siampu* is called for to perform ritual ceremony to appease the evil spirit which is believed to be causing the illness. This ceremony is called *Kithoih*. The priest would identify which spirit is responsible for the illness and perform the ritual ceremony accordingly. The following kinds of ritual ceremonies are usually performed by the priest.

1.   Khawbawl Kithoih (ritual)
2.   Sumtawng Kithoih (ritual)
3.   Nuhpi Kithoih (ritual)
4.   Gampi Kithoih (ritual)
5.   Muallam Kithoih (ritual)
6.   Ui-ha Awh Kithoih (ritual)
7.   Lou Tuibawl Kithoih (ritual)

Khawbawl Kithoih: This ritual ceremony is performed by the village priest for asking to the evil spirit to give the entire village a good harvest, to give good health to the people and to bless the whole villagers with all kinds of fortune. Since this rite is specially meant for the entire village, it is also called *Tangbiakna* which means public worship. The animal needed for such ritual ceremony is a gibbon or black monkey which they called *Zou-ui* or *Saha*. But if black money is not available, dog also can serve the purpose.

In the *Khawbawl* ritual, every household is involved. Each household would prepare the image of a mithun out of mud, which is to be brought to the house of the village chief along with some food. The representatives of each household would meet in the house of the chief, and take all the image and food to the country-yard of the village where the priest would perform the rite. After performing the rite, bunch of leaves would be hanged over the road leading to the village, so that the strangers coming to the village might know that the village had performed *Khawbawl* and avoid entering the village as the village which performed a *Khawbawl*, is not to be visited by any stranger till the completion of 2 to 3 days. During this period, the village is under *Zehsah* which means the village performed *Khawbawl*, and it is unlawful to enter the village. If any stranger happens to enter the village during this period, he would be fined with a mithun.

Sumtawng Ritual: This ritual ceremony is performed by a particular clan among the Paite society who are believed to be the descendants of a legendary orphans, *Liandou* and *Thanghou*. When *Liandou* and *Thanghou* were to be left by their grandmother, she asked them to worship her at *Sumtawng* (the verandah where mortar is kept). After telling this, she disappeared at **Sumtawng**. The ritual ceremony is performed by the lineage of the family for asking comfort and happiness to the spirit of the grandmother of *Liandou* and *Thanghou*. Therefore, it is not in anyway, connected with illness or natural calamities. The animal used for such ritual ceremony is pig. The animal is killed late in the evening, and the meat is ate at night. When the meat is properly cooked, the priest would take pieces of meat and kept at the beneath of the roof over *Sumtawng*. Then only the meat is eaten. After performing *Sumtawng Kithoih* the house is under *Zehsah* which means entering of the house is unlawful.

A bunch of leaves would be hanged in the front wall of the house, so that people would know that the house is under *Zehsah*. If any person entered the house during this period, he would be fined with a mithun and the ritual ceremony performed would have no meaning. However, after four or five days, the priest would take away the bunch of leaves kept in the front wall of the house, and the house would be free from *Zehsah*. After this, the *Sumtawng* ritual is over.

Nuhpi Kithoih: This ritual ceremony is performed by the village priest who is believed to have the knowledge of communication with evil spirit causing various kinds of illnesses. It is meant for curing those people who are today, believed to have been suffering from tuberculosis, typhoid, fever, dysentery, etc. When any person suffered from these kinds of illnesses, the priest is called for to perform ritual ceremony. The priest would ask the patient to abstain from eating meat, specially the meat of mithun for seven days. This is called *Zehthang*, and if the patient happened to break the order of the priest, the ritual ceremony would have no meaning, and ceremony would have to be repeated.

Gampi Kithoih: This ritual ceremony is specially meant for curing those people who are having sudden illness like high temperature. The Paites considered this kind of illness to be the act of evil spirit who burn the forest. It is said that the evil spirit burns the forest, and the heat of the fire caught the patient, thereby, causing illness. The animal used for performing this ritual ceremony is usually a pig of three palms (*Tuk thum*) big and a cock. It is performed at the country yard where the priest slaughtered the animal. After performing this religious rite at the country yard, the priest would tell the patient to abstain from taking certain meats and from doing certain works. The priest would also put a bunch of leaves in the front wall of the patient's house which means that no guest should enter the house for certain period, normally 7 days. If any guest happened to enter during this period, he would be fined. Therefore, no guest should enter the house of the patient during this period which may be 7 days.

Muallam Kithoih: This ritual ceremony has similarity with *Gampi Kithoih*. It is performed mainly for curing those suffering from severe illness. People believed that the patient is caught by the evil spirit called *Gamkha*. The animal killed in *Muallam Kithoih* is pig. Like other ritual ceremony, the priest asked the patient to abstain from eating certain meat for some days, usually 7 days. During those seven days, no stranger is allowed to enter the house of the patient.

Ui-ha Awh Kithoih: The ritual ceremony is purely meant for children. Whenever children are suffering from any illness, this ritual ceremony is performed. In this ritual ceremony the animal to be killed is a dog. A dog will be killed, and its lower jaw teeth should be taken out. This lower jaw will be put in a string, which is put by the child around his neck like necklace. Like any other ritual, the patient is instructed to abstain from eating certain meat and from doing certain work as the priest may consider necessary.

Lou Tuibawl Kithoih: This ritual ceremony is also meant for curing patient who is believed to have caught by the spirit dwelling in the stream near the jhum he cultivates. Here, a fowl is sacrificed at the spot where the patient got ill.

As mentioned earlier, the Paites believe that there exists different kinds of evil spirits, which they believed to be dwelling in thick wood, streams, rocky mountains, etc. They worshipped this evil spirit out of fear of their wrath. They were in the past in constant fear of evil spirits which caused illness, calamities and misfortunes to the people. However, Christianity from the western missionaries entered their land in 1910, and thereafter, many Paites are converted into Christianity. As a result of their conversion into Christianity they are no more in a constant fear of evil spirits. Almost the entire population of the Paites converted into Christianity. We will discuss the details of the coming of Christianity from the West and its impact on the socio-economic and political life of the Paites in the next part of this chapter.

6. THE ADVENT OF CHRISTIANITY:

Following the footsteps of the British imperial army, Rev. Pettigrew of American Baptist Mission landed at Imphal in 1894. His first intention was to work among the Meitei of the Manipur plain areas, but as the Maharaja of Manipur did welcome any Christian missionaries to work among the Meitei, he went to Ukhrul and started working among the Tangkhul Nagas since 1894.

Regarding Chin Hills, Chin Hills fall into the hands of the British in 1896. In 1898 Rev. Arthur Carson and his wife reached Haka to work for the kingdom of God. They were helped by Thra Sam Win, Thra Shwe Fen, Thra Po Ku and Maung Cone. In 1902 Dr. F.H. East reached Chin Hills. After two years of working he was compelled to go back because of ill health. On the 21st December, 1908 Rev. Dr. Cope reached Chin Hills, and in 1910 Dr. J.G.Wood reached Haka in Chin Hills. In Teddim Rev. Dr. Cope and his wife worked for the spread of Christianity while Woodin worked in Haka for the same. In the meantime, two missionaries from American Baptist Mission, Rev. Dr. R.J. Johnson and Rev. F.D. Nelson reached Chin Hills.

Though the Zo Chiefs were against the conversion of their subjects into Christianity, the progress of missionary work was remarkable. Many new convert Christians were tortured and punished, yet many more were converted each year. By now, in Chin Hills of Myanmar, some 95% of the Zo ethnic tribals are Christians professioning different Christian denominations.

In the meantime, Rev. F.W. Savidge and Rev. Lorrain reached Aizawl on the 11th January, 1894 under the sponsorship of Arthington Baptist Mission. As Lushai Hills was already under the British rule, the two Christian missionaries worked under the protection of the Government. On the 1st September, 1897, another missionary Rev. David E. Jones reached Aizawl under the sponsorship of Welsh Mission. He was in fact the first missionary from Welsh Mission. In the following year in1898, another missionary, Rev. Edwin Rowland reached Aizawl. In 1908 two missionaries, Dr. Peter Fraser and Mr. Watkin Roberts of Calvinistic Methodist Mission reached Aizawl. During that time two books from the Bible, St. John and the Acts of Apostles were already translated into Lushai dialect by Dorrain and Savidge. Dr. Fraser and Watkin Roberts bought 104 copies of these books and distributed in Manipur Hill areas bordering Lushai Hills. Mr. Kamkhawlun, Chief of Senvon Village bordering Lushai Hills, got a copy of St. John and was not able to understand what was it. Therefore, he requested them to personally come and explain what was there in the book. The two missionaries were happy with the request of Mr. Kamkhawlun. They went to Senvon village along with Thangkai and Lungpau who were at that time in Aizawl for studies and explained to the people about the Gospel of Christ. The people admired them so much that they requested them to remain in the village. But the two missionaries went back to Aizawl with Mr. Thangkai and Lungpau. On their way to Aizawl, Thangkai and Lungpau were converted into Christianity, and they were the first people to convert into Christianity in Manipur South.

After reaching Aizawl, Dr. Fraser sent the converted natives Savawma, Thangchhingpuia (Taitea) and Vanzika to work as missionaries in Manipur South. They reached Senvon on the 7th May, 1910, and this day is recorded and observed each year as Missionary Day in Manipur South District. They opened a missionary school at Senvon village, and they themselves served as teachers. They started working among the tribes of Manipur South in the face of stiff protest from the chiefs. However, they were successful in converting more and more people. They formed a church Association called, Thado-Kuki Pioneer Mission.

The name of the Mission was changed in the year 1924 from Thado-Kuki Pioneer Mission to North East India General Mission with the aim to widen its scope. By this time the number of Christians in Manipur South had come up to 2,000. As the population of Christian had increased it was found necessary to re-organize the administrative set up of the mission in the following ways:

1. Simsak Biak Presbytery
2. Simkhang Bial Presbytery

3.   Malsak Bial Presbytery

4.   Malkhang Bial Presbytery

5.   Vangai Bial Presbytery

The Simsak Bial Presbytery was constituted mainly for the Paite-speaking community. On the 5th March, 1948 the Simsak Bial Presbytery decided not to join the General Assembly of the N.E.I. G. Mission at Saikot. Accordingly it did so when the General Assembly was held there in 1949, but had the assembly of its own at Kaihlam village the same year. This was the first Christian assembly ever held in the name of Paite. In the following year 1950 its assembly was held at Songtal village in Manipur South, and changed the name Simsak Bial Presbytery to Manipur Christian Convention which was again changed to Evangelical Convention Church in 1973.

The other Presbyteries informed the Home Board in America about the refusal of Simsak Bial Presbytery and Vangai Bial Presbytery to join the Assembly. Mr. F.C. Benson, the General Secretary of the Home Board visited Churachandpur to have a spot inquiry into the matter. The time when F.C. Benson came to Churachandpur coincided with the Manipur Christian Convention assembly at Pearsonmun in Churachnadpur in January 12, 1951, and Benson too joined the assembly. The leaders of the M.C.C. informed Benson about their willingness to directly join the Home Board in America without joining the Assembly of the NEIG Mission. Accordingly, Mr. Benson gave the permission to directly join the Home Board in America. Following this, all the other Presbyteries also wanted to do same, and each joined the Home Board directly.

At present the following church organisations are under the NEIG Mission (now the Evangelical Congregational Church of India since April, 1986):

1.   The Evangelical Convention Church (Paites)

2.   Kuki Christian Association (Kukis)

3.   Manipur Christian Organisation (Vaiphei)

4.   Evangelical Assembly Church (Hmars)

5.   Evangelical Synod Church (Gangtes)

6.   South-East Manipur Anal Christian Association (Anals)

We have seen that Christianity entered among the Paites of Manipur in 1910 and at present almost 100% of the Paites in Manipur are Christians. In 1948 the total number of Christians among the Paite was a little over 2,000; but according to 1986 Evangelical Convention Church census, the number of Christians among the Paite has increased to 31,110, and now in 2012, Christian population of the Paite tribe is over 50, 000 which is same as 99% of the total Paite population.

The above figures include the Paite Christians in Mizoram and Karbi-Anglong of Assam. This figure, however, do not include the Paites belonging to other Church denominations like Lutheran Church. Church of Christ and Seventh-Day Advantist, Etc.

We have just seen that Christianity works among the Paites in particular and among the tribes of Northeast India wonderfully that within a short span, almost the entire population of the Paite community converted into Christianity. Christianity in fact, succeeded among the tribes of Northeast India in general because of the fact that, apart from Biblical stories, the teaching of Christianity, the western social life and ethic of the tribes were identical with their animistic belief. Under such favourable environment, Christianity took its root and spread rapidly with the personal dedication, and philanthropic spirits and works of the Christian missionary.

The other factor responsible for the rapid growth of Christianity among the Paites is the opening of western educational institutions and dispensaries. Prior to the coming of Christian missionaries, the Paites did not know what education is and what its uses are. But the Christian missionaries opened mission schools and sponsored students to study in the schools where they learned western way of life, Christian value and belief. The students were in the beginning animists, but they gradually changed their thought under the influence of missionaries and western education. When going back home from studies, they became missionary in their homes, villages, and areas and thereby

Christianity developed rapidly. However, the basic intention of Christian missionaries was not to educate the people, what they wanted was a workable literacy among the hill men. But Mission schools had become the chief agency for imparting education to the Paites till today. Those who had received education were sent out ot villages to teach as well as to preach the principles and beliefs of Christian religion.

The other factors responsible for the speedy growth of Christianity among the Paites was the humanitarian services rendered to the poor Paites by the Missionaries. The missionary rendered medical services by dispensing medicine to the people. In appreciation to such humanitarian services, many Paites became Christians. Therefore, Christianity had really spread like a wild fire among the Paites.

7. IMPACT OF CHRISTIANITY:

The coming of Christianity in 1910 had brought great changes in the Paite Society. With the coming of Christianity, the Paites ceased to perform their traditional festivals like *Mim Kut, Pawl Kut, Taptal Kut*, etc. They ceased to celebrate *Thangsuah* feast which was considered to be the feast of honour performed only by a well-to-do family. In fact, they had discarded all their traditional way of life, festivals, etc. Though many of their traditional way of living are not contradictory to the Christian belief, the presence of drinking rice beer in the festival is against the teaching of the Bible. The Paites discarded everything that is against Christianity. Christian hymns, western songs and small tea parties replaced their traditional music, war songs and celebration of feast. The bachelors' dormitory system had been stopped. For centuries, the Paites, like any other tribes of Northeast India had been living in a world of their own, leading a traditional life, constantly warring against each other. After their conversion into Christianity wanton killing was realized as a sin in the light of the teaching of Christ, and hostility was replaced by love and understanding. Some of their evil practices like head-hunting and bloody warfare amongst them had virtually ceased.

8. EDUCATION AND LITERATURE:

The Christian missionaries introduced western education among the Paites as a result of which, there are changes in all areas. Before the advent of Christianity, the Paites did not have script; they did not know what education is and what are its importance. But the Christian missionaries brought in the idea of education among them, and many Paites began to learn how to read and write. Not only that, they are also able to publish books in their own language using Roman script having 24 letters as their alphabet since 1903:

a	aw	b	ch	d	e	f	g
ng	h	I	j	k	l	m	n
o	p	r	s	t	u	v	z

Using Roman script mentioned above, they began to publish books, magazine, journal, newspapers etc in their own language. At present, there are more than 750 books published in Paite language. There are also 2 daily newspapers, The Lamka Post and the Manipur Express, each having a circulation of more than 5000 copies, and a number of periodical journals and magazines which includes among other The Lamka Chronicle, Tongluang and Christian Thukizakna.

The Paite language has become the most advanced and most developed tribal dialect in Manipur. In literary production the Paite stands second only to Manipuri. The Board of Secondary Education, Manipur, Council of Higher Secondary Education Manipur and the Manipur University have recognised the Paite language as one of the Major Indian Languages (MIL) for HSLC, Council of Higher Education (Class XII)) and Degree Examinations respectively.

The Christian missionaries, along with the British administrators took a leading part in bringing an end to evil practices among the Paites like head-hunting, making sacrifices to appease evil spirits, waring, etc. by teaching them how to live together in peace and love with other neighbouring tribes. It can also be said that Christianity was in inward mechanism which brought the modernization and westernization in dresses and lifestyle and education. Besides, Christianity also brought social reforms. It was Christianity that brought out the Paites from the thought of seclusion and isolation from which they were suffering for centuries into opening ideas, ideals and civilization of the people of the world.

The missionaries also brought about numerous changes in fundamental constitution of the Paites, in particular and of Mizos/Zomis in general; and improved their lots by translating of Christian hymns and other literary works into Paite and other Mizo/Zomis languages and distributing the evangelical literature and other literature by introducing the Roman script in the absence of their own, by preaching Gospel and church history, political, economic, social and historical ideas of the west, and by establishing schools, hospitals and Churches in order to make the life of the people more orderly, more civilized, more comfortable, more peaceful and more cultured.

Religion:

Before the coming of Christianity among the Paites, the Paites were animists and live in a constant fear of demons and other evil spirits. But with the introduction of Christianity the Paites begun to doubt their animistic belief as a result of which the observance of rigid traditional religious practices and taboos were loosened specially among the educated people. In the Christian community they experienced a loving concern and care which they had not experienced before. They were free from the fear of evil spirits. The Church gathering replaced the traditional festivals. The spread of Christianity also paved the way for moral improvement. The old war songs and traditional love songs were substituted by western hymns. The old religious ceremonies of marriage involving heavy expenses and marriage price systems were not encouraged. Love marriage became a normal practice and marriage has become a sacred ceremony with a deep significance. Divorce is not sanctioned by the Church as marriage according to Christianity means a life long partnership.

Besides, the dead were no longer buried with doubts of future life. They began to experience a new religion which assured them of better life after death. When people received the Gospel of salvation and accepted Jesus Christ as their Lord and Saviour, their lives got changed, morally and spiritually. Therefore, the conversion of Paites into Christianity does away all their evil practices.

9. SOCIO-ECONOMIC LIFE:

The living conditions, the family and the community lives of the Paites were much influenced by Christianity and its teaching. Both through the influence of Christianity and contacts with the western civilization, they built better homes and made modern furniture.

The Paites began to learn the importance of cleanliness from the Christian missionaries. Before the coming of Christianity the Paites did not know holidays. They worked all the seven days of the week. But when Christianity was introduced they have the chance to take rest on Sunday. On Sunday, instead of going to field for work, they go to Church services with their best dresses. They realized that cleanliness is godliness. The teaching of the importance of the purity of heart pre-supposes the purity of the body. As a result, the general standards of sanitation and community health have been improved among the Paites.

The prohibition of drinking wine by the Bible reduced drunkness and constant quarrels and reduced the consumption of corn for making rice beer. Christianity taught the Paites a unique relationship with their neighbours. Inter tribal warfare is replaced by inter-tribal and inter-village marriages. The position of women has been improved in the society in many respects through the teaching of the Bible. Mrs Louise Paw, the one time Secretary of the Myanmar Baptist Convention wrote in 1969 about the overall impact of Christianity on the Chins as a whole. The spirit of Carsons, the Copes, the Straits, the Nelsons, the Johnsons and many others will continue to inspire the present question of Zomi/Chin as the Judsons spirit does the Church of Myanmar. The lay leadership, specially from the rank of the ex-servicemen, is strong. There is also a definite material progress from reports of others who had visited the Chin Hills some time or ten years ago. I had expected to see windowless bamboo juts prapped on stilts, roofed with thatch and black on the inside with smoke. Instead, I saw a sturdy pine woods, fruits and vegetable gardens in the near. Apples, peaches, damsons, oranges are being grown on the increasing scale and have again the ex-servicemen may be credited with bringing new and modern ideas of life into the hills. Many of them served on local official bodies. The government has built some very good schools in all the large towns and villages along with demonstration centre for agriculture and animal husbandry. There is much to be done, but there is definite progress in all aspects of life.

10. SOCIAL CUSTOMS AND CULTURE:

Taylor says "Culture or civilization is that complex whole which includes knowledge, belief, art, moral, law, customs, and any other capabilities and habits acquired by man as a member of society". Kroeber is of the opinion that culture is "that which the human species has and other social agencies lack. This would include speech, knowledge, beliefs, customs, arts, technologies, ideas and rules". Thus culture embraces a wide range of subjects and not merely dance and music.

Christianity has a far reaching impact on the culture and customs of not only of the Paites, but all the Mizos/Zomis. For the Paites and other Mizos/Zomis tribes, participation in the traditional dancing and singing is a taboo. Even in the remotest villages the traditional festivals like *Khawdou*, *Sialsawm* etc. are no more observed and celebrated throughout the land of the Mizos/Zomis tribes.

Thus it was Christianity which has really transformed the Paite society into a modern society. It brought changes in the general outlook of the people who are now able to enter into the world of competition. It was Christianity which brought the ignorant Paites to the path of knowledge and wisdom resulting in more comfortable and more meaningful living. Had not the Christianity entered among the Paites they would have still been in the world of seclusion and isolation constantly fearing the wrath of evil spirits. But now, with the dawn of Christianity, they need not be in a constant fear of such evil spirits.

Though there are many positive impact of Christianity, there are also at the same time negative impact too. There are some circle among the Piates who feel that Christianity had destroyed the rich culture and tradition of the people. They said that Christianity destroyed the romance of communal life by forbidding the joy of feasting at the time of success in hunting and harvesting. They also claim that the bachelors' dormitory system, which if still continued can serve as an impartant centre for the village had been discarded with the advice of missionaries. However, it should be noted that those who are in favour of the continuation of traditional custom and culture are not against Christianity. What they feel is that traditional custom can be modified in accordance with Christian beliefs and principles. For instance *Khawdou*, one of the traditional festivals of the Paites can be observed by replacing the role of zu rice beer by tea. In this way, most of the feasts and festivals of the Paites can be modified so as to accord with Christianity.

On the other hand, there are some other circle among the Paites who are of the opinion that with the progress of mankind people of all corners of the world had to live according to the change of time. In this changing process every social system also undergo certain changes. In such changing situation, the Paites must also change some of their traditional culture and way of living so as to a tune with the changing world. They feel that what was practicable in the past may not be practicable today, and what is practicable today may not be practicable tomorrow. Therefore, they are of the opinion that the Paites also should not be too rigid and inflexible about their culture and tradition. In the past, those who are able to kill ferocious animals like tiger and those who are able to take the heads of enemy are honoured and respected in the society. But now, those who are able to come up with flying colour in various examinations are honoured and respected. Therefore, the whole system had totally changed, and to meet this changing system, we have to change our outlook, our social system, our culture and tradition.

Domestic Life:

The influence of Christianity on the life of the Paite over the seventy-five years is of tremendous worth. Christianity brings a broader concept and philosophy of life to the community. The gospel of Jesus Christ since its coming in 1910 has been a great force affecting the life of the Paite for the better.

Christianity has given a new outlook to life as a whole. The effectiveness of the Gospel as a life – changing force is seen in the status of women who previously did not hold the high level of esteem which they enjoy today. Now they are treated as equal to men as "capable of sharing all man's intellectual, social, emotional and physical aspects, a 'mirror' image with which man could find true communion" for there is neither male nor female in Christ.

In the Paite family of the pre-Christian culture, the husband took pride in divorce and then married another. Such an act was looked upon, by men, as a sign of superiority and popularity in society. Wives were considered the property of their husbands. Great changes were noticed in the family when Christ came into the hearts of a couple, and brought the spirit of Christian Marriage. They could both appreciate their respective positions in the light of the Gospel and, as such, their new life became richer and more meaningful in care of family life and in social life as well.

There is now a shared Christian life; a Christian love expressed together and a Lord served together.

Oh, the love that sought me:

Oh, the blood that bought me:

Oh, the grace thaqt brought me to the fold;

It is a love which does not regard the wife, consciously or unconsciously, as simply the one who cooks his meals, washes his clothes, cleans his house and brings up his children for the whole relationship is in the Lord.

Mutual Help:

In the pre-Christian life of the Paite, whenever the husband was doing some kind of work which was supposed to be that of the housewife, he was often called, thai neh-lou, a henpecked husband, which is a derogatory term in that society. But under the influence of Christianity, husbands who help in household chores do not consider this below their dignity. Christianity taught the Paite to realize that Christian life in one of its important facets means corporate living, corporate search and corporate discovery.

One notices a difference between the life of children who have been brought up in a Christian home and those from a Christless background. The love for ungodly stories or legends in the unChristian home is replaced by life-moulding Bible stories in the Christian home. The respect they have for their parents and superiors is rooted in the Bible, accompanied by a God-fearing attitude.

Right Relations:

By becoming Christian, an invisible line of honour that exists between husband and wife, between parents and children, between sons and daughters, between family and neighbours become more marked and meaningful in Paite Christian life compared to what had been in their pre-Christian life. Thus, "the rights of each are the obligations of the other". Now the joy they experience is becoming more enhanced and deepened depending upon right relationships with people.

A Lasting Joy:

It is common knowledge that doing our part in life makes us happy. But the Paite Christians experienced that a Christian spirit and sacrifice makes us more joyful. By playing their part in the cause of Christ, they receive joy that lasts a lifetime, not a joy that depends on outside things but on what cannot be taken away like our health, money, belongings and good times.

Sanitation:

Since the Gospel has enlightened the hearts of the Paite the remarkable social institution, *sawm* or *ham*, gradually disappeared. Every man preferred to sleep at his own house. One may find such change more healthy than many people sleeping together at one and the same place where certain diseases can easily be communicated.

With the coming of the Gospel of salvation a Mother's chewing of food for their babies and unhealthy mouth-to-mouth feeding was replaced by special cooking for babies and spoonfeeding. The Practice of having a latrine attached to the house and letting human refuse freely fall for pigs, dogs, and chicken in the open ground below was stopped. A separate construction at some distance from the house with a simple septic tank is preferred now. One canot but take such a complete change in the Paite family life as coming from above.

When the Paite came under the influence of Christianity, they began to realize the importance of personal cleanliness and community health. Teaching the importance of purity of heart finally bought forth cleanliness of body. Consequently the standard of sanitation of the community has been greatly improved. "Just as Jesus found it necessary to sweep the money-changers from the temple porch, so we ourselves need a lot of house-cleaning".

House Building:

Compared to patterns of older houses which are dark, stuffy and unwholesome with no ventilation, houses built after Christianisation have several windows. Although there is no change in shape of the building, the traditional pattern has been replaced in several villages by modern material such as tin C.I. sheet roofs, etc., with modern furniture. A chicken coop is built near the house and some even have pigpens.

On Religious Life:

As seen earlier the Paite who believed God to be like some cruel and indifferent monster inflicting punishment upon them through the devil were dominated and oppressed by demons and evil spirits until Christianity came to them. With the coming of faith people who worshipped the devil became doubtful of their pagan beliefs and became receptive to the preached Gospel and put away their former erroneous beliefs.

Better Practice:

The practice of food offering to the spirits of their dead which they believed remained one full moon in the house, was totally given up ever since they understood that human spirits do not roam the earth. Killing of mithun, fowls, goats and pigs at burial ceremony on the belief that the spirits of these animals accompany the dead on the way to *pialgal* also stopped. Christians now condole with the family of the dead person by giving firewood, clothing, rice, sugar, salt and money, according to the ability of the mourners. Voluntary grave-digging by young adults took the place of paid labourers.

The Gospel helped to eliminate evil practices; it condemned magic, sorcery and witchcraft. It also produced Christians who were truly concerned with the welfare of others, with their spiritual and physical lives. In doing so, Christians produced harmony and fellowship where it previously did not exist.

This is true with Paite Christians. Christianity now freed the Paite from their ageold spiritual bondage. The Gospel of Christian has created a cultural revolution.

Worship in Ones Culture:

The Paite Christians of a younger generation were brought up with inspiring songs and hymns translated from English. Along with this, other hymns based on Christian experience composed by native Christians with indigenous tunes are highly favoured. The Paite are known for their love of lyrical poems. Hymns and songs play important parts in their life and worship. The former group is used mostly in formal worship while the latter for individual and group devotions and fellowship, and condolence or celebration in private homes and chapels. Western Christian hymns and tunes and music have been firmly rooted in this area and it is believed they will stay. There is always the danger of identifying western culture with Christianity. Paite culture is a fertile soil for the Gospel.

Now hunting and fishing for human souls has taken the place of intervillage feuds and fighting for superiority. Scriptural principles now guide in settling disputes amicably. The Paite have become new creatures and realize what is meant by the term Christian:

A mind through which Christ thinks;

A voice through which Christ speaks;

A heart through which Christ loves;

A hand though which Christ helps;

Scott and Coote reflect this, " it was impossible to be a Christian and live as one had formerly lived. The new faith led to a new way of life". These days, bells of devotion service ring before sunrise in every church on every Sunday, wherever there is an Evangelical Convention Church.

The spread of the Gospel of salvation paved the way for moral enlightenment. The old patriotic songs and traditional love songs based on Paite social life are now replaced by western tunes, hymns with indigenous ones as well. As such, traditional dancing and *Kilangseh*, responsive singing, accompanied by rice beer has become incompatible with their new found faith.

On Socio- Economic Life:

Socio-economic life of the Paite community has been greatly influenced by Christianity resulting in leading a better way of life. Drunkenness that was widely prevalent in pagan life and which consequently produced constant quarrels vanished altogether as a result of the prohibition of *zu* drinking by the church. Hence a considerable amount of rice and corn consumed every year in *zu* production has now turned into regular food for the family.

A Day of Rest:

In the old way of life, the Paite did not have a holiday. Their everyday life was occupied with work from sunrise to sunset, except in the case of either sickness or observance of certain festivals. With the coming of the Gospel, the church was organized and Christians observed one day of rest in a week, Sunday, by attending church services. Even if they spent weekdays and nights in the field, they never failed to come home on Saturdays for Sunday rest and services.

The old belief that not working on Sundays meant poverty was now proven wrong for Christians wore better clothes and ate better food, enjoying health through God's blessing.

It was the season of protecting ripened grain in the fields from birds and monkeys. It was reported that a farmer who had been protecting his field came home on Sunday leavinghis field open to birds, monkeys and animals. But when going back to his field on Monday he found to his amazement that it was completely safe on that Sunday from birds and animals.

With More Clothing:

In the old way, Paite women spent their evenings in spinning cotton for clothing far into the night, not to mention the other work that occupied their entire day. Even then people hardly had enough clothing. Because of the Christian influence, the villagers were found with more clothing in spite of less labour in weaving clothing. Every Christian now has spare clothing.

The *meleng* in washing clothes was replaced by factory soap.

Application of the Philosophy of Paul:

Smoking has been almost inherent in the blood of the Paite from generation to generation. A smoking-pipe, made of bamboo, was replaced by cigrattes rolled themselves with homegrown tobacco in small pieces of old newspapers. By this time, habitual practices such as smoking and *buktui* are gradually given up by Christians with reference to the philosophy of the Apostle Paul on Christian life as recorded in 1 Corinthians 8.8-13 and 10.23-24.

In pre-Christian culture, the conversation between women filling water or collecting firewood was mainly ill on someboy, but the conversation among Christians now turns to the Gospel of Jesus Christ.

Steward of Life and Time:

Being Christians the Paite could put themselves at the disposal and call of the Creator. Their Knowledge of life, which is from the Scriptures, is brought home by Dr. Cook:

When man is given life, it is in the form of a loan.

Our lives do not belong to us. The created man is a steward of God.

We are answerable and accountable to God for life itself and how we use that life. We are not free to return the loan whenever we feel like it.

In line with the challenge of Paul to Christians to redeem time because the days are evil, the Paite Christians are convinced they must make best use of the time that God has allotted:

I have only just a minute,

Only sixty seconds in it.

Forced upon me – can't refuse it.

But it's up to me to use it.

I must suffer if I lose it.

Give account if I abuse it.

Just a tiny little minute,

But eternity is in it.

On Social Customs:

Christianity has a far-reaching influence on Paite customs. Community festivals and ceremonies like *Sawmzunek*, *Khawdou*, *Khuai-aih*, *Sa-aih*, *Ton*. Which were accompanied by considerable beer-drinking were now replaced by Christian celebrations, Christmas, New Year's Day, Good Friday and Easter Sunday, and Thanksgiving Day, with tea-drinking.

The total disappearance of animal sacrifices which consumed a considerable portion of all the earnings of the people, several superstitious festivals and ceremonies which sucked material possessions promoted the economic growth of the Paite. "Belief in Christ does not eradicate all other powers (of culture) rather it places him above all powers".

Burial Rituals:

Grave digging by about eight men of family council was replaced by free voluntary labour by men over fifteen as a social obligation and a Christian privilege. A priest who consecrated gravesites in pre-Christian life is now unheard of. The dead are buried either by a pastor or an ordained elder, with no doubt of a future life, and with a comforting message from Scriptures and prayer in the presence of the church congregation.

As soon as burial is over a cupful of clean rice and three sticks of firewood are collected from each house which is a help to the bereaved family.

Hanmung, Burial Pole:

This part of the old way of life is replaced by a wooden cross epitaph. After sometime, a memorial stone is erected ont the tomb.

The dead are mourned for at least three nights singing together; however the duration of this varies from village to village. On the first night boys and girls sang through out the whole night. During mourning, boys and girls are assigned different tasks, such as carrying water and cooking a meal for the bereaved. "Christ has power to transform cultures and social orders".

Haithak-lop, Thanksgiving:

This new festival was brought by Christianity which was never celebrated before. It is observed in August. Agricultural produce, like cucumbers, melons, watermelons, etc. are collected. A thanksgiving service is held in church. After service, those fruits were distributed among those who sang together, *lengkhawm*, in praise of God for His blessing.

Witnessing:

What Robert E.Speer wrote about the Gospel in 1900, "whenever it goes, it plants in communities of men forces that create new social combinations" is true in the life of Paite. Being Christian they have come to realize that what Christ does in them and for them is something that others are bound to know and not kept to themselves; they ought to let others know about it for the glory of God.

Some portion of Scripture translated into Paite before World War II went a long way in helping them to edify them, foor them firmly in their faith and religious life. Today the Paite, young and old, are actively engaged in witnessing the immeasurable love of God by conducting Gospel Crusades, organizing camps for all ages, and revival meetings as well, sending gospel teams and even by broadcasting the Gospel of salvation through the air. The reality of Paite Christianity is best proved by the fact that they help others to be Christians in obedience to Christ. "When a person is saved, God gives him a knower to know with" (Paul Rader).

On Moral Life:

Moral life of the transformed Paite is, in short, contained in what the Apostle Paul, who was transformed from Saul of Tarsus, said "Christ lives in me" (Gal. 20.20). In a new life in Christ, the following worthwhile moral life marks are typical to the Paite:

1. "The man who loves needs no law to impel him to action which works on both sides of the moral line. The man who lives right and righteously will do what is right, law or no law, while the man who loves wrong will do wrong in spite of all law".

2. The Paite Christians have come to know more of that self-respect or self-knowledge which comes from the shining of God's light makes one safe and healthy.

3. In the face of problems the Christians are able to see the bright side of things. They do not believe bad stories about other people, instead they try to think the best of everyone.

4. Once an issue is settled, they unite in a common goal that is worthy of Christ's cause.

5. They use the Bible in their decision-making of moral questions. The Bible is a source of moral principles.

6. Love and respect become fundamental in every discussion. As against the idea of non-Christians they came to knw that the Christian goal is not victory for the other side in

a church matter, but finding God's will and unity for all in an issue.

7. They experience preaching of the Gospel always divides: unsanctified associations and doubtful practices have to go; wherever Christ is, there the dividing process goes on dividing good from evil, the holy from the unholy, the spiritual from the carnal. Moreover, Christian life involves obedience, an expression of faith, which is seen in every walk of life, in every area of life and so affects characters, conduct, career-positively, not just negatively.

8. They come to realize that prayer is a life-line between God and Christians which differentiates them from the non-Christian. There is a restraining influence upon evil which finds expression politically, personally, socially, morally and spiritually.

9. In building their characters, the Paite Christians found life to be creative (Gen.1.28); selective (Mat.7.24-25) and decisive (Mat.7.26-27).

10. As a result of the Christian influence they are guided by Christian fellowship which involves the basic elements such as loving (Jn. 13.34-35); caring (1 Cor. 12.25-26, Gal. 6.2); forgiving (Eph. 4.32); forbearing (Eph.4.2); submitting (Eph. 5.21-22; Heb.13.17; Rom. 12.10; Phil. 2.3); communicating (admonition, Rom. 15.14); comfort (1Thes. 4.18); encouragement (Jam.3) and disciplining.

On Literacy:

The Paite had no written literature in their language until the advent of Christianity in Manipur except Paite Sintung (the Paite Primer) co-authored by David E.Jones and T.Vialphung. The introduction of written language in the Roman Script was a great factor in the spread of Christianity through literature.

The important of literature was realized early. Boys and girls were taught how to read and write by beginning with the alphabet. This was at Sunday School or informally at home. One or two slates given by missionaries and brought from Aizawl were used by learners to practice writing. They manufactured slate pencils from stones brought from the river. Even grownups learned to write in the evenings by firelight. One man printed a few lines or letters and passed the slate to his friends sitting beside him and so they began to learn to write.

On Self-Help:

Christianity gave the early Paite Christians a sense of responsibility. They were aware of the necessity to buy basic requirements for the church not available in their areas such as kerosene oil, lamps, etc. Hence they were instructed to contribute whatever they could for upkeep of the church. The menfolk were encouraged to produce handiwork materials in the areas each were skilled in while the womenfolk contributed firewood. Women often brought one stick each when attending Sunday service, both morning and evening. These contributions were sold for money which went a long way to meeting the basic needs of the church. One hundred sticks were bought for one rupee; these days one rupee fetches three sticks.

"The Principal means by which the missions and churches influenced society can be categorized as-

1. The Gospel and new life-style.

2. Humanitarian service

3. Literature and

4. Education.

Culture Retained:

1. The traditional way of cultivation has been largely retained. No food habit is changed.

2. Kinship systems are not touched, such as taking mate, formation of household council, *innsungta.*

3. Brideprice is retained with no fixed rate. With this *moutam* and *sialkhumsa,* are also retained.

4. *Tou-sa* is retained.

5. Killing of domesticated animals as *langkhet* ritual is replaced by tea as a Christian practice.

What Joshua Daimol wrote about culture and Christianity is found meaningful in the changed Paite lifestyle:

The death of Christ has redeemed all things, including our cultural heritage. We are saved by Christ in a given culture. When we give our lives to Christ as his servants we also offer to him our cultural heritage. Our lives and our culture come under Christ's direct lordship. Christ as Lord of our lives and cultures is responsible for what we ought to keep and what we ought to put away.

Prof. Roy expressed what Christianity has been in the life of the people, including the Paite, in the Northeast India:

Christianity, as it has been preached by the European and American missionaries, has succeeded in modernizing the tribal people of Manipur. Indeed it has unlocked and opened up the closed doors of those primitive villages to the light of the modern world. In promoting the modern education, reforming the social ills and curing diseases, the helping hand of those philanthrophic missions are always there. Christianity has not only brought these hill-men from darkness to light but also has earned for them prestige and regard from others which they never had before.

Thus, from the above discussion we came to the conclusion that in spite of various criticisms against Christianity, it is understood that it was Christianity and Christian missionaries who brought in Christianity that made all ignorant Paite masses a civilized and cultured men.

CHAPTER IV

Social Institution

1. INTRODUCTION:

Man has a natural social instinct and is referred to as social animal. This social instinct of man is natural because man has natural needs which could be satisfied only as a member of social institutions. Man needs food, clothes and shelters among others, for his survival and sustenances. A man who lives in isolation without the company of others, is either a beast or a deadman. Therefore, social institutions are a basic necessary and inevitable for human survival. Family, consisting of man woman and Children, is the first and smallest unit of social institutions, and all other social and political institutions are the product of family. A member of families together, formed a village and society, and a many villages together formed state or political institution. Therefore, the basis of all social institutions, including political institution is man's natural social instinct.

2. INSTITUTION OF FAMILY:

Like in any other society, family is the smallest unit of social institutions among the Paite tribe. They follow the patriarchal system in which the father is the head of the family. He is the chief administrator and his words are heard and obey by all other members of the family. However, if the grandfather is alive, he is respected even by the father. The father represents the family in all matters effecting the family. As a head of the family, the father shoulder all responsibilities for the well-being of the family including social and economic well-beings. He has to see that sufficient food grains and other necessity of life are stored for the year. He led other members of the family in all day to day works and has to train younger male members of the family in works relating to economic activities., while the mother train the female members in both domestic and jhum works.

The role of the mother is no less important in the family life of the Paites. While doing all other jhum works, except clearing the jhum site, the mother has as her primary duty to keep the family in order. By looking after the youngones of the family. She has to keep sufficient fire-wood stock for the year, keep the food grain ready for consumption each day, has to do all kitchen works of the family. She is assisted in her domestic works by female members of the family. It is the mother who makes all the clothing needs of the family. The mother is expected to have the expertise in traditional handlooms, right from cultivation of cotton upto the stage when raw cotton is put in a finished form for clothing. It is the mother who has to train her daughters in all social dealings. She too has much in matter of marriage of the sons and daughters of the family.

3. BEH LEH PHUNG (CLANS AND SUB-CLANS):

The division of the Paites into several clans and sub-clans is called *beh leh phung*. These clans and sub-clans are the product of family expansion. The origin of the clan is, therefore, family and the name of the clan is usually taken from the name of the head of the family from which the clan originated. For instance, the Guite clan, the dominant clan of the Paites is believed to have originated form a man called Guite. Since all the Paite clans and sub-clans are the product of family expansion, all separate clans regard themselves as of the same family. Whenever a family of a particular clan is having household functions like marriage ceremony, death ceremony, etc. other members of the same clans are expected to take the initiative. If a person of the Guite clan is killed by a man belonging to another clan, it is the responsibility of the other members of the Guite clans to take revenge for the killed. Therefore, the Paites belonging to the same clan share happiness and sorrow together. However, within the same clan, there can be smaller sub-clans. For instance, within the Thawmte clan of the Paites there are group of Thawmte- Thawm-puang sub-clan. Likewise within the Guite clan, there are a group of families belonging to Guite Mangzo. This means that the various clans of the Paite tribe are further sub-divided into smaller sub-clans. Though the Paites belonging to the same clan considered themselves to be of the same family, they do not necessarily live in a group; but scattered among the other clans. Therefore, the various clans of the Paites live together in a village. For instance, the Mimbung village in Mizoram, bordering Manipur consists of almost all the clans of the Paites. The Paites believed that even after death, a person of a particular clan would join his own clan even in the abode of the dead. This means that when a person belonging to a particular clan dies he would join his fellow clansmen in the abode of the dead. But for joining his own clan at the abode of the dead one must know his clan song as all the clans have each of their clan song.

Some clans of the Paites are also found among the other tribes of the Mizos/Zomis ethnic group. For instance, the Valte clan of the Paite tribe are also found among the Hmar and Lushai tribes with slight variation in spelling. The Lushai and the Hmar put 'r' in place of 'l' and thus *Varte* in place of *Valte*.

Likewise, there are also a group of people among the Kukis belonging to Guite clan. This is a clear proof of the fact that all the tribes belonging to Mizos/Zomis sub-nation belonging to the same origin.

We have mentioned that the Paites are divided into several clans and sub-clans. Paite, in fact, is the result of the combination of several innumerable clans and sub-clans of which some are as follows:

1. Guite	2. Phuaizang	3. Sianthuam
4. Munsong	5. Hiangzung	6. Thangpum
7. Thawmte	8. Hauzel	9. Mangzou
10. Haulai	11. Kullai	12. Leivang
13. Sona	14. Biangtung	15. Khumlai
16. Thansing	17. Tunglut	18. Totak
19. Dousel	20. Valte	21. Vualnam
22. Tombing	23. Hangzou	24. Hanghal

25. Khuptong	26. Khuphil	27. Zalut
28. Tonsing	29. Hatzaw	30. Hatlang
31. Samte	32. Phaipi	33. Langel
34. Nunthuk	35. Chilthat	36. Laingek
37. Songput	38. Tangpua	39. Buansing
40. Naulak	41. Munluah	42. Vangteh
43. Mangte	44. Soute	45. Suante
46. Phualte	47. Hangtal	48. Insun
49. Vangoh	50. Hilsia	51. Vualzong
52. Bawngmei	53. Sumai	54. Kipging
55. Douthuk	56. Simhang	57. Matvung
58. Luisuk	59. Elthuam	60. Luhsong
61. Zilom	62. Kimlou	63. Ellu
64. Tongluai	65. Lethil	66. Sukte
67. Hausing	68. Tungdim	69. Neihguk
70. Suantak	71. Sangen	72. Akmei
73. Doungel		

4. INSTITUTION OF BACHELORS DORMITORY SAWM):

Bachelors' Dormitory is a social institution that was in existence not only among the Paites, but also it has existed among different tribes of North-East India. The Institution and its functions being the same, different tribes had given different names to the institution. The Tangkhul (Nagas) called it, Longshim, the Angami Nagas, Kichukir and the Ao Nagas, Aviju. Among the Zo ethnic families, the Lushai and the Dapzal Paites called, it 'Zawlbuk' while Lamzang Paites refered to it as, 'Sawm' or 'Ham'.

The origin of Bachelors' dormitory (Sawm/Ham) could be traced back to the time when the Paites, like any other tribes were in a state of constant and perpetual war. The creation of such a social institution was necessitated by the need for defending, the village from sudden and surprise enemy attack, which usually happened at night. In order that male Bachelor members of the village, on whom the safety and security of the village rests, slept at night in a common dormitory, usually built at the centre of the village. It is basically a sleeping place for all male bachelor members of the village, so that they could be in a state of ever-readiness to meet any emergency situations like sudden and surprise enemy attack, natural calamities, etc. In such eventualities, the safety and security of the people entirely depends on the male bachelor members of the village. Therefore, they have the social and security obligation to the villagers to defend the village from enemy attack, and also to give safety to the people in the event of nature's fury be falling on the village. The members of dormitory are collectively called, 'Sawm'. It also function as the most effective mechanism for social control.

Functions of Dormitory:

The Primary function of the dormitory among the Paites was to serve the purpose of common sleeping place for the boys. It also served as a rest house for a stranger who could not find a kin in the village. It also has an important function in socializing the boys by giving the opportunity to mix freely with other boys. This developed a sense of cooperation and important qualities of life which can be developed in such group activities. Thus, the dormitory in the society served an important purpose of socialization. It served as a centre of social life and the bachelors were trained to behave well and respect the elders. It also enforced strict discipline to the youngsters which is the need of the hour. By enforcing strict discipline to the hoys, the young boys played an effective and important role in shaping the Paite society.

The *Sawm* is also a charitable institution. It helped the orphan, the weak, the widow, the poor and the needy. Because of the existence of this charitable institution no single beggar could be found in the Paite society. It served as the most important institution for enforcing the spirit of *phatuamngaihna* which is very wide in its connotation, an omnibus for any acts or services I that it is selfless philanthropic, benovelent, charitable and chivalrous. There is no exact work equivalent to the term in English language. Thus, the term *phatuamngaihna* can be expressed in this way. It is a peculiar connotation embracing all aspects of humanitarian services rendered either to an individual in particular or to the society and public in general. The institution of *Sawm* has imparted the spirit of *phatuamngaihna* to its members. The *Sawm* also served as the club house of young men where they usually organized their recreational activities or take counsel with one or other for undertaking any joint enterprise. In fact, the *Sawm*, was a boarding house of modern public school, the main difference being the activities and discipline prevailing therein, it was indeed a highly instrument for the overall social education of the village folk and succeeded magnificently to weave out a pattern of their personality where in the claiming and requirements of the family and those of the village as a society were nicely fabricated.

The members of the *Sawm* were responsible for the defense of the village from the attack of the enemy and that the *Sawm* served as a soldier barracks. The *Sawm* being a philanthrophic institution the members did not hesitate to come out of the *Sawm*, even at midnight if there arose emergency like surprise attack by enemy. The *Sawm* provided the much needed services to any house or individual in the village such as chasing of wild cat or pursuing a leopard or any other wild animal to save domestic cattle or fowl from their attack or in carrying sick person to a place of medical attendance or upto the boundary of the village in case the patient belonged to other village or transporting the dead if he belonged to other village.

The *Sawm* also organised and celebrated a number of annual festivals of which mention may be made of the *Khawdou*. The *Khawdou Kut* is an annual festival initiated by the *Sawm* in which the whole village should feast. It was generally celebrated after harvest every year and generally, the host provided rice for the occasion. Each *Sawm* member was required to contribute one pot of rice beer. Usually, pigs and in some occasions even mithun were killed in the occasion. In some cases, the festival lasted for several days during which the people had rice beer, sing songs and dance with various musical instruments, such as gong, drum, horns of mithun, etc.

In spite of its educative value, its valuable social services and its significant, the *Sawm* institution had completely disappeared today. Therefor, it is found necessary to examine why and how this social valuable institution gone out of existence today.

There are two obvious reasons for the extinction of Sawm institution from the Paite Society which are:

a)   Modern system of administration introduced by the British, and

b)   The introduction of Christianity by the missionaries.

5.   MODERN SYSTEM OF ADMINISTRATION INTRODUCED BY THE BRITISH:

Prior to the coming of the British, the village chief was the sole administrator of the village: and he has a great influenced on the *Sawm* which he needed for the safeguard of the village and overall development of the village. However, in the late 19th century the British subjugated Manipur which also affected the village administration of the hill people. After the Independence of India in 1947, the administration touched even the remotest area of the country. As a result, the chiefs lost their powers and today they can be said to be totally disappeared or extinct. Thus, with the extinction of chiefs, the *Sawm* institution also extinct.

Introduction of Christianity:

The most important factor contributing to the extinction of the *Sawm* was the advent of Christianity. Early in the last century, Christian missionaries form the West began to spread Christianity among the Paites. The vigorous activities of the Christian missionaries in converting the Paites into Christianity brought into play a strong resistance to the *Sawm* way of life. The converted Paites began to think that their past way of life with their *Sawm* discipline was not conducive to their spiritual and material growth. They began to feel that the only way to improve their lot was to break away from their old way of living and imitate the Westerners; not only embracing of Christianity, but also their external way of life. As a result, they began to undermine their traditional way of life and discipline without gaining substantially the constructive features of Western life. The establishment of educational institutions by Christian missionaries was also responsible for the extinction of *Sawm*. Parents resisted sending of their sons to Sawm at an early age on the pretext that the home provided a better place for study than the *Sawm*. The outcome of this was the fast erosion of *Sawm* life till it completely disappeared.

Today, in place of Sawm there exist a large number of social service organizations such as the Young Paite Association (YPA), the Siamsin Pawlpi (SSPP), local clubs, Zomi Youth Association (ZYA), etc. We will discuss them in the later part of this chapter.

6. THACHIAL AND LAWMPI:

This is a sort of philanthrophic service rendered to those who are in need of help. When any household of the village is not able to finish his jhum work due to illness or any other unavoidable inability, he would make a request to all or some households to assist him to finish up his jhum work. When any household is in need of such collective service of the people, children would be sent to each household to make a request for help saying, *"Tha K'ong Chial"*, which means "I invite your service", However, theis request is only obligatory on the part of the people to help or not to help. The householder making a request for such collective service must have to throw a feast by killing fowl, pig, etc. Rice beer is also served at the feast in the past. Though this sort of request for collective service is still practiced even today. Rice beer is no more served as people are converted into Christianity. Instead, red tea (without sugar) is served.

Lawmpi:

This is a sort of collective service by about 20 to 30 young boys and girls. A group of young boys and girls would work in the jhum of each of the member on a rotation basis. When one rotation is completed, they will start from the beginning till the work of all the members of the group is finished. After the work of each member of the groups is finished, a feast would be thrown by killing a pig. When the young boys and girls work together they have much joy and pleasure as their existed cordiality among them.

This sort of group activity develops a sense of responsibility among the youth which inturn contributed to social upliftment in the society. However, this institution has lost its importance as a result of the change in the social system and a pattern of the economic activity in the society.

7. THE YOUNG PAITE ASSOCIATION (YPA):

With the disappearance of bachelors' dormitory system, it had been felt necessary that a new social institution be formed which would be responsible for the social upliftment of the Paite society as a whole; and which would have as its objective 'labour for humanity' irrespective of caste, creed, sex, race and religion. Therefore, a new social institution called The Young Paite Association was formed on the 3rd March 1953 at Churachandpur in Manipur under the able presidentship of T.Vungsiam. The strength of this newly formed social organization has increased considerably within a span of 34 years of its existence. There are at present over 10, 000 members, 21 life members and 16 patrons. It is basically a community based non-political organization which had earned the appreciation and cooperation of the Government. It is a voluntary social organization of young men and women dedicated to the cause of humanity and its welfare. It is, indeed, a laudable organization which deserves blessings and cooperation from all sections of the society. It has a large number of programs and activities in all spheres of life and 'altruism' is the watchword of the organization.

Founded on the porinciples and philosophy of altruism, the YPA is basically a philanthropic organization extending helping hands to the needy, the poor, the widows, orphans, those who are effected by natural calamities, etc. Its guiding principle is 'Tlawmngaihna' or (selfless service). The word 'Tlawmngaihna' means something more than selfless service, altruism, or philanthrophism. It is the word used for selfless service with dedication without accepting anything, in kind or cash, in return for the service rendered. Being founded on this principle, every time, anyone in community dies, or suffers physical injuries, or anyone in the community is in dire need of help, the YPA, stepin and extend help in whatever form, physical, financial, etc.

As it is non-profit making and non-political organization, it has a standing principle of non-interference in the electoral politics of the Paites. Members of the organization are strictly advised to adhere to this standing rule of the organization. Therefore, the organization, as an organization of social service, is extending help to all irrespective of their political affiliation. Members are also free to join any political party or free to support any candidate in the election in their personal capacity, yet they are not to do so as a member of YPA. As a matter of fact, it would not be an exagaration to say that all the Paites from the age group of 18 to 45 are the member of YPA, unless otherwise expelled from it. Therefore, its membership is extensive as well as inclusive.

The jurisdiction of the Young Paite Association extends to the Paite inhabited areas and localities irrespective of sex, creed and territorial jurisdiction, and also to person who subscribes to the YPA'S principles and objectives. The YPA, a non-political social organization, has a wide range of functions to perform. Each unit is responsible for cleanliness of the unit. It has to see that the Village Street and footpath are clean. It has also to see the drainage systems of the village are well dug. The YPA unit in its own jurisdiction has to work for the general cleanliness of the unit locality.

The YPA is also responsible for the social equality in the society by uplifting and helping the poor and the needy. As there is no class distinction in the Paite Society, everyone is equal in the eyes of YPA. The YPA unit helps the widow, the poor and the needy. If a widow does not have a son of 14 years, the YPA unit looks after the widow. It builds the house of the widow, cuts and clears the jhum of the widow. In short, the YPA unit is helping the widow in all aspects.

It is the YPA which always extends various kinds of relief work. It extends relief work to the fire victim, famine affected people, cyclone victim, etc. The YPA have been helping those affected by natural calamities through donation and services.

The YPA unit acts as an organ of the village authority in eradicating social evils and anti-social elements. In the village where YPA unit is established, the unit is responsible for removing social evils and anti-social elements in the village. It is suppose to book the thieves, the murderers etc. It also sometimes serves a notice for prohibiting intoxicating drinks and smokes like drinking alcohol, smoking of heem, etc. and using of nicotine drug in the locality.

Again, the YPA is a social organization, which aims at enforcing the spirit of *phatuamngaihna*. As we have already discussed what *phatuamngaihna* is, we need not repeat here. So, every unit of YPA is expected to work for the society, for the poor and for the needy without expecting any reward from them. For instance, when a person dies in the jungle, the YPA boys and girls are responsible to carry home the dead body without expecting reward from the family of the deceased. But once any reward is given to them, their services are not counted as selfless service. Therefore, it is strictly that no reward should be accepted for the services rendered.

Out of the numerous social and selfless services rendered to the society and individuals, the following are worthwhile mentioning:

Social Welfare:

1. Serving, helping, relieving and providing assistance to the needy in time of adversity as a charitable service irrespective of caste or creed without discrimination.

2. A special bell of alarm is kept by every unit for use in time of emergency like fire accident, etc.

3. Adopted measures to eradicate social evils among the youth and teenagers in particular since 1962 till today.

4. Initiated the establishment of the Citizens Welfare Association (CWA) for eradication of social evils in 1977 in collaboration and in consultation with other organizations.

5. Arranged placards like 'WELCOME TO LAMKA' and 'KEEP LAMKA TOWN CLEAN' and placed them in suitable location and bridges in the remote hill areas.

6. Constructed thatched houses for the poor and homeless persons as rehabilitation measures in times of natural calamity.

7. Prevented the villagers and litigants from lodging cases for petty and minor disputes.

Health and Sanitation:

1. Cleaning of street and drainage on social work since 1972 till today particularly within the Municipality area (Churachandpur).
2. Maintained cemetery (common to all) in Lamka Town and in rural areas. Traditional conveyance of the sick and disposal of the dead are being carried out voluntarily.
3. Distributed drinking water in time of drought and scarcity and also arranged for water supply in rural areas by digging wells and tanks.
4. Contributed furniture like benches, waterpot and dustbins for use in places like Civil Hospital, etc.

Social Education:

1. Making 'Arrow Marks' to show water points along the inter-village paths in rural areas.
2. Making 'Arrow Marks' at the junction of roads indicating distances and directions.
3. Installation of 'Letter Box' at the entrance of villages in rural areas to enchance better communication.
4. Launching campaign for prevention from fie accident since 1954 till today.
5. Marking of traffic signs within Lamka Town area in 1972, 1977 and 1979 consecutively.
6. Tree plantation in Lamka Cemetery areas, public places and institutions in 1973, 1980 and 1982.
7. Constructed street lamps (lamp posts) at Singngat small town (where there is no electricity as yet) in 1978.

Relief Works and Assistance:

1. Fire victim relief works at Teisiang village in 1962.
2. Fire victim relief works at Mualnom village in 1962.

3. Mautam Famine relief works in Guite areas in 1963.

4. Fire victim relief works at Singngat town in 1967.

5. Cyclone victim relief works at Singmun village in 1967.

6. Moreh fire victim relief donated towards Chief Minister's Fund.

7. Provides utensils like benches, cups, pots, petromax and tarpouline for use during condolence meetings.

8. Distributed blankets and baby foods to the needy persons and motherless babies.

Shooting of Documentary Films:

The shooting of a documentary film entitled *Khupching* leh *Ngambawm*_based on traditional folktale has been under taken under the supervision of the Manipur State Kala Akademi.

Publication of Works:

1. Published the YPA Annual Magazine in 1979 and 1982.

2. Published the YPA Constitution and documentary film script entitled *Khupching* leh *Ngambawm*.

3. Publication of YPA Magazine and Journals.

Government Assistance:

1. Shri L.P.Singh, Governor of Manipur donated Rs. 1000 in appreciation of the YPA activities.

2. The steel industries of Crissa donated Rs. 1000 towards construction of the YPA Hall.

3. The Manipur State Kala Akademi granted sanction of Rs. 500 and Rs. 700 respectively as recuring grant towards publication assistance and also management subsidy for establishement of 'Songs, Drama and Cultural Institutions'.

Construction Work:

1. Constructed YPA hall at Lamka Headquarters at the cost of Rs.35, 000 only with the fund solely donated by well wishers of the Association.

2. The Association has constructed YPA Hall at Singngat small town and Sinzawl Village (Thanlon sub-division) respectively at unit level.

Project at Hand:

1. Construction of the YPA Theatre Hall-cum-Rest House at Lamka with the estimated cost of Rs. 3 lakhs only. The Government of Manipur and the Ministry of Culture, Government of India is likely to cause sanction of financial assistance towards the same.

2. Construction of Night Shelter-cum-Kitchen for attending patient within the Civil Hospital campus, Churachandpur, etc.

It has been seen in the above discussion on the various activities of the YPA that the Association is a social organization which has as its primary objective, the upliftment of the poor and the needy in particular and the society in general. Its activities are not concentrated only in the Paite dominated areas, but it has also been extended to other areas inhabited by other tribes of Mizos/Zomis family like fire victim relief works at Teisiang village in Churachandpur District in 1962. It is really a useful, praiseworthy and charitable social organization of young Paites in Manipur. It is one of the most prominent, well organized and one of the largest organization of young men and women organized on communal basis in Manipur. It has been playing an importang role in shaping the Paite Society, Therefore, it is our hope that this valuable social service organization go forward and do more useful works in the time to come.

8. THE SIAMSIN PAWLPI (SSPP):

It was on the 13th January 1947 a few members of Paite students held a meeting with Dr. K. Liankham, in the chair and late Mr. Khatchin Dousel as secretary at Mission Compound, in the then South District of Manipur. It was in this meet that the Paite Students Association came into being. But after a lapse of 7 years in 1953, it was felt that the inclusion of the word 'Paite' in the name of the Association was narrow in scope as well as in intent, and hence the present name *Siamsin Pawlpi* (SSPP) in short was adopted as the name of the Association. The word *Siamsin Pawlpi* is a combination of two words having different meanings, *Siamsin* meaning students or learners and *Pawlpi* is equivalent to organization or association in meaning. The word *Siamsim Pawlpi* though founded with the initiative of a few Paite students it is such a beautiful name which does not exhibit any communal colour except it is derived from Paite words. It is a rare coinage of phrase as the name of the Association is without inserting the name of any particular community.

The *Siamsin Pawlpi* is purely a students' welfare association which has been running its own constitution smoothly unpolluted with the banes of communal politics as we see prevalent among the tribals in Manipur. As it is a student's welfare association it has never been involved in politics and it has been maintaining peace and tranquillity. In spite of the fact that students' organization are used as a political tools by certain political parties in other parts of the country, the *Siamsin Pawlpi* has never follow a violent and revolutionary part for the fulfilment of its demands.

Aims and Objects:

As embodied in the preamble to its constitution, the aims and objectives of the *Siamsin Pawlpi* are as follows:

1. Furtherance of the pursuit of the various fields of education.

2. Enrichment of literature.

3. Emphasis on co-curricular activities.

4. Moulding of character including building up of honesty, perseverance, faithfulness and religiousness.

5. Infusion of nationalism and patriotism among the youngsters.

6. Building of sociability among its members.

7. Building of the idea of fraternity and friendship with the other students' organisation.

8. Helping of the poor and the needy in the society.

Activities and Achievement:

One of the most worthwhile mentioning achievement of the organization is that it instituted Meritorious Award since 1963. It has been instituted as a part of the program for the fulfilment of the aim and objective of the organization and as a means of giving encouragement and incentives to the young learners belonging to the organization. This award is meant only for those who have outstanding performance in the University or Board examination by securing first division grade. The Award has usually been derived from donation by well-wishers and from annual fund of the organization. The first award which was given to Mr. Haulianthang Hanghal of Lamka was donated by Capt. V. Dongzathang. It was called 'V.V. Award' in memory of his late father *Vualnam Vaialvum Award*.

The other worth mentioning activity of the organization is the publication of an Annual Magazine for the last 24 consecutive years. The publication of the Magazine gives opportunity to the members for improving their writing capacity. It serves as the source of information about the organization, its activities, program and achievement.

9. ALL PAITE STUDENTS UNION (APSU):

The All Paite Students Union was formed on the 18th September, 1982 under the Presidentship of E.Vungkholian. It was formed mainly with the aim to pressurise the government for the realization of the following demands:

Remaining of Churachandpur
Township as Lamka Township:

The APSU claims that the present name 'Churachandpur' is an imposed name, the original and indegineous name of which is LAMKA. Therefore, it has submitted a memorandum to the Chief Minister on the 27th October 1982 for pressing the Government to correct the name Churachandpur Township as LAMKA TOWNSHIP. The memorandum goes-

That, the present Churachandpur town came into being as township following its declaration as a small town with nominated membership in the year 1963 with the then S.D.O Churachandpur, as its ex-officio Chairman. That, never before its declaration as a small town, the present Churachandpur town was known as Churachandpur. It was and have always been known as Lamka by the original inhabitants who had founded it and raised it to the status of a Municipal Township.

That, the real Churachandpur, which was named after His Highness Maharaja Sir Churachand Singh, is the present Mission Compound Headquarters, which was the only settlement worth the name then, as it was a Mission Headquarters of the NEIG Mission. It was large establishment and there were-

a)   A Mission High School with residential hostels for boys and girls.

b)   A residential Bible School.

c)   A Printing Press.

d)   A Mission Hospital and Post Office.

That, at that time Hiangtam Lamka (Churachandpur now wrongly called) was a hamlet with half-a-dozen houses and Shri Phungkhothang as its chief.

That, when the country became a democratic Republic in January 1950, the Thanlon Circle and Tamenglong Circle were merged to constitute the present Churachandpur Sub-division, with its headquarters at New Churachandpur.

That, the said New Churachandpur was a newly found place situated west of the hill town village and the Tipaimukh road, north of the Chiengkonpang Village, south of the Chiengkonpan stream and east of the Gelmol Loubuk village in the Churachandpur Sub-division itself.

That, since it was a new Administrative Headquarters set up admits a jungle, it was called New Churachandpur by way of retaining the name of the late Maharaja after whom the Mission Compound was first named. And so the Mission Compound remained Old Churachandpur and the Sub-divisional Headquarters was named New Churachandpur (1950-58).

That, in the entire settlement of the New Churachandpur there was not a single private house; they were all Government quarters of S.D.O'S Office, and the Office building of the established only.

That, New Churachandpur (in name and style) was never imposed on settlements east of the Tipaimukh Road where village like-

a) The Hill Town (Thangzam Veng)
b) Hiangtam Lamka (Phungkhothang)
c) Bizang Loubuk (Zenhang)
d) Sielmat (Lhunkhothang)
e) Bizang (Soulhunkhua)
f) Phailian (Dal-a khua)
g) Chiengkonpang (Khuppau khua) and
h) Bungmual (Thangtual khua) were already in existence.

That, these settlements were collectively known as Lamka (Road-crossings) whereas the allied villages came to be known as 'veng', viz., Thangzam veng, Zenhang veng, Khuppau veng, Dala veng, and in that order-as constituent localities.

Hence The Local Populace Call The Official Churachandpur As Lamka Till Today; and Churachandpur as the Revenue Sub-Division:

We, therefore, approach you to declare the Churachandpur Municipal area as Lamka and the revenue Sub-division as Churachandpur Sub-division to sustain the original identity of the township as well as to avoid confusion over calling name between the township as well as to avoid confusion over calling name between the township as well as to avoid confusion over calling name between the township and the Sub-division in the interest of the public at early date.

Dated 27-10-1982

Place : LAMKA

Sd/-G.Langchinkham   Sd/-E.Vungkholian
General Secretary   General President

All Paite Students Union

As there was no positive reply from the Government, the APSU had called a bundh in Churachandpur in the month of January 1983. However, the Government is still reluctant to change the present Churachandpur to Lamka, and it is continued to be called Churachandpur though the Local people often time called LAMKA instead of Churachandpur. It is our hope that there is an agreement between the Government and the APSU on the matter.

Removal of Churachandpur Municipality Board:

The APSU felt that the imposition of Municipality Act in the Churachandpur area do not serve the tribal people, instead it is a dangerous step as no special provision has been given for the protection of the tribal people against the over-domination of the plain people of the area. It is, therefore, felt that Churachandpur is yet too a small town and the Municipality is yet impracticable. Therefore, the APSU had pressed the Government for the removal of Churachandpur Municipality Board by submitting memorandum to the Government of Manipur. But as there was no positive reply from the Government it has made an appeal to the Secretary (LSG) Government to the Manipur on the 20th January 1983 for early action.

However, in spite of such appeals and request to meet the demand of the APSU, the Government issued an order for Municipality election. On the other hand, APSU made an unsuccessful attempt to boycott the Municipality election in March 1983 which resulted in clashes between the students and the police. Though Municipality election was held in March 1983, the APSU still continued its demand for the removal of Churachandpur Municipality, When the term of the office of the members expired n 1987, the Government had finally removed the Municipality Act from Churachandpur in 1988.

Besides the above discussed demands, the APSU has also made other minor demands like the extentions of Radio program in Paite in All Inda Radio Station, Imphal. Though it is a very new organization, due to the strong will of its leaders, the organisation survived till today. It also demanded that more autonomy should be given to Village Authority in the Hill Areas of Manipur with regards to the maintenance and control of village schools, so that the Village Authorit may have the power to initiate the appointment, suspension and termination of teachers of the school concerned.

CHAPTER V

Economy

SELF-SUFFICIENT VILLAGE ECONOMY:

The Paites, prior to the introduction modern system of market economy, have a self-sufficient village economy. With the exception of salt, which they procured from Silchar in Assam and Imphal in Manipur, all their material needs for survival and sustenanced are produced within the village by the villagers themselves. They have thick woods and forests which supplied abundance of fresh vegetable and a construction materials like cane, bamboo and woods. It has to be noted that the construction of house is completed with cane, bamboo and wood, and not even a single construction material of modern house like nail, tin, etc. are used. Bamboo and cane are the raw materials needed for making different kinds of basket for different purposes. There are streams and rivers in the vicinity of the village which supplied fresh drinking water and fresh fish and other water-borne delicacies. Every household produces sufficient food items (rice and other staple food) for the year from his jhum land. For the supply of clothing needs, every household has a cotton field for the supply of raw cotton, which, female members of the family, after going through different stages of production, provide the house with all clothing requirements. There is a village blacksmith who manufactured and repaired all agricultural and other implements including weapons for hunting wild animals and wild enemies. There is also a village potter who made earthen and aluminium pots, plates etc. required for cooking. Mill made cooking oil like mustard oil, soyabean oil etc. are unknown to the Paites in the past. They have their own oil, the oil derived from pig, for cooking as well as for hair oil.

Therefore, as discussed above, a Paite village was a 'self-sufficient, self-reliance' village in all areas. Politically, a Paite village was a small independent and sovereign entity. The Chief of the village, assisted by his nobles (Hausa Upa) were the chief administrator including administration of justice. Economically also, a Paite village, as mention preceding discussion, was independent of others. What the villagers produced was sufficient for the village; and incase, any household was unable to produce sufficient foodstuff for the year, others who had in surplus help them, so that nobody in the village suffered was starved, except great famine which is beyond human control. It is for all these reasons that we referred a Paites village as a 'self-sufficient' village and the economy as 'self-sufficient village economy'.

1. AGRICULTURE:

Agriculture and the allied sectors constitute the primary occupation of the hill people of Northeast India. About 90% of the total population of Northeast India are rural and over 75% of the population are directly dependent on agriculture. An average of 60% of the population are cultivators, 9.25% are agricultural labourers, while nearly 8% depends on live-stock, fishery, forestry, plantation and orchards etc. The bulk of the cultivated areas have been devoted to rice and other food crops. In Manipur 84% of the cultivated land is devoted to rice and other foodgrains. Regarding the hill tribes of Manipur South District including the Paites, except a few educated and business classes, the rest of the population are directly involved in agricultural activities and are dependent directly on agriculture. The method of cultivation too is primitive, unproductive and wateful shifting cultivation. Except a few Paites practicing wet rice cultivation in the Khuga Valley of Churachandpur, the rest of the Paites including the allied tribes, are shifting cultivators.

Jhum or Shifting Cultivation:

Not only the Paites, but all the hill tribes of Northeast India are familiar with shifting cultivation. Shifting or Jhum Cultivation is the first step in the transition from hunting culture to food production. In India it is known in different areas by a variety

of local names. The Bhuija of Orissa call *Dabi* and *Komon* while
Mania of Bastar call it *Panda*, Khound as podu and different hill
tribes ofNortheast India call it in their own local dialects. The
Paites of Manipur, Mizoram and Chin Hills of Myanmar call it
Tang-lou or *Singtang-lou*. Tang means 'mountain' and *lou* means
'field'. The Lushais and the Hmars call it Tlanglou. *Tlang* means
mountain and *lou*, field.

The cycle of agricultural operation of jhum cultivation is
marked by the following stages:

1. Selection of the site;
2. Clearing of forest tract by cutting down the jungle;
3. Burning of the dried forest into ashes;
4. Dibbling and sowing of seeds;
5. Weeding of unwanted wild plants;
6. Watching and protecting the crops;
7. Harvesting of crops;
8. Carrying home the harvested crops;

Selection of Site (November):

Before the existence of Village Authority in Manipur and Village
Council in Mizoram, the village chief was the sole owner of the
village land. The village chief with the help of Hausa Upas (elders
or nobles of the chief) allotted jhun land to each household who
in return give 5 to 7 baskets or tins of paddy to the chief. However,
with the existence of Village Authority in Manipur, and Village
Council in Mizoram the allotment of jhum sie to each household
is done by the Village Authority under the Chairmanship of the
Chief; and the chief no more enjoyed his share of paddy called
buhsun. The selection of jhum site is normally done in the month
of October.

*Clearing of Forest Tract by Cutting down the Jungle (December to
February):*

The clearing of the jungle by felling trees and lopping off the
undergrowths begins in the month of November. The clearing
off the undergrowth is finished before the end of December; and

the falling of abig trees is done during January and February. It is the belief of the jhum cultivator includint the POaites that, if the clearing off of the undergrowth is finished before the end of December the jhum can burn better. Therefore, every effort is made by each household to finish the clearing off of the undergrowth before the end of December. Among the Paites, the clearing off of forest is left to the male members of the family. Except widows, no woman is employed in cutting the forest.

Burning of the Dried Forest into Ashes (10 to 15 March):

When all the households of the village finished the clearing and cutting off of forest, the fallen trees and plants are exposed in the sun to dry up for one month. Every effort is made by each household to get ready for burning the forest before 15th March as it is likely that rain may fall in the later part of March.

Sowing of Seeds (Haichituh) (April to May):

The sowing of crops, like maize, cucumber, watermelon, variety of beans, peas and pumpkin is started right after the burning of jhum. But rice is sown normally from the middle part of April till the middle of May. The work of sowing crops, other than rice is done by the women while the sowing of rice is done by the entire adult members of the family. After sowing of rice, there is a time for taking rest for about half a month normally the later part of May.

Weeding of Unwanted Wild Plants (Loukhawh)-(June to August):

The weeding of unwanted wild plants in the field is started from the early part of June and is continued for two to three months till August or September. During this period, two or three round of weeding is done. Since the weeding or clearing of wild plants (*lou khawh*) is time consuming, the entire adult members of the family are involved in the work. If rainfall happens to be heavy, the weeding or clearing of grasses is more difficult as the grasses grow faster than the crops.

Watching and Protecting the Crops (Louhon):

After finishing the weeding or clearing of grasses from the jhum, the cultivators have to wait for about one month for harvest. During this period, the cultivators have to protect the ripening paddy from birds, monkeys, and other wild animals. The Paites call this period of resting as *phavang awlleh*, which means 'Resint period of Autumn'.

Harvesting of Crops (Later part of November to December):

The harvesting of paddy is started from the early part of November. The Period of harvesting paddy is considered the happiest and joyous of all agricultural activities. The entire famil, except small kids and the old grandparents are involved in harvesting, and except the mother with baby, the rest of them slept at the jhum in a small hut called *lou buk*. Each jhum is supposed to have a small hut or *lou buk*. Since the ripening paddy cannot be delayed, every effort is made to finish up harvesting before 15th December.

Measure of Grain (Buh Tehna): The amount of grain just collected on the threshing floor was measured by height of the heap as follows:

Dungtan: the full length of a grownup man as he lay on the heap of garain, his feet touching the ground at the base of the heap.

Khutsiktup: height his outstretched hand reaches as he lay on the heap as above.

Kawitetup: height his sickle reaches in his outstretched hand as above.

Temsat: height his big knife in his outstretched hand reaches as above.

Sipzawn: the height of a fullgrown man standing upright on the ground.

Khutkazawn: height a fullgrown man can reach with out stretched hand, standing upright himself.

Tugazawn: height a fullgown man can reach up with his hoe in his outstretched hand, himself standing upright.

Meithalzawn: the height of a fullgrown man can reach with his gun in his outstretched hand, himself standing upright.

After the harvesting of paddy is finished, the annual cycle of agricultural operationis also finished and the clearing of jungle for the following year is started forth-with.

It has been seen that the jhum cultivation is a continuous process Exept the month of October, there is no time for resting and doing other profession however profitable it may be. When the annual cycle of agricultural operation is finished, the next cycle has to be started. Therefore, it requires a continuous and unending work.

1. Agricultural Implements:

The jhum or shifting cultivation being confined to cutting down the jungle, burning it and dibbling in the seed among the ashes which does not require sophisticate implements. The agricultural implements used by the Paites are:

Dao (Tem): The dao used by the Piate jhum cultivators is normally $1^{1/2}$ ft. long and the broad end of which $3^{1/2}$in. It is one sided sharpened dao, and is used mainly for cutting and clearing off of the undergrowth of the forest.

Axe(Hei): It is about $3^{1/2}$in. at the broad end which is sharpened. The handle of the axe is made of elongated bamboo of which one side is the root. The head of the axe is thrusted throught the tough root portion of the bamboo handle. This is mainly meant for cutting down the big trees or overgrowth of the forest.

Hoe (Tu): The hoe used by the Piates very closely resembled the axe. But the head is much lighter and the bamboo portion of the handle is shorter and smaller. This is used for weeding of wild plants and grasses from the jhum land.

Kawite (Sickle): This is the implement common to all paddy cultivators both shifting cultivators and wet rice permanent cultivators. It is used for harvesting of paddy in the month of November and December.

1. PRINCIPAL CROPS:

In the past, most of the Paites and other allied tribes of Mizos/ Zomis family grew crops only for their own consumption. Because of the lack of road communication and marketing facilities, they could not sell what they have in surplus. Therefore, whatever they grew, it is meant only for their own consumption. However, since the Indian Independence they have a little chance of selling their own production like chillies, ginger, etc. But as road communication has not reached them, they have to carry on their back to the market place like Tipaimukh, Churachandpur andAizawl in Mizoram. With the small amount of money the got by selling those items, they were able to buy their basic needs like salt, mill-made clothes, etc. The following are the main crops grown by the Paites from time immemorial till today:

Rice, yam, Mize, beans of various varieties, joh's tear, sesame, pumpkin, gourd, banana, cucumber, ginger, pineapple, orange, lemons of various varieties, chillies, aunglauk bean, sweet potatoes, potatoes, marrow, garkin, onions of different varieties, brinjal, wild variety of spinach, etc.

Of the above mentioned crops, rice, joh's tear, maize and yam constitutes the food grain. Rice is the main food of the Paites while Maize, job's tear and yam are the substitute of rice in case of the shortage of rice. Grams, varieties of peas, small bean, soyabean, aunglauk bean constitute the main curry of the Paites. Root group of crops includes sweet potatoes, yam, turmeric and ginger. Lastly, vegetable and herb group includes pumpkins, onions, chillies, brinjal and wild varieties of spinach.

Working in the Jhum Site:

Jhuming needs every day hard labour. Immediately after taking a morning meal, they set off to the paddy fields to work, carrying their lunch, **'buhtun'**. At noon they take lunch in the hut of the field. After having rested sometime, they continued working. They returned home just before sunset.

The co-operativeness that characterised the activity of tribals like the Paite constituted one of the most striking aspects of their social life and pattern of labour. Many kinds of work were done by them collectively. Edwin Dalton says, the low-level technology, combined with small size ... results in ingrained mutual dependence among people sharing many relationships; those with whom one is economically involved are the same as those with whom one is involved through neighbourhood, religion, kinship and polity. The primitive economy in that sense is 'embedded' in other community relationships...

This is true of the Paite.

Lawm, Corporate Weeding:

Men and women did the weeding in a labour called lawm. There was a male leader, (1) *lawm upa*, and a boy attendant, (2) *lawm naupang*, and a female leader, (3) *lawm nupi*, and a girl attendant, *lawmnu neu*. The *lawm upa* was the commander, and was given high respect in all matters relative to the lawm. There could be one or more *lawms* in a village, each consisting of about thirty to forty members. However, there was no limited number.

In the morning, members of *lawm* waited together at *khawmual*; women or girls carried baskets, seng, with bundles of lunch, *buhtun* or *sun-an*, plus curry with working garments and hoes for the men. On the field the menfolk, *lawmpate*, started work first and the females, *lawmnute*, took positions alternately between the *lawmpate*. Everybody used to take the same positions each day. Change of position was viewed as fickle-mindedness, and other members might be offended.

Role of Lawm Naupang:

In the field, the fetching of drinking water in a gourd or bamboo pipe was assigned to the *lawm naupang* who served the *lawm* with water nay time the need arose. The role of *lawmnu neu* on the other hand was to collect *buktui* just after lunch to give it to *lawm nupi*. After having apportioned it in equal shares, the *lawmnu neu* gave each of the members, one after the other.

In order the lawm could work on the field of widows by way of helping, they let even children of widows participate in the lawm, irrespective of their youth. Any family which could not do enough on the field because of sickness or other reasosn were helped by the lawm. The lawm was responsible for the need of the weak and the poor.

Thus, the lawm was weeding each day, working one day in each member's field. After one round, they started another from the beginning until the end of the season for weeding.

Ka gal a lawmpite aw,

Ka u sonlai na mu uam?

Mu ung e mu ma hung e,

A pahtang uah siam a gan.

Yonder working young people,

Did you see my beloved sister?

We did see her, we did see her,

She was weaving on the front-platform of the house.

When they were going to have their communal feast or drinking, lawm-zu, after the end of weeding, every household prepared beforehand a pot of beer each. The beer pots were collected, according to their convenience, by the lawm naupang at one house in evening where they feasted on zu, for only one evening. They danced, and sang. One man danced in the centre while the others sat around him. They all sang lawm la the dancer in a high pitch and the others in low pitch, making beautiful harmony.

This collective labour is knitting the people into a close and harmonious society.

Thathot: This was another kind of collective labour in weeding with full vigour, and was the initiative of young men and maidens. To do this, the consent of Lawm upas was to be obtained first. On obtaining the consent of lawm upas, the host family invited the public in tha-thot. Labour was provided by as many young men and maidens as possible. Each carried buhtun, and the host family fed them with pork and zu, in the field at noon. However, those who were not in a position to feed the helpers in the field, could do it later at home.

They chanted 'hei-ha' in unison, as they worked. Whenever full vigour was exerted, the maidens withdrew for a little distance from the position and did the collecting of weeds the young men cut down. Also engaged in weeding were the khuangpu, drum-beater, and sialki-khen, mithun-horn beater. Both were beating theirs in unison with the 'hei-ha' chanting all the time while they were weeding with utmost strength all day long. There was a rhymthmic motion to the beat of a drum, a horn, and a shout of 'hei-ha'. At noon lunch was served, followed by the giving of zu, to one after another. Then they got to weeding in the same manner. Whether they finished the weeding or not, they went home before sunset.

When the feeding of tha-thot was held, youngmen and maidens danced singing Latawm La. It lasted two days and two nights.

Harvest: When the ears of the paddy appeared, wild animals and birds also appeared to feed on it. All day long and sometimes all night long, they have to shout and make noises to drive birds and animals away.

When the grain turned to golden ears the people's hearts were full of joy.

The plants are cut down with sickles and left to dry. When the cutting was done, neighbours were asked to help in gathering grain. The grain in stalks were gathered at a place where tey were threshed or beaten out. This collective work was given to families in turn. The more well-to-do families would make a feast on the field.

When the fields were three or more miles away from the village, the grains were stored in the road midway between thatched huts and then brought home. They carried the grain on their backs in big baskets. Seng.

Since people have to work all the year round on the fields, the working members ate most of their meals, lunch at least, in the fields or jungles.

Kisawlseh:

These are signals using little boughs or leaves at crossroads, lamka-thuam, just ot indicate that the other friend had gone home. Sometimes it indicated the path to be followed. The Paite cultivators used to practise this in order to show who went home first by putting some leaves on the path of those who followed.

(Zawl La)

Tuanglam nih a ka aw e, zawitui tuanglam,
Vual nuhsawl she sunni hai vul aw;
Na tongdam ka san sikin tutkhawl veng,
Lambom nuhsawl na seh in tong dawng mawh.
The path folks in two, the paths to jhums.
The signal leaves you, my beloved, place has dried up;
In place of having your word, I just sat down,
And the leaves you placed could not hear me.

(Lakhiang La)

Lungtuaknu sawl na seh ni'n zau lamthuam ah,
Sing zatam in zalai ah honlel hi;
Sing zatam in zalai ah honlel zong.
Lungtuaknu sawlseh ka bang lou ding hi.

When I place signal leaves on the path for my beloved,
All people speak ill of me;
Though all people speak ill of me,
I shall not stop giving signals to my beloved.

(Lunglen La)

Lengvan tuanglam a kalai ah
Von aw, nuhsawl na pai aw;
Lengvan tuanglam tou-ding vangla,
Banzal in tangbang kai aw.
At the crossroads of heaven,

Place a signal of fresh leaves, my son;
Through the steep path to heaven,
Lead me on by the hand.

Hunting and Fishing:

Hunting is a pastime most males relish and is a most competitive game. Killing wild beasts such as tigers, leopards, bears, elephants, dear, boar, etc. was a great honour, bringing social status. Their longing to kill wild animals was so intense that it was almost impossible to differentiate between their songs about animals, Sa La, and songs about girls they loved, Ki Ngaih La. Therefore, the most honoured members in society were those who could kill many animals. They enjoyed, by and large, a higher status in the community and thus could find and marry a girl of their choice. Having a great longing for the kill, they dreamed it even in dreams:

Ka zalmang in nuaizin tunnu'n,

Von leh sang tel aw chi e;

Von lah ngai sang lah ngai ing,

Von momnou mah tel ing e.

In my dreams the spirit mother said,

"Choose between children and beasts";

I love children and I love beasts,

So I choose young children.

Just before going hunting, there were times when they cast lots using eggs. When the lot fell in their favour, they used to set out hunting for two or three nights, in the wood. As to directions, only east and west were known to them, for they didn't even hear of a compass.

Sapi Khim:

When a tiger is killed, a most elaborate rite is performed. The legend says that there was a time when the tiger could talk like man, and man and beast were on good terms. Man and tiger made an agreement not to harm each other. However, since the nature of the tiger is such that it used to kill man's domestic animals, and sometimes even human beings, man had to kill the tiger.

When a tiger was killed by man, it was made to appear as if the tiger had been pierced by a reed and killed while out hunting a mithun.

Pu ngamtawn tawh tong ka chiamin,

Chiam pel aw sial tualdelh e;

Chiam pel dinga zangsa kamkei,

Amah lauluang in sun e.

I made a covenant with the tiger,

He who broke the covenant killed a mithun;

The covenant breaker, the tiger,

The reed pierced him through.

The carcass of the tiger was not cut up but brought whole upto the outskirts of the village. There, the entire village would come out to receive the trophy, bringing much beer and a bunch of coloured feathers and goats for each member of the hunting party to wear on their heads.

The head and lungs of the tiger was taken out by the village priest. The sacred parts of the carcass were buried in a small pit in the ground under a stone slab. Water and beer were also poured into the pit. A stick pierced the ears of the tiger. All this was done with incantation by the priest. It was believed that the spirit of the tiger was thus outwitted, *khim.* and would no longer roam and kill domestic animals nor hear the call of other tigers.

Killing of such wild animal brought a sense of dread also. So the one who killed the tiger would dress like a woman and would strike the carcass with a spindle rod, *muitung*, saying that a woman killed the tiger. Thus they supposed they would deceive the tiger and man would not be guilty of breaking the agreement.

When the carcass was brought home, it was accompanied by much merry-making, dancing and drinking. A feast was prepared also. The kind of musical instruments used were bamboo pipes, *phit*, with different tones and pitches played by several persons to make music. Interestingly, this music can be heard as a signal in the Paite program in All India Radio, Imphal Station.

Nahsing nuai kamkei aw e,

Na min lawibang thang aw e;

Na min lawibang thang aw e,

Sang deih tun siang ah tun e.

The tiger in the wild woods,

Your fame spread far and wide;

Your fame spread far and wide,

I brought the beloved beast home.

Tangpi Ngabet, Community Fishing:

In fishing, nets were also used sometimes, and fish traps were laid sometimes. But occassionally when poisonous weed was beaten and dipped in the river, fish that ate that juice died. When the day of distributing portions came, the chief went to the spot and got one share, and each member of the party got one share per head.

Sources of Income:

Mithuns: Mithuns were kept by almost all households for trading and festival purposes. They were allowed to wander freely in the jungle, but were made perfectly tame by giving salt when they came home. The price of a full grown mithun varied from forty to fifty rupees. Among the Paite, the value of property was often spoken in terms of a number of mithun. They were considered an economic resource. In addition to the price paid the buyer had to pay one or two rupees more as *sumdawng*, which was to go to the *tanupi*. Other saleable domesticated animals were the pig, goat, dog and fowl. When a fat pig was killed for sale, the flesh with the fat was apportioned by a bushel, *lawh*; a bushelful was brought for a rupee.

Agriculture Produce: Cotton was grown in the hills. The crop was planted in April and was gathered in December. The price of raw cotton per maund ranged from three to four rupees. Cotton from which the seeds had been extracted was far more expensive.

As its demand was great among the Meiteis in the plains, they used to come to the hills people in search of it. It was weighed by seer, the rate being four seers for one rupee.

Sale of Grain: Surplus food grain was sold to anyone who might need it. It was measured in a basketful called *dan* same as seng, being equivalent to one and a half tin of kerosene these days. Three *dans* of paddy were bought for one rupee.

In those days, a man's daily wage was one anna. In 1905 common rice was sold for 15 annas a maund, and unhusked paddy was only 5 annas a maund. With three rupees in hand one could go to Imphal town and do good shoping. One shirt of a very good quality was bought for three fourths of a rupee.

Salt: Salt was the only household necessity one had to purchase from outside. One could get sufficient supply of it for a few seers of wax gathered in the jungle or a maund of raw cotton. When resold in the locality, it measured by bowl, *belhbu*, and was bartered with any article.

Since everything was to be carried on the back through the hillside trails, salt was particularly dear. In 1895, only three seers were procurable for one rupee; in 1904 the price fell to eight annas per seer.

In the past when land was abundant, and when the population was small, shifting cultivation was considered to be good, and the Paites have self-sufficient village economy as they were able to produce sufficient foodgrains for themselves. However, with the growth of population, land has become scarce and the same plot of land has to be cultivated only after the lapse of 3 to 4 years. In the past, land was abundant, and each year each family of the village could select a fertile land which was left uncultivated for 10 to 20 years. As a result, except in case of destruction of crops by natural calamities like hail, storm, draught, etc. and the damage of crops by pests, wild bears, wild elephants, monkey, rats, etc., the people were able to harvest sufficient foodgrains for the coming year. However, with the growth of population, land has become scarce and the jhum cycle in the same plot of land which extended upto 20 to 30 years in olden days has now been repeated only after 3 to 4 years. The shortening of jhum cycle has also resulted in the decrease of the productivity of land as a result of which bigger land have to be cultivated to get sufficient foodgrains. Therefore, shifting of jhum method of cultivation is now considered to be impracticable and wasteful. However, as mentioned earlier the Paites and other hill tribes of Manipur South (District) remain much dependent on jhum cultivation as a result of which famine has become a yearly occurance.

Table 5: 1

Item	Sex	Paite			
		Total	Rural	Urban	Total
1	2	3	4	5	6
		MANIPUR (Excl. 3 Sub-divisions)			
1.Scheduled Tribes Population (Including institutional and houseless population)	P	49,271	47,545	1,726	571
	M	24,679	23,843	836	286
	F	24,592	23,702	890	285
2. Population in the age group 0-6	P	6,610	6,382	228	97
	M	3,339	3,236	103	51
	F	3,271	3,146	125	46
3.Literates	P	33,685	32,357	1,328	272
	M	18,172	17,488	684	159
	F	15,513	14,869	644	113
4.Total Workers	P	18,487	18,052	435	199
	M	10,467	10,176	291	113
	F	8,020	7,876	144	86
5. Main Workers	P	15,316	14,923	393	151
	M	9,305	9,022	283	80
	F	6,011	5,901	110	71
(i) Cultivators	P	7,746	7,742	4	126
	M	4,286	4,283	3	62
	F	3,460	3,459	1	64
(ii) Agricultural Labourers	P	2,062	2,062	-	1
	M	1,101	1,101	-	1
	F	961	961	-	-
(iii) Household industry workers	P	438	433	5	2
	M	183	181	2	1
	F	255	252	3	1
(iv) Other workers	P	8,070	4,686	384	22
	M	3,735	3,457	278	16
	F	1,335	1,229	106	6
6. Marginal workers	P	3,171	3,129	42	48
	M	1,162	1,154	8	33
	F	2,009	1,975	34	15
(i) Cultivators:	P	1,053	1,052	1	30
	M	427	427	-	28
	F	626	625	1	2
(ii) Agricultural labourers	P	431	430	1	-
	M	218	218	-	-
	F	213	212	1	-
(iii) Household industry workers	P	677	664	13	4
	M	79	79	-	3
	F	598	585	13	1
(iv) Other workers	P	1,010	983	27	14
	M	438	430	8	2
	F	572	553	19	12
7. Non-workers	P	30,784	29,493	1,291	372
	M	14,212	13,667	545	173
	F	16,572	15,826	746	199

Shifting Cultivation:

It is an established truth that shifting method of cultivation, though still practiced by the Paites and other hill tribes of Northeast India at large, is considered to be a wasteful, rimitive and defective to the fertility of the soil. We will discuss the defects of shifting cultivation as follows:

The shortening of jhum cycle from 2 to 3 to 6 years resulted in manifold problems not only of accelerating the surface run off and soil erosion, but also have an adverse effect on the present economic system of the people. As a result of this, the Paites and other jhum cultivators of Northeast India live below poverty line. Shifting cultivator is much dependent on rainfall which is beyond human control. This always causes a failure to jhum cultivator, if it rains just before the burning of jhum land, then the burning of jhum land might be disturbed leading the cultivator to a difficult situation as he would not have the chance to cultivate that year. At the same time, if it does not rain during April-May, then the cultivator would face another problem as he waould not be able to sow seeds. Therefore, too much dependent on rainfall which always is uncertain causes famine in the following year.

The level of agragrian technique is very low and tools and implements are primitive in nature and inefficient. This resulted in low yields per acre, and obviously little or no surplus for further investment. This subsistence level of cultivation leads as a consequence, to low income per head and probably zero saving for the large mass of jhumias.

As mentioned earlier, shifting cultivation requires cutting down of forest and burning them to ashes. Obviously, the burning of such valuable forest resources every year is a setback to the economy of people. If one make a comparative study of the value of the grain produced in the jhum in a particular year with the expected value of the forest burnt down for the purpose of jhum cultivation, one would find that the expected value of the forest burnt down may be greater than the value fof the grains produced in the year.

The practice of shifting cultivation led to an extensive deforestation causing a large scale denudation of hill tops and slops, thus leading to undesirable ecological changes and elimination of water shed area of the region. The extensive deforestation also causes a large scale erosion of soil which have an adverse effect on silting of streams, river beds and marshy areas resulting flash flood in the plain areas and loss of fertility which is not easily built up, causing low productivity and subsequently expanding the denudation of forest zone.

The practice of shifting cultivation by the Paites and other hill tribes of Northeast India has no scope for development of sources of subsidiary income. Besides these, there are also other aspects which adversely affect social welfare, the public health, education, communication and such other facilities. It is difficult to develop the society when there is no permanent settlement. When the available land in the vicinity is getting exhausted, the tribe migrated to another location for jhuming. Such scattered and small villages are a great empediment to the provision of modern eminities to the people, such as school, dispensaries, drinking water supply and the like- agreat handicap indeed for the developmental and administrative machinery to function.

Jhum cultivation upsets the balance of nature. It reduces rainfall precipitation from the rain beating clouds which pass over the area where there is no obstruction of trees, etc.

Thus, we have seen that the continuation of shifting cultivation by the Piates and other hill tribes of Northeast India is a setback to the economy of the people.

The system of land ownership among the Paites and other Mizos/Zomis tribes has been a setback to the development of their economy. The system of land ownership among the Piates and other Mizos/Zomis tribes in the past was primitive in the sense that the village chief was the sole owner of the village land, and he allowed any household to cultivate in the village land on payment of annual fee of paddy. The village chief welcomes any person to cultivate the village land as he was to get paddy from each household cultivating the land. Therefore, he did not permit any one to set fire toe the forest. He was interested to protect the village land from fire so long as he was getting the customary payment of paddy and meat from the villagers.

However, the situation has now been changed since the enactment of the Manipur Village Authority (in the hill area) Act 1956. The villagers are no longer willing to pay the customary payment of paddy to the chief. As a result, the village chief is no longer interested in protecting the village land. The village chief would not interfere the village land. The village chief would not interfere to any person who sets fire to the village land. Instead, the village chief has the motive of selling the forest trees to someone in order to get benefit which will compensate the lost of the annual payment of paddy. When this is done, it is destructive to the villagers not because of the deforestation, but because of the fact that such an area is rendered useless for jhum cultivation. Now, the village authority is responsible for protecting the village land, but as none is getting extra benefit or profit by protecting the village land, the village land becomes unprotected.

Thus, we have seen that the continuation of shifting cultivation is a serious setback to the economic development of the Paites and other hill tribes of Northeast India. But, in spite of this they have to continue as along as there is no substitute to that. The educated section of the Paites are aware of the adverse effect of shifting cultivation, yet they are in a helpless condition as there are problems confronting the people from changing the system of cultivation which are discussed as follows:

1. PROBLEMS FACED BY THE PAITES FOR CHANGING THE METHOD OF CULTIVATION:

If the shifting cultivators among the Paites are to start wet-rice cultivation, they will have to wait two to three years before the production under the new system started. But, they are too poor to sustain themselves for two to three years without any production. Therefore, it has become absolutely difficult for the poor Paites to change their method of cultivation in the absence of financial helf from the Government.

There are suggestions that since the system of shifting cultivation is no more considered to be practicable, it would be desirable for the cultivators to change from rice cultivation to some other long term horticultural cultivation like planting of orange, coffee, tea, etc. But, to switch over to such long term horticultural cultivation, the poor cultivators find it difficult to sustain themselves for the time gap between the planting and actual production. Therefore, this cannot be followed in the absence of financial assistance from the Government.

The other problem faced by the j humias for changing the method of cultivation to permanent wed rice cultivation is the scarcity of water in the area, particularly in the South District of Manipur and in Mizoram, water is so scarce that it is not even sufficient for drinking purpose. There are streams where plenty of water is available, but those water cannot be utilised for the purpose of cultivation without the use of water pumper which no single cultivator could afford to buy. Therefore, the scarcity of water in the region remains the unmitigated problem for changing the method of cultivation. To enable the poor jhumias to start wed rice cultivation in the hilly region of Manipur South District, the State Government must make an arrangement for providing water pumping set to rural farmer free of cost or which they can pay on instalment basis.

As discussed above, the main approach to solve the problem of shifting cultivation is to bring elements of permanent cultivation by a gradual process, because the people are very much sensitive about ownership of land and forest. In 1956 the Manipur Village (in the hill) Authority Act was passed to abolish the chieftainship in some way or the other, which was strongly opposed out of fear that this would affect the ownership of land by the tribal people. Chaturvedi andUppal observed that "the correct approach to the problem of shifting cultivation lies in accepting it not as social evil practice but recognising as a way of life, not condemning it as evil practice, but regarding an agricultural practice evolved as relax to the pohysiographical character of land".

It can again be suggested that with the financial assistance of government the present agricultural occupation can be changed to animal husbandary. Livestock and poultry rearing are perhaps, most of promising and untouched field, particularly in Northeastern region. Therefore, a unit of cattle or goat, pig or poultry or even mized units may be reared by a family of jhumias either to substitute jhum cultivation or to supplement their economy.

As discussed earlier, the method of shifting cultivation was practicable in the past when there was abundant of land and when the population was small. But with the growth of population this system is no more practicable and now it is considered to be wasteful and unproductive. However, the shifting cultivators among the Paites in particular are too poor to start any other method of cultivation. Unless the Government takes steps to assist them, they are bound to continue till the entire hilly areas of Manipur South District becomes a desert. It is regrettable to note that the State Government scheme under department to accelerate the living condition of the poor farmers are not reaching the poor farmers as it goes astrayed before reaching them. If this state of affairs remains unchecked, there will never be improvement in the economy of the poor tribal jhumias.

Thus, shifting cultivation, as it is no more practicable and is now considered to be the cause of tribal poverty must be eliminated by encouraging the tribal to start wed rice cultivation, horticultural crops and to start animal husbandry. This would be the only way to remove poverty and to develop the economy of the tribals of Northeast India as a whole, and the Paites in particular.

2. COTTAGE INDUSTRIES:

The cottage industries have been playing an important role in the development of the economy of the hill people of Northeast India. There are various types of small scale and cottage industries in the region. These industries are the major suppliers of consumer goods to the rural and the urban areas. The small scale and cottage industries play a vital role in providing additional income and employment to the rural and urban people of the region. The industries in the urban areas of Assam, Manipur, Meghalaya and Tripura are developing in market view, but in most of the hill areas the productions are mainly for domestic consumption. The village and cottage industries include handloom, handicrafts, smithy, manufacture of brass utensils, etc.

Though small scale industries play a vital role in the economy of the hill tribes of Northeast India, the Paites and other allied tribes of Manipur South District have a very little chance of developing their village industries. This is a partly due o the fact that there is no market facility, and partly no sufficient financial assistance is given as yet to fully develop. Therefore, they have to produce only just enough for their domestic consumptions and requirements.

However, it should be remembered that the Paites have the skill to produce to meet their requirements. Prior to the coming of the British, there was no contact with outside world, and that they produced everything that they needed. In other words, they had self-sufficient village industries. There is a village blacksmith who makes and repairs agricultural implements and arms. Each householder is expected to be well versed in making all kinds of cane and bamboo works for his household. The womenfolks are expected to know the art of weaving loom, and making of all kinds of clothing for the household. Therefore, the Paites in the past had self-sufficient village industries. Except iron and salt which they needed badly, everytything they needed was available in their own land. With regard to iron and salt they exchanged their human captives from the plain with iron and salt. Sometimes they also exchange bee-wax far salt and iron. Some of the main cottage industries among the Paites, and for this all Mizos/Zomis tribes can be discussed as follows:

3. MANUFACTURING OF ARMS:

Before the advent of British, all the weapons and implements needed by the Paites were manufactured by themselves. With the coming of gun from Myanmar, they were able to learn how to manufacture guns. The typical fun is generally of the length of two to three feet with a wooden bud, a clapper to strike and ignite the gun powder inside the barrel. They were able to manufacture gunpowder which is having the power to shoot at a distance of 200, 300 and 400 yards. It is not known as to where from the Paites learnt the method of manufacturing gunpowder. The manufacture of gunpowder is affected in the following manner, which is the most curious of all Mizos/Zomis customs.

In the remote past, the Paites built their houses in such a manner that the pigpen may be beneath the house and the household's latrine immediately above the pigpen. The sides of the pigpen were banked up so that no rain may fall and wash away the surface of the soil so that the ground of the pigpen may get a good thick crush of excrement. The nitrate produced from this area is used for producing gunpowder, and the pen is left untouched by the pigs for at least three years, and the latrine being used constantly during this period, and the pigs beneath doing their duty by way of eating, trampling etc. all the time. Then, there was about one inch of artificial deposit on the surface of the soil. This faecal and urine impregnated the deposit in them trowled upon and placed in a basket, which is suspended above receptacle, water is poured into the deposit and allowed to filter through, the deposit assuming a reddish colour, and was passed through and through, time and again, until all the nitrates are dissolved. When the water after passing through the deposit remains quite clear and colourless, the process is considered complete. The deposit is now thrown away and the reddish water is boiled until most of it has evaporated; the remainder is kept in the receptacle until it is cold, when it is passed through a sieve and the water drain into the other receptacle. The nitrates are taken from the sieve, crystalised out and mixed with an equal weight of charcoal, which has been so carefully pouned up that it is all dust and contains no lumps and then the powder is ready for use. The sulphur used for making gunpowder is obtained from a particular bean called by the tribe *ga* or *gatam*. The other weapons like dao, bow, arrow, axe, etc. are made by the village blacksmith. However, the iron used for making them was imported from Myanmar. The main duty of village blacksmith is to make and repair agricultural implements and weapons for hunting and killing enemy.

The forge of the village blacksmith is placed in the middle of the widest street to lessen the risk of fire; it is only a rough shed with a log platform in front, which is as favourite as a resort for loafers as in the forge door in England. The bellow consertd of two bellow wooden cylinders in which pistons, fringed with feathers are worked up and down. The lower end of the cylinders are buried in the ground, side by side and from them two bamboos tubes converge, meeting just behind a stone through which there is a hole. The charcoal fire is placed in front of this stone and when the pistons are worked smartly, a very strong drought is obtained. The main duty of village blacksmith is to make and repair agricultural implements and weapons for hunting wild animals and for killing enemy. There are also some specialized blacksmith in the past who were capable of making gun.

4. POTTERY (BELVEL):

In the early days the only kind of pot that the Paites used was earthen pot known as *lei bel*. The work of making pot was left to the women. The Paite women were expert in making earthen pots according to the requirements of the family. The average size of pots the Paites made was 6 to 8 in. diameter at the mouth. There is another peculiar kind of pot known as *zubel* which is 24 in. height and 15 in. in diameter with a pipe of about 9 in. at the mouth. This kind of pot is specially meant for keeping and preparing rice beer, and the pipe at the mouth is used for brewing rice beer. Besides these, there are also different kinds of earthern pots which they produced according to the requirements. The process of making earthen pot can be discussed as follows:

As we have mentioned that the task of making pot was left to the women, the women of the household took a basket full of clay from calypit and poured water on the clay. When the water gets thoroughly wet, she pounds it in the mortar until it is thoroughly soft. Then she moulds a small pallet in her right hand and a smooth stone in her left hand, then she hits slowly the small stone against the uneven portion of the pot until the pot gets thoroughly smooth all over. The finished pot is then kept in the sun for a month of two after which it was burnt in an open furnance until it is burnt red-hot. When the burning is finished the process of making the pot is completed and the pot is ready for use.

5. BRASS WORK:

With the coming of brass, the Paites soon began to learn brass work. It is however not known as to how and when they learned the art of brass work. It is believed that they learnt it from their captives from Myanmar or India or from a person who had learnt from them. Today earthen pots had been totally discarded and it is replaced by brass pots which is more lasting. Brass pots are extensively used today and each village have an expert in making brass pot. They are now able to modify and update the kind of pot they produced, and are now able to make a sort of pressure cooker, though not exactly matched with the factory made pressure cooker.

6. CLOTH MANUFACTURING:

In the past the Paites were not dependent on mil made cloth nor were mill made cloth available. They produced cotton according to their requirement. They grew cotton in the jhum or cultivate a separate land for cotton production. But what they produced was meant only for domestic consumption and not for sale in the market.

Cotton is gleaned in a home made gin, consisting of a frame holding two wooden rollers, one end of each being carved for a few inches of its length into a screw, grooved in the opposite way to the other, so that on the handle being turned the roller revolves in opposite directions, and the cotton is drawn between them, the seeds being left behind. The cotton is then worked hard into rolls of a few inches long when it is spun into spindle of a rough spinning wheel, on occasionally a bobbin is used, which as being given a sharp twist, draws the cotton into a thread by its own weight. This method admits of diligent ones spinning as they go to and from the jhum. The thread having been spun is thoroughly wetted and then hung in looms some three or four feet long over a horizontal bar and stretched by several heavy bars being suspended in these looms.

Every Paite woman is expected to know art of weaving looms (*siamgat*). A Paite girl is trained by her mother in the art from her attainment of teenage period, and is expected to be having a thorough knowledge of weaving loom. The making of cloth is left to women, and they ae expert in weaving different kinds and different designs of clothes to meet the clothing requirement of the household. Every Paite girl is expected to keep a sufficient stock of clothes which she has to take to her husbands's house as a dowry. In the past Paite woman weaved puanpi which is a very serviceable from guilt. It is made by passing round every fourth or fifth thread of the warp a small roll of raw cotton and drawning both ends up. A raw of these cotton rolls is put in after every fourth or fifth thread of the woof, so that on one side the quilt is composed of closely placed tufts of cotton. However, today the people found it more practicable to make a simple ordinary mattress than making of *puanpi* with great difficulty. *Puanpi* is rarely to be found in the urban areas and it can only be found in a remote rural villages.

Regarding the process of making cloth, it is along process to transform a raw cotton into a finished cloth. The wrap (*siambu*) is prepared by passing the thread round two smooth pieces of bamboo wood one of which is fastened to two upright, while the end of the other are attached to the end of broad leather band, which passes behind the back stretches the thread to the requistic degree of tightness. The woof is formed by passing to and fro bamboo round which are wound different coloured threads which are beatened home with a well polished (balten made) of sago palm.

7. DYEING CLOTH:

The Paites, and for this all other Mizos/Zomis sub-tribes knew the art of dyeing cloth from time immemorial. The process and method of dyeing was very simple. To obtain red colour, they boiled the cloth with alkalin turmeric in a bowl for an hour or so and remove the cloth well dyed. Sapling and skin of different tress are also used for getting seven colours of the rainbow. But, they are not permanent as they can be washed away. To obtain permanent colour, it required many times immersion. The method of dyeing cloth as practiced in the past is no more practiced now. This is chefly because of the fact that more varieties of dyed and cotton yarn have been imported and colourful clothes are woven with magnificent designs and pattern on the handloom.

8. BAMBOO AND CANE WORKS:

Bamboo and cane work occupies an important place in the day today life of the Paites. No house can be built and no furniture can be made in the absecence of bamboo and cane. Cut of the many items made of bamboo and cane the following few can be mentioned:

Basket (SENG): The Paite men are very expert in making different kinds of basket out of bamboo and cane. Here, we have to bear in mind that where bamboo is used, cane is also required for binding together the splitted bamboo. The work of making basket is left to the work of the householder of the family. Exept widow, no woman makes basket. The householder makes different kinds of basket with different sizes according to the requirement of the household. Of the different kinds of baskets made by the householders mention can be made of *lelpi*, *seng, lawh* and *bawm*.

Lelpi: Lelpi is a basket with four legs, about 12 in. square at the bottom, widening till the mouth is circle with a diameter of about 30 in. The outer layer is of finely split bamboo closely woven. *Lelpi* is usually used for keeping the most valuable articles the household possessed. In early days, it was considered a must for the bride to take one lelpi to the groom. It is now considered not absolutely essential to take lelpi to the groom's house. *Lelpi* can still be found in rural Paite villages. It has not yet totally extinct.

Seng (dawron): Seng occupies an important position in the agricultural activities of Paites. In the absence of seng, no harvest can be done and no grain can be brought home from jhum. *Seng* is used or carrying goods and foodgrains from jhum to the village. It is also extensively used for harvesting, collecting paddy from the site of the jhum hut (*loubuk*). The size of seng varies. The bigger ones are called sengpi, which are menat for male bachelors of the household and the smaller ones are meant for woman and children of 10 to 15 years. The material used for making *seng* is only cane and bamboo. It is used till today both in urban and rural areas.

Bawm: The bawm, an open basket with oval mouth, 15 in. by 12 is used for carrying goods on long journey. As the making of *bawm* is simple the user donot preserve it for the next use, but throw it away after one use. It is made of bamboo and cane. Besides the above mentioned items there are a lot of aticles used by the Paites which are made of bamboo and cane alone. It should however be remembered that whatever the Paites make out of bamboo and cane, they are meant only for domestic use and not for sale in the market.

Table 5:2   Number of Artisan Householders among the Paites in Various Professions in Churachandpur District

Profession	No. of Households	Total
Gold/Silver Smithy	Nill	
Blacksmithy	23	
Carpentary	104	
Weaving	834	
Tailoring	46	
Bamboo/Cane Products	54	
Pottery	Nill	
Knitting	Nill	
Others	18	
Total	**1, 079**	

Source: Tribal Bench Mark Survey, Manipur South (Churachandpur) District 1982.

Thus, in order to develop the economy of the Paites and the hill people of Manipur, main emphasis must be put on the development of agriculture and small scale industries. Agriculture is the main occupation of the people, and except a few educated employed in the Government and few businessmen, the rest of the Paites are agriculturists, depending directly on agriculture. But the system of agriculture they practiced is primitive, wasteful and unproductive, and can no more support the population. As a result, every year thousands of families are starved and have to depend on roots. Therefore, a herculean task is on the shoulders of the agriculture department in playing a key role for the economic development of the people.

Besides this, the development of the existing small scale and cottage industries like bamboo and cane work, blacksmithy, weaving, etc. can play an important role in the economic development of the Paites and other hill tribes of Churachandpur District. Therefore, the industry department has also a role to play for the economic development of the people. Small scale and cottage industries should be encouraged so that production will not only be meant for domestic use, but it will also be meant for sale in the market thereby supplementing their income.

It is true that the tribal development department under scheme like IRDP and ARDA sanctioned a huge amount of money each year for the upliftment of poor people of the rural areas, but whatever amount given out is never utilised for the purpose for which it is sanctioned. If this practice continues, there will never be any improvement in the economy of the poor rural population. Therefore, it is necessary for the field officer to go to the spot and select the right person for the right trade. This will bring improvement to professional trades like blacksmithy, carpentary, bamboo and cane work, piggery, fisheries, goatry, duckery and cattle farming.

At present the whole amount under the Tribal Development Department appears to be centrally utilised resulting in depriving the benefit to the real poor and needy because the poor cannot afford to go to Imphal for a grant of Rs. 500/- or so which when not paid in time is all wasted on the to and fro journey. Besides, officers at Imphal cannot make proper selection of schemes of either individuals or otherwise. Therefore, the allotment whatever it may be should be proportionately allocated to the tribal districts according to their living condition and population. In other words, allotment of fund should be decentralised at district level. This will speed up the economic development of not only the Paites, but of all the tribals of Manipur.

Thus in conclusion, we can sum up that to achieve economic development of the Paites and the hill tribes of Manipur, encouragement should be given to them:

1. To change their method of cultivation.

2. To start the cultivation of horticultural and cash crops.

3. To start animal husbandary.

   On the other hand the Government must-

   1. Give adequate financial assistance to the rural population.

   2. Encourage the tribal to develop cottage industries by giving financial assistance.

   3. Provide marketing facilities to sell their produces.

   4. Improve road communication in the hill areas of Manipur.

   5. Decentralise the allotment of fund at the district level and

   6. Ensure that no political faourtitism play a role in giving grant-in-aid.

1. IMPACT OF MODERN ECONOMY:

The overall impact of Modern Economy on the Paites is manifested in the change of their material cultural habitats. Most of the Paites in the urban town of Lamka, Churachandpur, have the aspiration to have modern homes and furniture and many new wants like car, jeep, bus and many more have become necessities of tribal life. In order to have these, money is needed and since their traditional way of life and occupation is not money oriented, the people have to change their way of living and occupation in order to earn money. The growth of Lamka as important urban centre of Manipur has brought a major change in the economic life of the People. In Lamka the commercial activities are highly developed. In fact, money economy has brought transformation in the social economic life of the Paites. In the past, selling of agricultural produces was impossible because of the lack of marketing facilities and because of lack of road communication facilities. However, with the little improvement of road communication between urban and rural areas, and with the availability of urban centre like Churachandpur, the Paite agriculturists have now the better chance of selling their agricultural produces to the market. Besides, there are also many Paites working in the government offices and running hotels, shoops, etc. thereby earning their live a new social economic class namely 'elite' which has become a new threat to the development of the economy of th poorer section of the people.

2. EMERGENCE OF SOCIO-ECONOMIC ELITE:

One of the most important factors determining the nature of economic and socio-political development in the Paite Society is the emergence of a new but relatively small elite formed out of colonial rule. The introduction of Western education and the impersonal monetised market system resulted in the emergence of this new elite group. This new elite group includes professional elites sush as politicians, bureaucrats, doctors, etc. and the non-professional elite includes the wealthy merchants and the wealthy contractors.

Of the above mentioned elite groups, the professional elites directly influence the decision making process of the government, and economically they are in a better position. They are dependent on the Government for their livelihood, and are the priviledged class of the society. They live mostly in the urban town of Lamka, Churachandpur and Imphal.

The second elite group, the non-professional elites indirectly influence the decision making process of the Government. They are wealthy merchants, traders or businessmen and Government contractors. With their money they are able to contro the representatives of the people who make decision in their favour. The non-professional elites are economically in the best position. Most of them are now becoming private money-lenders charging a high rate of interest which varies from 8% to 15% per month, as against 12% per annum changed by banks. The non-professional elites have now almost virtually control the economy of the urban population of the Paites. It has been realised now that the non-professional elites are threatening the economic development of the society as a whole, and an attempt have been made to check this trend by forming the Private Loanees Association at Lamka. This association which was formed on 1st October, 1987, feels that unless something is done to check the private money-lenders in Lamka, Churachandpur from charging a high rate of interest per month, the poor wil become poorer and the rich become richer and richer which may result in the rigid stratification of the society into the haves and have-nots. Therefore, in pursuance of the resolution passed in its meeting held at Zougal Hall in Lamka, Churachandpur on 1st October, 1987 it has made an appeal to the public and money-lenders in the following words:

Our Churachandpur District Headquarters, Lamka is popularly known as the second town of Manipur. Outwardly, all the inhabitants seem rich. Actually, 95% are poor and 5% are rich. In the district the most popular one is that of lending money on high rate of interest to the poor families by the capitalists. The lenders charged 15%, 10%, 8%, 7%, 5%, etc. interest rate permonth against 5%, 6%, 7% charged by the Banks per annum. This system is very popular in the district which is not practiced in other districts of Manipur.

The high interest rate charged to the poor loanees by the lenders affected a good number of families. In most cases, the interest exceeds the actual amount of the capital taken to two folds; three folds so on and so forth. A number of families virtually become bonded labourers in one way or the other to the money-lenders, which is not only the problem of the person in question but social disorder at large.

The persons under such condition could not give their children proper education, medical care, clothing and fooding of their families. Many children become thieves, teachers and office workers could not function their duties. Tht it is true to say that the Money-lenders are the blood suckers of the poor people, because even in the condolence ceremony the money-lenders collected the condolence gifts from the borrowers. Sometimes, such case has happened in somewhere. From the above circumstances, the grievances of the loaness are too high in the district.

This trend, if not checked timely, will check our socio-economic condition at a point of no return.

In the light of the above cited facts, the association would like to approach the good co-operation of all political parties, Ministers, M.L.As., D.C., Public leaders, social organizations, Government Officers, Mahajons and general public of Churachandpur district ot remove the public grievances in the district by finding a general acceptable solution between money-lenders and the borrowers. Why the Law of Dampupat should not be introduced in our district, and then in the state.

Sd/- (Siakpi Pamngai)   Sd/- (Yamsei Haokip)
        President   Secretary

Private Loaness Association

The emergence of this elites among the Paite society has an adverse effect not only on the economic development of people, but it also has an adverse effect on the developing Paite society. In the past, there was no social stratification of society based on economic wealth; and the society was marked by equal respect to each individual. However, with the growth of urbanization, there came into existence the economic superiors which resulted in the emergence of social stratification between the have and the have-not. It is now becoming such that socil interaction is now gradually confined to the ellite group themselves. Exchange of social visits are common within the group. The person belonging to this new elite group will consider intermarriage between the poor and the rich elite unwise. It is becoming true as an educated Paite seeks educated girl for his life-partner, and he considers the uneducated girl not match for him how beautiful she may be. In the same way, incase of condolence meeting, marriage ceremony, etc. the rich and the educated people have attracted more people whereas the poor and unpriviledged people have only exceptional sympathiser. This widens the gap between the rich and the poor.

Thus, apart from the economic domination the elite will have over the poor the society will be stratified into the upper class and the lower class in which is harmful to the society as a whole.

CHAPTER VI

Political Institutions

1. INSTITUTION OF CHIEFTAINSHIP:

The institution of Chieftainship is the oldest political institution among the different tribes of North-East India. However, there are differences and variations with regards to the origin, powers and functions of the chief among these different tribal communities. Authoritarian type Chieftainship exists among the different tribes of Zo ethnic group, whereas, among majority of the Naga tribes, there exists a kind of republican. In other words, there are two forms of Chieftainship-Authoritarian and Republican, of which the Paites have the authoritarian form.

2. ORIGIN OF CHIEFTAINSHIP:

Originally, the right to rule was with those who have the power and ability to command sufficient number of subjects, so as to be able to repel any attack by other chiefs. It implies that Chieftainship has its origin in the physical and intellectual power of a person. It also implies that a person who has sufficient physical power, supplemented by mental and intellectual power to control and command maximum number of people, so as to be able to provide safety and security to the life and property of his subjects, becomes the chief. Therefore, it is established that chieftainship, as a political institution, originated in the physical power of the individual chief.

A traditional Paite village is a tiny sovereign independent political entity, ruled over by a village chief who is the sole owner of the village and village land. He was not an elected chief, but was a hereditary chief, and who became the chief by virtue for being the eldest son of the chief. If the Chief has more than one son, the traditional custom is that, the eldest son inherits the chieftainship of his father, and if sufficient land is available, other sons of the chief will be sent out to establish villages of their own in which they become the chiefs of their newly established villages. As a result of the practice of this tradition, most of the Paite chiefs belong either to Guite or Sukte Clan. The Guite and Sukte clans are the ruling clans of the Paite Society.

Among the Paite Chiefs of the Guite and Sukte clan, Goukhothang, who ruled over almost the entire southern part of the present Manipur, and Kamhau, who ruled over the whole present Northern Chin Hills of Myanmar, are worth mentioning. Goukhothang was the most powerful Guite Chiefs. He was treacherously captured by Manipuris with the help of the British and who, ultimately died while he was in captivity. Carey and Tuck, in their book, 'The Chin Hills' p.124-125, narrated the story which goes-

"The land inhabited by the Kamhaus or Sooties lays to the south of Manipur and east of the Toorool or Manipur River, that is, between the country inhabited by the Lushais proper and the territory of the Raja of Kuba, a tributary of Myanmar. They were a constant source of trouble for Manipur, and had at times, made the southern part of Manipur uninhabitable. Col. Johnstone thought, the cause of this constant raiding was that the Sooties were being driven forward by the Shindus, a powerful confederacy living to the southeast of Chittagong Hill tracts. The Lushais held the Sooties in great dread, and were falling back before them. The Sooties were well supplied with fire arms and ammunitions procured from Myanmar. Though the Sooties had no direct dealing with the British Government, in between 1857 and 1871 they made seven raids into Manipur. During the Lushais expedition of 1871, the Sooties agreed to help the Maharaja. But in spite the Maharaja's instructions to them not to attack the Lushais, they engaged a Lushai tribe, killed some, carried off a large number of the rest, and sent the heads of the four men killed to Manipur. At the close of the expedition the Sooties under the chief Kokatung (Goukhawthang) while carrying away 957 captives from two Lushais villages, were intercepted by the Manipur troops and treacherously captured. Gen. Boucher stigmitised this as an act of treachery, though it had been admitted that Kokatung had committed a raid on a Manipur village in 1871 and in retaliation of which the Manipur contingent took resort to foul play".

In 1877, a Sootie deputation came to Manipur for negotiating Kokatung's release. But they were informed that no proposal of any kind could be entertained while a single Manipuri subject remained in their hands and that, if the captives were not released, the Maharaja would punish the Sooties. Kokatung died shortly afterward in the Manipur jail. In August 1872, the Maharaja pressed the political agent to obtain the sanction of the Government for the supply of four mountain guns with elephant gear complete, to be used in an expedition against the Sooties. But the government declined. The mediation of Col. Mowbrey Thomson, who was then officiating as Political agent in Manipur and the Sooties (Sukte), and gradually many captives were exchanged. Through Col. Thomson's good will, the tribe swore allegiance to Manipur. Kokatung's son was released, and then skull and bones of his dead father were made over to them in March 1973. Peace was established. But some captives still remained under both sides yet to be exchanged.

Though in November, 1872, Col. Thomson, the officiating Political Agent, after his examination of Pemberton's map and the treaty of 1834 (by which Kabo Valley was ceded to Myanmar) came to the conclusion that the country belonged to Myanmar and that, if threatened or injured by the Sootie, the Manipuris should refer their grievances to the Burmese Government of India. The imperial records prove that the Burmese Government did not exercise any control over the Sooties to the south of the Manipur boundary, and as such the whole tribe was practically independent and uneffected by the Treaty of 1834. Moreover, the Sootie not only raided into Manipur, but also into Myanmar. In the administration report for 1872-73 Dr. Brown said that the frontier Burmese authorities generally repudiated the idea of their being under the Burmese control. He also observed that for all practical purposes, these tribals should be considered as independent and liable to punishment from either power it raided upon.

In 1874 when the Sooties attacked the Manipur Villages of Kumsol and Munkoong, the Maharaja of Manipur decided to send an expedition and the Government of India too approved of it. The expedition 2,400 strong started on February 19, and came back on 14th April 1875. According to the Manipur Authorities the expedition had few light engagements with the Sooties as a result of which the latter surrendered.

Dr. Brown, however, in referring to this expedition in his *Administrative Report for* 1874-75 stated that from the past experience he was led to doubt the correctness of the Manipuri version and made independent enquiry regarding the achievement of the expedition. He learnt from some members of the expeditionary force that not a single shot was fired on the Sootie village of Mombie, each party seeming to be afraid of the other, and remarked that the Sootie would not be deterred from committing further raids on Manipur from any fear of Manipur troops.

Though, for the time being peace was maintained, the Sootie raids were frequent from 1876-1878. The Maharaja of Manipurwas anzious to subdue the Sooties, but he required the British help in arms and ammunition, and the Lushai also afford their assistance against the Sooties, their deadly enemies. But the British Government was always ancious to avoid any engagement with the hill tribes on frontier and always dissuaded friendly state like Manipur from attacking any hill tribes without provocation, for a chaos in the hill area might make all the hill tribes restless.

The Sokte version is that the Manipur army entered the hills by following the course of Tapai (Chakpi) stream, and they were at once met by a Sokte (Sootie or Sukte) deputation, and it was arranged that their differences should be discussed with a view to an amicable settlement. The Manipuri river was chosen as the place for the parley, and on this river just north of the mouth of the Yangdum *Lui* (Jangdum river) the Manipuris encamped. The Major declared that Yetal (Zatual)'s sword had been placed in their hands as a token of submisision of the Sukte (Sootee or Sukte) tribe. But the Chins denied this and said that as far as they understood the whole proceeding, the Major never intended to fight, but merely to treat in a friendly manner, and that the only weapon which changed hands was that with which a dog was killed by the Manipuris to cement the friendship of the two independent rulers, the knife or sword was given to Kanvial (Kamvial) of Teddim who, with the Manipuri priest, performed the ceremony of swearing friendship over the blood of the animal.

The negotiation ended in the exchange of captives and promises of peace in future, which the Suktes did not for a moment respect, and the next year the Political Agent described them as more aggressive and arrogant than before, and to prevent their inroads, four new thanas were constructed on the south of the plains.

The Soktes account for their conduct by explaining that they were kept fully informed all that was going on in Manipur, and that they had received incontestable information that the Maharaja was seriously discussing the question of annexing the Sokte tract. As they had no intention of submitting to Manipur yoke, Kochim, in council, directed all who acknowledged his overlordship to kill every Manipuri whom chance or design might deliver into their hands.

No more expedition was sent against the Soktes who, however, never ceased until 1872 to raid on the plains in a spasonic manner. Some years, the Maharaja's territory was entirely free from raids and during the others, a serious agreesion occurred. Gradually, however, the raids became less fierce and les frequent. This was due to the fact that the Sokte tract being overpeopled, which necessitated migration northwards.

From the above account, it is evident that the relations between the Paite chiefs and the Maharaja of Manipur were not cordial ever since the treacherous capture of Kokatung, the then Guite Chief of a Paite clan. To avenge this, the Kanhaws (people of Kamhaw, chief of Sokte clan of Paite tribe) raided Manipur in 1874, and several times between 1876-78, and until 1892, the Paite did not cease their raids on the plains of Manipur.

Therefore, from the above discussion on the relation of the Paites with the Maharaja of Manipur, it is obvious that the Paite chiefs were not subjugated by the Manipuris in the various expeditions sent against them. They were able to maintain their independence, and were neither under the direct control of Manipuris nor the Burmese. From time immemorial, the Paite Chiefs were the sole owners of the village land.

3. POSITION OF A PAITE CHIEF:

A Paite chief was an authoritarian chief, having enourmous administrative and judicial powers. Being the absolute owner of the village and village land, he was holding the final and ultimate power over citizens and subjects. However, the chief, like any other, was bound by customs and conventions of the Paite society, which was in existence from time immemorial, and which has been observed, followed and practiced in the society. It was these customs and conventions which really restrained the chief to behave and act arbitrarily. Though the chief is supreme in the village, people are democratic and they have a simple remedy if the chief suppresses them viz..., to move to other village, thereby, render him to become a powerful chief without subjects. Therefore, a village chief, though powerful he might be, seldom acts arbitrarily.

The chief's house is a store house of the village, and all orphans and others, who have no means of support, are received there and get food in return for their labour. In the past, a Paite chief was responsible to look after the poors and the needies who had no means of support. The orphans and the poors lived in the house of the chief as slaves, worked for the chief and were looked after by the chief.

The house of a chief is a harbour of refuge to anyone taking shelter therein, but the person so doing becomes the chief's bondsman. Each man is bound to labour three days yearly for his chier, each house in the village furnishes its share of any expense incurred in feeding or entertaining the chief's guest.

If a person commits murder and is chased by others for revenge, the criminal has no alternative, but to run inside the house of the chief, and embrace the biggest wooden post which extands at the middle of the house near the fire place inside. When a criminal is in such position, no one by custom, can assault him physically.

Thus, until and unless the case is settled by the chief court, the criminal is legally free from physical attack by others.

4. POWERS AND FUNCTIONS:

From the above discussion on the position of a Paite Chief, it is evident that a Paite chief occupied an important place in the village. Therefore, it would be worthwhile to discuss the powers and functions of a Paite chief in the past.

One of the most important functions of a Paite chief was to appoint the members of his council or *Upas*. The chief has the discretionary power to appoint and remove the members of his Council. He had the power to remove any member of his council any time without assigning the reason thereof. Therefore, no member of his Council could risk his membership by opposing the chief. Like the chief of any othe Zo tribes in relation to his council, his power was absolute and unlimited. Regarding the size of the Chief's Council, it was not fixed, and the chief appointed as many members as he felt it necessary. The chief presided over the meeting of his Council which was usually held in his house. The meeting of the council was held as and when necessary.

Hausa Upas (Chiefs Council):

The members of *Hausa Upa* assisted the chief in the performance of his functions. Though the *Hausa Upas* had the right to advice the Chief on certain matters effecting the village, he (the Chief) was not bound to obey their advice. In other words, the chief holds the veto power on the decision of *Hausa Upas*.

The *Hausa Upas* in the past, enjoyed the following rights and priviledges:

1. They were exempted from the payment of Buhsun (payment of the chief's share of paddy each year) to the Chief.

2. They were exempted from force labour (during the British period).

3. They have the privilege to select their jhum site before ordinary villagers select their own.

4. They participated in the eating of *Sasat* (when a case is tried and settled in the Chief's Court, a fine is imposed on the guilty in terms of *Sasat* which means that the guilty has to kill a pig for the eating of the Chief and his Council who settled the case).

Siampu (priest):

The second important function of a Paite chief was to appoint a *siampu*. The chief had no religious function other than the appointment of village priest. Once the chief appointed the village priest, it was the duty of the village priest to perform all religious rituals, ceremonies and sacrifices. The priest was believed to have the knowledge of communication with evil spirits. When any person in the village became ill, it was believed to be the work of evil spirits, and the *siampu* was required to perform sacrifice on behalf of the sick person. The *siampu* acted as the doctor and nurse of the present day.

In return to his services the *siampu* enjoyed the following privileges:

1. He had the right to collect paddy annually known as *phaidam* from the sick persons for whom he preformed sacrifices.

2. He was exempted from the payment of *buhsun*.

3. He was exempted from force labour (during the British period).

4. When a sacrifice was made with four-footed animal, he gets the shoulder of the animal killed.

5. He had the priviledge to select the site for his jhum before any ordinary villager selected his own.

Tangkou (Village Crier):

The next important function of a Paite chief was to appoint *Tangkou*. The main duty of the *Tangkou* was to proclaim and made known to the villagers the decision of the *Hausa Upas* and the order of the Chief.

The chief has several advisers, who are called Upas. They have the first choice of land, and sometimes the chief allows them to get a basketfull of rice from each house. The other village officials are the crier, who goes round the village after dark, shouting out the chief's order, the blacksmith, and the *Siampu*, priest who performs sacrifices in case of illness. These persons generally receive a donation of rice from each house in return to their services.

The village crier received a fixed quantity of paddy from each household each year. The quantity of paddy given to the village crier varies from village to village; in some villages the crier received one kerosin tin of paddy from each household, while in some other villages the quantity of paddy the village crier received exceeds two kerosene tins. Besides, he was exempted from force labour, and also from the payment of *Buhsun*. Lastly, he had also the privilege to select the site of his jhum before any ordinary villager selected his own.

Siksek (Village Blacksmith):

The next function of a Paite chief was to appoint village blacksmith or *Siksek*, whose duty was to make and repair weapons and agricultural implements. The chief appoints anyone whom he feel talented in the job.

The following privileges were enjoyed by the village blacksmith:

1. He had the right to collect one *Phaidam* (one basket full of rice) from each household annually.

2. He was exempted from the payment of *Buhsun* to the chief.

3. He was exempted from force labour (during the British Period).

Distribution of Jhum Land:

The next function of a Paite chief was the distribution of jhum land to each household of the village. The chief, the members of his council and other priviledged persons had the right to select the site for jhuming before distribution to the villagers every year. After the priviledged persons selected their jhum land the ordinary villagers could select the sites for their jhum within the land set apart for a particular year. The one who first reached the site became the first selector, after making a sign on a tree which was called *Temtak*.

Defence of the Village:

The next important function of a Paite chief was the defence of the village from the attack of the enemy. In the past, war between village and village and between clan and clan was frequent occurance. There was absolutely no peace. Any village can expect the attack of the enemy at any time, day or night. Therefore, every chief had to put his village in a state of ever readiness to meet such eventuality. The chief had no standing army as such, but all the male bachelors of *Sawm* (Bachelors' dormitory) were assigned the task of protecting the village from certain natural calamities like fire, hailstorm, etc. and they were the defence force of the village from the attack of the enemy. The chief was also the chief administrator of the village and was responsible for the overall administration of the village. Being the chief administrator of the village, he had to see the general welfare of the people of the village as such.

5. PRIVILEGES ENJOYED BY THE CHIEF:

Like any other Chief of Zo tribes, the Paite chief also enjoyed a number of priviledges which were, however, mostly in kinds. These privileges were given to him in return to his services to the people. The followings are some of the rights and privileges enjoyed by the chief.

Buhsun (*the chief's right to collect a male load of paddy from each household of the village*):

It was given to the chief by each and every household of the village at the time of harvest. The quantity of paddy given to the chief was normally, a male load that is equal to 3 to 4 tins. But if anyone wanted to cultivate a better and larger land, he might go to the chief at the time of the distribution of jhum land,

and promise him to give more quantity of paddy at the time of harvest. In this case, he could even ask the person to pay a double of what was given by others.

Saliang (Share of Flesh): The second important privilege received by the chief was *Saliang*. When any villager killed a wild four-footed animal within the limit of the village boundary, the chief had the right to claim hind leg or the shoulder of the animal killed. The Chief also had the right to impose a fine of Rs. 40 to a person who did not give *Saliang*.

Khuaisiah (Share of Honey): The next privilege enjoyed by the Paite Chief in the past was *Khuaisiah* when any person in the village collects honey within the limit of the village boundary; he had to pay certain quantity of honey to the chief as a tax, which is called *Khuaisiah*.

Sai-mawl or Sakei-ha (Tusk of Elephant or Tooth of a Tiger): The next privilege enjoyed by the chief was, he had the right to claim the tusk of elephant killed by any villagers. If a tiger is killed, he would get one tooth of the tiger killed.

Hausa Innlam: (Constructing Chief's House): The next privilege enjoyed by the chief was that his house was constructed by the people of the village without any cost or payment. Since the chief was pre-occupied with the administration of the village, he had a very little time to do his own work. Therefore, the chief received the services of the people as and when necessary.

Inn-le-lou Khak (Confistication of House): The last right the chief enjoyed was the right to confisticate the house, garden or foodgrain of the villager. When a village migrated from the village to another village without the prior consent of the chief, the chief has got the right to confisticate the property of such person.

Administration of Justice:

The personal and customary laws of the paites envolve through a long process, encompassing generation of both static and the migrating families living in Manipur , the Sialkal Range in the else where Lushai hills (now Mizoram), karbi-Anglong (Assam) and Chin hills (Burma). These laws were enforced by the Chief-in-Council so far as the civil and criminal aspect are concerned. The personal laws relating to marriage, divorce, inheritance, adoption, etc. are normally administered by the *Inndongta* or Household Council. This implies that the Paites have certain established customs according to which, all criminal and civil cases are decided. Though these customary laws are unwritten, they are adopted by most of the Paite Chiefs while deciding cases.

The chief settles all disputes in the village, arranges where the jhum are to be, and when and where the village is to move. The Chief's house is a store house of the village, and all orphans and others, who have no means of support are received there, and get food in return to their labour.

As mentioned above, the chief of each village, assisted by his *Upas* (nobles or Council) was the one and the only court of justice in the village, and from their decision, there was no appeal, but nevertheless an unsuccessful litigant found a way of getting case reached. The Chief's Court therefore, has been the only court of justice so far as criminal cases is concerned. The village chief with the help of his *Upas* decides all cases within the village according to the customary laws of the people, and as long as a man remains under the protection of the chief he is bound to conform the village customs. Mrs. M.Coobe says, "as long as a man remains under the protection of Raja, he is bound, whether he be a Poi, Kuki or a Lushai to conform the village custom". Though there is no abosolute uniformity in the customary practices of the Paites, there are obviously some commonly practised customary codes of conduct.

6. TRADITIONAL CUSTOMARY PRACTICES:

In any social system, administration of the system, both the traditional and conventional, has to do much on the successful working of the system. As far as the traditional customary practices are concerned, they are not written, yet they are still followed and practiced. They are normally orally transmited from generatioin to generation.

The Paite Customary Court was instituted in 2002 to decide cases in which the disputing parties are from Paite Community. The Court has its jurisdiction over all Paite speaking people who wished to appeal in the court. This implies that nobody, no party to the dispute could be forced to approach the PTC Court for the settlement of disputes i.e. any party to the dispute can approach any other courts of the council.

Simultaneously with the establishment of PTC Court on 1st February 2002 the Paite Tribe Council published the Paite Customary Laws which was amended in 2013, and which has provided the maximum details of the customary laws and practices of the Paites including offences and penalties thereof. The purpose for instituting the PTC Court is to decide cases involving the Paite people on both side according to the customary law of the people. So far, the Paite Tribe Council has tried and decided more than 152 cases out of which 148 cases were settled. Petitions with reference to Marriage and Divorce are not treated as Court case, and therefore, are not referred to PTC Court Judge Team, the President and Secretary (Customs & Culture) are only the Certificate Issuing Authorities for Marriage and Divorce (When any party submit cases relating to Marriage and Divorce, PTC Court, though accepts the petition, does not decide the case, but issues Certificate after the family council of both party amicably settled the matter).

7. THE PAITE CUSTOMARY LAW & PRACTICES (2ND AMENDMENT, 2013)

PRELIMINARY

1. **Title**: The tilte of this Code may be called 'The Paite Customary Law&Practices (Second Amendment, 2013).

2. **Extent**: This Code shall extend to all Paite People.

3. **Code Enforcing Authority**: The Provisions of this Code may be applied and enforced to any person belonging to Paite tribe by the following authorities:

    i.   Houeshold Council;

    ii. illage Authority;

   iii. Paite Tribe Leaders;

   iv. Court of Law setup by the Government.

4. **Commencement:** The Paite Customary Law & Practices (2nd Amendment, 2013) shall come into force from January 01, 2013.

5. **Over – riding**: In case the provisions of this Code contradicts any law made by the Government on the same fact or case, this Code will prevail on any person belonging to Paite tribe.

6. **Contravention**: Any person belonging to Paite is not allowed to use separate family laws or clan rules in contravention of the provisions of this Code.

7. **Residuary Power**: For setting cases for which rules are not laid down under this Code, any decision arrived at on the case by any competent authority may be accepted to be in conformity with this Code.

8. **Amendment**: The power of amending this Code by taking away the existing provisions or adding a new one making any other changes as and when required is vested with the Paite Tribe Council (PTC) Assemblt with the consent of two-third members present and voting.

9. **DEFINITION OF WORDS**: The definition of words found in this Code is as follows:

   i. *Ganta Kheli Nei:* In case of domestic animals, a four-footed animal includes dog, goat, pig, sheep, cow, horse, mithun and buffalo; in case of wild animals, any four-footed animal, bigger and larger than a barking deer, including a barking deer.

   ii. *Gang:* The husband of a woman, who is the real (blood) sister of a father is called 'Gang'.

   iii. *Chief:* The Chief is the owner of the village and its land, guardian and administrator of the village.

   iv. *Mi:* A person belonging to any sex, male or female, called 'Mi'.

   v. *Naungek:* A baby of any sex below three years of age is called 'Naungek' (baby).

vi. Naupang: A child of any sex below thirteen years of age is called 'Naupang' (child).

vii. Ni: A father's real sister is called 'Ni'.

viii.Nungak: A girl of eighteen years and above till she gets married is called 'Nungak'.

ix. a). Nupi: A married woman is called 'Nupi'.

b). Nu-pi: Children born to a younger sister will called the elder sister 'Nu-pi'.

x. Pasal: Any male person is called 'Pasal'.

xi. Pisal: A male person, after marriage, is called 'Pisal'.

xii. Pi: The mother one's own father or mother is called 'Pi'.

xiii.Piching: Any person belonging to any sex who is 18 years and above of age is called 'Piching'.

xiv.Pu: The father of one's own father or mother is called 'Pu'.

xv. Sanggam: Sons and daughters born to the same parents are called 'Sanggam'.

xvi.Sisan pal/ Nawitual: If a married woman or unmarried woman conceived and has a child, it is called 'Sisan pal or Nawitual'.

xvii.Sisan pallou: A married woman who has not yet produced a child is called 'Sisan pallou'.

xviii. Tangval: A boy of 18 years and above till he gets married is called 'Tangval'.

xix. Teilol/Teirol: Any person belonging to any sex who is between 12 and 17 years of age is called 'Teilawl' or 'Teirawl'.

xx. Tuailai: It refers to any person in between the age of 19 and 35.

10. **PAITE:** Anyone fulfilling any, or all, of the following three conditions will be called 'Paite'.

    i.   A person whose father is Paite, is Paite by birth.

    ii. A woman who gets married to a Paite husband is Paite by marriage.

    iii. A person who opted to be Paite himself becomes Paite from the date of taking such an option

11. Definition of words relating to OFFENCES, CRIME AND JUDGEMENT ON THEM:

A definition of words relating to offence and judgement is as follows:

    i. *Gilou:* Any criminal or illegal action against living being and non-living things constitutes an act of offence of 'Gilou'.

    ii. *Guta:* Anyone who takes something which belongs to somebody else, without the knowledge or permission of the owner is called a 'Thief' (Guta).

    iii. *Hiamkham:* If someone who commits an offence against another person, kills a four-legged animal in acknowledgment of his guilt and to express wish that there should be no counter offence, is called 'Hiamkham'.

    iv. *Inn Sian:* If a person dies or if a woman gives birth to a child or if a man and a woman engage in a sexual act, inside a house that belongs to another person, it will amount to defiling the house and when the offender prays for forgiveness through customary laws, it is called 'Inn sian'.

    v. *Khelhna:* When a person does something that he should not do, and he did not do something which he should do, it is called 'Khelhna'.

    vi. *Khutkhial:* If a person, without having any intention, causes harm or injury, or even death, to any person or animal, or any other object, it is called 'Khutkhial' (Accident).

    vii. *Min Sesak:* If a person accuses another person dead or alive, of committing something which the accused person never committed, it is called 'Min Sesak' (Defamation).

    viii. *Pawngsual/Sualluih:* If a man forces a woman to have sexual intercourse with him without the woman's consent, it is called 'Pawngsual' (Rape).

ix. *Sasat:* A pig killed by a convicted person when the dispute is settled by the Village Council as a fine, it is called 'Sasat'.

x. *Sialding:* When a mithun is given as a fine for some offence, it is called 'Sialding' (the standing mithun) and in lieu of Sialding Rs. 5,000/- (Rupees five thousand) is accepted.

xi. *Tualthat:* If any person intentionally causes death to another, it is called 'Tualthat' (Murder).

xii. *Zawlgai:* If any male person engages in a sexual intercourse with a woman/girl outside marriage and if the woman conceives, it is called 'Zawlgai'.

xiii. *Zawltai:* If a man elopes with a girl without the knowledge and consent of the girl's parents, and living together as husband and wife somewhere, such kind of an act is called 'Zawltai'.

xiv. *Zehphi:* If a priest prohibits anyone from entering or leaving a house or village, which sacrifices are performed with the sign of prohibition, i.e. leave or branch of a tree stuck to the walls, or village entry point, and if somebody knowingly violates the prohibition, it is called 'Zehphi'.

xv. *Zehtang:* If a priest prohibits anyone from leaving his home or village while sacrifices are offered for the health, or well being, of a person, or the entire village, it is called 'Zehtang'.

xvi. *Zu:* A home-brewed wine from rice and hush, fermented with leaven in a pot and later mixed with water, the liquor so derived is called 'Zu'.

xvii. *Zubel tung:* When a case relating to some dispute is brought before the Village Council, the proponent of the case has to bring one pot of home-brewed wine for the Council members, which is called 'Zubel tung'.

Constitution of Inndongta:

12. **Inndongta:** When a man gets married and sets up his own home, his father will constitute a Household Council called 'INNDONGTA' for him, as follows:

i. ***Inntek:*** The householder is known as 'Inntek'.

ii. ***Thallouh:*** The eldest brother or other close related brother of the householder is appointed as his 'Thallouh' if the householder is the eldest son, he may take his father's elders or younger brother for the post.

iii. ***Thallouh Mang/Thallouh Thusa:*** One of the brothers of the householder or any other relative from within the clan may be appointed 'Thallouh Mang' or 'Thallouh Thusa'.

iv. ***Thusapi/Vengthusa:*** A close friend or another person who enjoys the confidence of the householder is generally appointed as 'Thusapi/Vengthusa'.

v. ***Beh Thusa:*** Anyone from within the householder's clan may be appointed as 'Beh Thusa'.

vi. ***Tanupi:*** The householder's sister or his eldest daughter is used as 'Tanupi'.

vii. ***Tanu Nihna:*** The householder's sister or nay of his father's sisters or even is married daughter, may be 'Tanu Nihna'.

viii. ***Tanu Thumna:*** The householder's sister or any other woman within his clan, or even his married daughter may be appointed 'Tanu Thumna'.

ix. ***Tanu dante:*** Any other women who are eligible to be 'Tanu' may be appointed upto seventh 'Tanu'.

x. ***Nuphal:*** The husband of the householder's wife's sister is called 'Nuphal'.

xi. ***Pu Pi:*** Mother's father or eldest brother of the householder is known as 'Pu Pi'.

xii. ***Pu Nau:*** The wife's father or eldest brother of the householder is called 'Pu Nau'.

xiii. ***Zawl:*** A good friend of the householder, who belongs to another clan, is appointed as 'Zawl'.

13. Functions of Inndongta: The Household Council has Executive and Judiciary powers in the matter of death, loss, joy, marriage and celebrations at the householder's house and they execute all works pertaining to these occasions as and when necessary.

14. Distribution of Animal Flesh: In the event of killing a domestic or wild animal by the house holder, a distribution of the animal flesh among the Household Council is as follows:

    i.   *Inntek:* The head of the animal, the heart, the liver and the inner parts.

    ii. *Thallouh:* A larger portion of hind leg.

    iii. *Thallouh Mang/Thallouh Thusa:* Shoulder.

    iv. *Thusapi:* A portion of hind leg.

    v. *Behthusa:* Lower portion of ribs.

    vi. *Tanupi:* A larger portion of ribs.

    vii. *Tanu nihna:* A lesser portion of ribs.

    viii. *Tanu Thumna:* Lower portion of ribs.

    ix. *Pu Pi:* Upper portion of hind leg/neck/ear.

    x. *Pu Nau:* A portion of flesh taken from inside back bone.

    xi. *Zawl:* A portion of flesh taken from upper portion of back bone.

    xii. *Nuphal:* A portion of flesh.

    xiii. *Tanu dangte:* A portion of flesh.

15. Sa-ik Delh: When 'Tanupi' got the larger portion of ribs of the animal called 'Sa-ik', she compulsorily performed 'Zuu lup' or Tea to the Householder, which is called 'Sa-ik delh'.

16. Satan Delh: In the Household Council, those who got the portion of the animal called 'Satan' they collectively performed 'Zu Lup' or Tea to the Householder, which is called 'Satan Delh'. But the case of getting a piece of meat called 'Sabak', there is nothing to do with 'Zu lup' or 'Tea'.

17. Householder's Authority: In general, the householder In general, the householder has to go by any decision arrived at in any cases by his Household Council, but he can make his own decisions on certain issues.

18. **Tou Sagoh:** This is a fest with a four-legged animal organized by a younger brother at his eldest brother's house, after he has set up his own home and his marriage, which is known as 'Tousa goh' and signifies respect for the elder brother and they are now se[arated households. On the day of performing Tousa goh, the younger brother who performed and throwing feast at his 'Thallouh', he brought his 'Sungpa' (the wife's father or eldest brother) as his one day Thallouh. On that day, the eldest brother presents household articles to his younger brother. He also arranges and sets up a separate Household Council (Inndongta) for the younger brother. The younger brother not organizing 'Tou sagoh' is taken to be disrespect for his elder brother; however, there is no fine for this lapse.

19. **Pu Zukholh:** As a sign of love and respect, a man/woman brings a jar of wine (or tea) at his/her maternal uncle's house, which is called 'Pu Zukholh'. The maternal uncle then blesses his nephew/tunu by invoking God's bounty in the form of 'Akmit Et' and a cock is generally presented to the nephew/tunu.

20. **Pu-Sa:** Woman cannot bring in her parent's traditional practices to her husband's family. However, when the Nephew caught wild animal, he gave 'Pu-sa' to his maternal uncle (Pute-Nu' Pa hiam sanggam pasal upa pen) like the neck, the tail or the ear. There is no hard and fast rule about eating 'Pu-sa'.

21. **Putawp Zukholh:** There are two types of 'Putawp Zukholh' i.e. Woman's Putawp Zukholh and the Husband's Putawp Zukholh.

    i.   *Woman's Putawp Zukholh:* When a woman gets married, she organizes this ceremony for her maternal uncle, as she now belongs to her husband's family, and the maternal uncle becomes the real 'Pu' for her children as her 'Nolam' is the original 'Pu'. After having performed 'Pu Tawp Zu' and in case of death, her brothers performed 'Pu Tawp Zu' and in case of death, her brothers performed 'Pu Zutawi' in condolence to the bereaved family on the following day of her burial. But her maternal uncle performed the said 'Pu Zutawi' if she did not performed 'Pu Tawp Zu' to her maternal uncle during her life time.

ii. *Husband Putawp Zukholh:* When the head of a family dies, his children shall perform Putawp Zukholh to Pu Pi of the deceased's father. It signifies that the wife's brother shall become Pu Pi to his children and that it is necessary to reconstitute the Household Council.

22. Langkhen:

i. *Langkhen:* When a nephew (tupa) dies, his maternal uncle (a Nu nolamte'n) will perform Langkhetna' ceremony with tea or wine and treat the 'Langbawlte'. The maternal uncle let him sit on this 'Lang' and conducted the burial ceremony. No one bury the dead body in the absence of 'Pute'. "Pute leh Lamsak nehzohlouh" is the Paites proverb that no one is buried without 'Pute'.

ii. *Pu Zutawi:* When the maternal uncle performed Langkhet, the nephew's brothers feed the deceased's maternal uncle with 'Pu Zutawi'.

iii. *Gunnman/Lukhawng:* If a nephew (tupa) died, his family performed 'Pu Zutawi' to his maternal uncle and he said, "Ka Sialpi sungsuak ka tupa khuai na hihchiang un, a mel ka muhna ding in," this saying and take one of the valuable items which the nephew's daily used materials. This is called 'Gunnman'. If the maternal uncle says nothing, the bereaved family gives the valuable item, which is called 'Lukhawng'.

23. Kosah: When a man expires, his brother (s) and sister (s) kill a pig, a cow or a mithun as a mark of their love, which is called 'Kosah'.

24. Procedures of Naming Baby:

i. If the eldest son produces a male baby, the baby will named after the father's father (Pa'Pa). If the baby is a girl, it will be named after the Wife's mother (Sung' nu). The second son or daughter will be named after the mother's father/mother (Pu or Pi) i.e the mother's side or the father's as the case may be.

ii.   The third son or daughter will be named after the father's sister (Ni/Gang or Tanupi) likewise, depending on the sex of the child.

iii. If the younger brother produces a male child, it will be named after his eldest brother (Tou). There is no mention about the rest of the children.

25. **Pudem/Simmoh**: If a nephew refuses to give due share of four-footed domestic or wild animal to his maternal uncle (Pu), it is termed as an act of dishonor (Pudem/Pusimmoh) and he is liable to pay fine of one standing mithun.

Chief & Village Affairs:

26. **Chief:** The Chief is the owner of the village and its land; and the guardian and administrator of the village. The Chief, with the help of the village Council, decides on cases and disputes in the village and pass judgments in accordance with the Paite Customary Code.

27. **Privileges of the Chief:** The following rights and privileges were enjoyed by the Chief in the past:

i.   *Rights of Confiscation (Innkhat/Loukhat):* When a villager migrates from the village without the consent of the Chief, the latter had the right to confiscate the villager's house/garden.

ii.   *Levy rights (Saliang):* When a villager kills a four-footed wild animal, the chief had the right to levy or take the shoulder of the animal.

iii. *Buhsun/Tangseu:* The village Chief had the right to collect some amount of paddy from the villagers as and when necessary.

iv.   *Construction of the Chief's House:* As and when needed, the villagers constructed the chief's house without labour charge.

v.   *Levy of Tusks/Teeth:* The Chief had the right to levy from the villagers the tusk of elephant or teeth of tiger or lion killed by a villager.

28. **Functions of the Village Council:** It is the duty of the Chief and his Village Council to look after the general welfare of the villagers, mode of earning their livelihood and the preservation of the village land in general, and the following in particular:

    i.   Allocation of sites for building dwelling houses and jhum field among the villagers.

    ii. Making and amending rules and laws for the administration of the village.

    iii. Hearing and adjudicating on cases and problems to those who violated the village rules in accordance with the Customary Laws.

29. **Privileges of Members of the Village Council:** In the matter of villages administration and settlement of cases and welfare of the villagers, the Members (Upate) are responsible for assisting the Chief, they have got the following privileges:

    i.   They are exempted from payment of Buhsun/Tangseu.

    ii. They are exempted from social labour.

    iii. They have the right to select jhuming fields of their choice every year.

    iv. They participate in the feast of 'Sasat'.

30. **Priest (Siampu):** There is a village Priest appointed by the Chief. There may be other Priests too, but such Priests are not entitled to the privileges enjoyed by the appointed Priest.

31. **Functions of the Priest:** The Priest offers sacrifices to god for, and on behalf of the sick in the village.

32. **Privileges of the Priest:** The village Priest appointed by the Chief, enjoys the following privileges:

    i.   He has the right to collect paddy annually, known as 'Phaidam' for the sick persons for whom he had performed sacrifices.

    ii. He is exempted from the payment of 'Buhsun'.

    iii. He is exempted from social labour.

iv. When a sacrifice is made with a four-footed animal, he gets the shoulder of the animal killed.

v. He selects the site of his choice for jhuming every year.

33. **Balcksmith:** There is a village Blacksmith appointed by the Chief. There may be other Blacksmith in the village, but they are not entitled to the privileges enjoyed by the appointed Blacksmith.

34. **Duty of the Blacksmith:** The village Blacksmith makes necessary agriculture tools and implements such as hoe, dao, axe, etc. for the villagers.

35. **Privileges of the Village Blacksmith:**

The following privileges are enjoyed by the chief's appointed village Blacksmith:

i. He can collect paddy of one 'Lohbeu' as 'Pum An' annually from the villagers whom he helped.

ii. He is exempted from payment of 'Buhsun/Tangseu'.

iii. He is also exempted from social labour.

36. **Village Crier (Tangkou):** There is a village Crier in every Village.

37. **Duties of the Village Crier:** When the village Chief has something to announce to the villagers, the village Crier makes the announcement at dawn or dusk so as to make all persons well-performed.

38. **Privileges enjoyed by the Village Crier:**

The Village Crier is entitled to the following privileges:

i. He is exempted from payment of 'Buhsun/Tangseu'.

ii. He is exempted from social labour.

iii. Like a Village Council Member, he can select the site of his choice for jhuming.

39. **Distribution of Jhum Land:** The Chief, members of the Village Council and the other privileged persons can select sites of their choice before the jhum land is allocated to the villagers; thereafter, the villagers make their selection of the

sites for jhum within the land set apart for a particular year, and the one who reaches the site first becomes the selector, and he earmarks that site with a sign on a tree, which is called 'Temtak'.

40. **Haam:** In a village, 'Haam' which is a dormitory for the boys of the village is established in the house of the village Chief, or any other person, which is constructed on one side of the courtyard (Sumtawng) of the house.

41. **Functions of the Boarders:** The boarders of 'Haam' are assigned the duty of protection of the village against attack from enemies or natural calamities like fire, etc. and they are a volunteer force.

42. **Haam Administration:** There are one or more Haam Upa (Elder) and the administration of the dormitory rests in the 'Haam Upa' who assigns the duties of the boarders and they executed accordingly.

43. **Establishment of New Village:** With the due permission of the village Chief, a new village can be established within the jurisdiction of the village by any person.

Marriage:

44. **Procedure for Engagement:** When a boy of a marriageable age intends to get married, his parents and their Family Council visits the house of the prospective girl with a jar of wine (or tea) and start negotiation. If the girls's parents agree to the proposal, they can accept and drink the wine or tea, and a date for marriage is fixed. If the offer is rejected, the wine (or tea) is returned to the boy's parents by the girl's Family Council.

45. **Zawlthu Kal a Sial Thawl:** After there is agreement between a boy and a girl for marriage, if any other boy or girl spoils the engagement, it is said to be 'Zawlthu Kal a Sial Thawl' or 'Sialkhau sattat' and the offender is liable to pay a fine upto one standing mithun, 'sasat' and 'zubel' or tea.

46. **Marriage:** If there is no breach of the engagement between the boy and the girl till the date fixed for the marriage, a

marriage ceremony is performed in the knowledge of the family Household Council and the public, and the boy and the girl become a couple. (With the coming of Christianity, Church Marriage is the general practice now).

47. **Mou Liah/Lawm:** There is a girl who is by the side of the bride while a marriage ceremony is performed. She is called the bride's maid or 'Mou Liah' or Mou Lawm'; there is no fixed fee, either in cash or in kind, to be paid to the bride's maid by the bridegroom. It depends on the mutual agreement between the groom and the bride's maid.

48. **Lawichal:** The leader of the party, who escorts the bride to the house of the bridegroom (usually a member of the Household Council of the bride's parents) on the night of marriage, is called 'Lawichal'. The bridegroom pays to 'Lawichal' something, in cash or in kind, according to their mutual agreement.

49. **Tukli Leh Thaman:** The term 'Thaman' refers to a fee paid to the bride's family by the bridegroom and it signifies the right to bury her in case of death. It is also called 'Tukli leh Thaman' – the value of four – palm sized pig being Rs 4/- and 'Thaman' being Rs. 2/- in the past, which have been increased to Rs. 400/- and Rs. 200/- respectively.

50. **Mou Man:** In the olden days, our forefathers spoke the bride price in terms of mithun which was their most valuable properties (domestic animal). Generally, the price of the bride is taken as two mithuns, and it is also called a mithun and a calf. The parice may also be paid in cash or in kind. Since everything and our livelihood changed and in the absence of mithun, the value of a mithun and its calf are accepted at Rs. 2, 000/- and Rs. 1, 000/- respectively.

51. **Precedure for Payment of Bride's Price:** When a man gets married a woman (bride), the following is the mode of payment followed in the olden days:

    i.   *Voktal Tukli:* When a youngman eloped with a lady to be his wife, his Household Council (Inndongta) killed a four-palm sized male pig and throwed feast to be the first procedure for negotiations or gave an equivalent value of Rs. 4/- in the ancient times, but now Rs. 400/- (Rupees Four hundred) is accepted. 'Tukli' is only used when a man eloped with a woman as fine but it is not compulsory at mutual understanding in marriage.

ii. *Thaman:* 'Thaman' is the basic right to have a bride and the right for burial,

Rs. 2/- (meaning one plus one) was given in the olden days, now accepted Rs. 200/-

iii. *Manpi:* It is a female mithun and a calf, valued at Rs. 40/- and Rs. 20/- respectively in the very olden days. Its present value of Rs. 2, 000/- and Rs. 1, 000/- respectively are accepted.

iv. *U Kan Man:* If the younger sister supersedes her elder sister in marriage, the elder sister can ask for a certain sum of money or a Traditional Shawl (Puandum) from the bridegroom which is known as U Kan Man.

v. *Pu Sum:* When the bride's maternal uncle (Pu) sends off the bride for marriage, he can take some cash or something in kind from the bridegroom as 'Pu Sum'.

vi. *Mou Tutphah:* At the time of payment of the bride price, the bride's parents return a certain amount of money from the bride price, back to the bridegroom, which is called 'Mou Tutphah'.

vii. *Min Man:* When a girl gets married, the person after whom she was named has the right to get something, in kind or in cash, from the bridegroom and it is called 'Min Man'. If it is in kind, it has to be Traditional Shawl 'Puandum' and if it is in cash, the amount depends on mutual agreement.

52. Payment of Bride Price-Exemption and Mandatory Payment:

i. *Exemption:* If the bride's parent insists that they would not take the bride price, there is no need for the bridegroom to pay it. But the right for burial which is called 'Thaman', is compulsory to take it.

ii. *Mandatory Payment:* If the bride happens to die before her price is all paid, the bridegroom is required to pay up compulsorily the remaining amount to the bride's parents, unless otherwise forgiven by them.

53. **Sialkhumsa:** When a mithun and a calf (Sial nuta) is paid to be the bridek's price, the bride's parents are compelled to kill a pig or a cow as 'Sialkhumsa'.

54. **Exemption of Sialkhumsa:** The bride price is mithun. In the olden times, the bride's parents then kill a pig or a cow to acknowledge that the bride price has been paid. This is called 'Sialkhumsa'. But when the parents of the bride do not accept bride price, it may not require for the bride parents to perform 'Sialkhumsa' and/or nothing is required in lieu thereof.

55. **Tanu Sagoh:** The bride's parents may kill a cow or a pig as a sign of their love and affection for their marriage daughter any time, and that is called 'Tanu Sagoh'.

56. **Articles Taken by the Bride**: The bride's parents can present her various articles on her marriage. During the send-off ceremony of their daughter, the following articles are necessary to her:

i. Blanket or Mattress.

ii. 'Seng' and 'Nam'

iii. Axe and Hoe without handle.

iv. Wooden box or cane box.

v. A pot of oil.

vi. A pot of wine, or tea (Mou Zupuak).

vii. 'Sa Sengsin' or Shawl (The Shawl meant for 'Tanupi' of the bridegroom).

viii. Moutam: The bride brings a number of shawls to distribute to her husband's family and their relatives to be a goodwill gift, which is called 'Moutam'.

The above items are the articles taken by the bride. Apart from the aforementioned materials, all materials given to the bride have beenr reckoned goodwill gifts and should be given on the other day. In case of crisis or divorce, all other than the seven-points are termed as nothing in vain.

57. **Sa Sengsin:** When the Parents of the bride gave her material (Mou vanken), the cover of the basket (seng) called 'Puandum (Traditional Shawl)' is known as 'Sa Sengsin'. The Shawl is given to 'Tanupi' of the bridegroom.

58. **U Kan Man:** If the younger sister supersedes her elder sister in marriage, the elder sister has the right to claim a 'Puandum' or cash equivalent to the value of the 'Puandum'. That is called 'U Kan Man'.

59. **Angpuan:** When the youngest sister is married, the bridegroom gives a Traditional Shawl (Puandum) to the bride's mother, which is called 'Angpuan'.

60. **Bride to Follow Bridegroom's Traditions:** In case there are differences in custom and practices between the bride and the bridegroom, the bride will give up the practices of her father and adopt of the bridegroom. Whether the bride price has been paid fully or not yet paid fully has no relevance here.

61. **Elopement (Zawltai):** If a boy and a girl, without the knowledge and consent of their parents, elope and live together like husband and wife, it is called 'Zawltai'. A fine of not less than one standing mithun can be imposed on the boy.

Divorce:

62. **Divorce:** By custom and tradition, a divorce between a husband and his wife is neither sanctioned nor allowed.

63. **Divorce due to Adultery:** In case there is separation or divorce between husband and wife due to adultery:

    i.   If it is the fault of the husband, the wife can reclaim the properties which she had brought with her at the time of marriage; she need not refund the bride price paidy by the husband, and if any due the husband shall make full payment of bride price unpaid.

ii.   If the divorce is due to the wife's fault, she cannot reclaim any property she ahd brought with her at the time of marriage except her own clothings; she shall refund the bride price already paid by her husband.

64. **Divorce due to undoundness of Body and Mind**: If one of the marriage partners is found to be physically and mentally unsound after marriage and there is no hope of recovery, the unsound partner may be divorced on payment of not less than two standing mithuns as relief and she shall be escorted to her parents.

65. **Breaking of Engagement**: If there is engagement for marriage between two persons but one of the partners withdraws from the engagement through deceit before the actual marriage, it will amount to cheating and the offender shall be fined atleast two standing mithuns for the same.

66. **Physical Disability**: If a husband or wife is found to be incapable of having sexual intercourse after marriage due to physical defects in the body, it will be deemed to be cheating of the other partner and such a person can be fined of atleast two standing mithuns.

67. **Fine for Divorce**:

1.   If a husband divorces his wife:

   i.   He shall be liabel to pay a fine of standing mithun (Sasat) and 'Zubel'/Singpi'.

   ii.   He will return back the properties as per the customary laws.

   iii.   He shall not be entitled to receive back the bride price paid to   the wife's parents.

2.   If the wife divorces her husband:

   i.   She shall refund, in cash or kind, the bride price paid to her by her husband.

   ii.   She shall not be entitled to get back any property brought to her husband at the time of marriage, except her own bare clothings.

   iii.   She will have no authority over her children.

3. Kipha Khen: If a husband and wife separate through mutual agreement and understanding, it is called 'Kipha Khen' and no fears or liabilities are imposed on any of the parents.

Adultery & Immorality:

68. **Adultery (Angkawm):** If a married person has a sexual relation with any person other than his/her own spouse, it is called 'Angkawm' (Adultery).

69. **Adultery with Married Woman:** If any man commits adultery with a married woman, he shall pay a fine of atleast five standing mithuns, 'Sasat' and 'Zubel'/'Singpi'.

70. **A Married man commits Adultery with a Woman:** If a married man commits adultery with a woman and takes her as his wife, he will bring her to his home. If the first wife refuses to live together with them, the man and his new wife will leave the house and live separately. All properties of the man will go to his first wife and children, and the man will have no claim over them.

71. **Stealing Wife:** If a man elopes with a married woman and take her to be his wife, he will have to pay a fine of atleast ten standing mithuns, 'Sasat' and 'Zubel/Singpi' to the first husband of his new wife. He will also pay bride price to the first husband as per Customary Law.

72. **Fine for Elopement:** If a man elopes with a woman without the knowledge or consent of her family, the woman's parents can impose a fine of atleast one standing mithun on the man, apart form bride price and other liabilities.

73. **Illegitimate Pregnancy:** If any girl/woman conceives a child out of wedlock, it is said to be 'Zawlgai'.

74. **Sisan Palman/Nawitual Man:** A woman who had produced children or 'Nawi tualsa' but the perpetrator (pasal) rejected to be his wife, that man will be fined 'Sisan palman or Nawitual man' in terms of the standing mithuns, killing a four-legged animal and 'Zubel'.

75. **Zawllei leh Zawlta**: If a man has a child from any woman out of wedlock, he shall be liable to pay a fine of two standing mithuns, 'Sasat', 'Zubel'/'Singpi' for the offence. The father will take the baby within three years and he will pay one standing mithun per year against the upkeep of the child. If the child is not taken within three years, the father will forfeit all claims on the child afterwards, then, the child will be of the mother.

76. **Illegimate child to wife**: If the father refuses or fails to take his illegitimate child from the custody of the mother within 3 (Three) years, the child belongs to the mother automatically.

77. **Khumpi Kaiman**: If a boy and a girl, or a man and a woman engage in sexual act on the bed of another man, it is called 'Khumpi Kai' (Climbing on a man's bed). The male partner is liable to pay a fine of atleast one standing mithun to the house-owner.

78. **Inn Subuah**: If an unmarried man and a woman engaged in sexual act inside the house of another person, it is called 'Inn Subuah'. The male partner is liable to pay a fine of atleast one standing mithun to the house owner.

79. **Nawi Mek**: If a man touches the breast of nay woman/girl without her consent, it is called 'Nawi Mek'. The offender is liable to pay a fine of atleast one standing mithun.

80. **Rape:**
    i.   If one or more person (s) makes an attempt to have a sexual intercourse with a woman without her consent by using physical force, it is called 'Rape'. Besides, a man has sexual intercourse with a woman without her consent is also rape. The offenders are individually liable to pay the fine of five standing mithuns, killing a four-legged animal called 'Sasat' and 'Zubel'/'Singpi' for the offence, even if he/they fail in the attempt to rape.

    ii. Rape of under-age girl: If a man engage in a sexual act with a minor girl, with or without her consenst, the offender is liable to pay a fine of not less than ten standing mithuns, 'Sasat'/'Zubel'/'Singpi' to the girl.

Succession & Inheritance:

81. **Gou**: A property, both acquired and inherited, movable and immovable, which remains at the time of a man's death to be succeeded by his son (s) is generally called 'Gou'.

82. **Gamh**: If the head of a family has no son at the time of his death to succeed or inherit his properties, both movable and immovable, then the properties shall be called 'Gamh' and it will go to the nearest male member of his relatives.

83. **Eldest son, A successor**: As per the Customs, the eldest son who looks after his father till death, is entitled to succeed the properties of his father at the time of his death. But the eldest son who refused to look after his father and shifted to another house has no right to inherit his father's property; one of his brothers who looks after his father till death will inherit the properties. In case, head of a family dies without making distribution of his properties, the inheritor if he agreed so, can make appropriate distribution of the properties to his brothers.

84. **Inheritance of Properties**: If a father has no son to succeed and inherit him, he can distribute the movable-immovable properties to his daughter (s). If there is no such proper distribution or deed (will) during his life time, the inheritor will inherit all his properties.

85. **Right to other Children**: If the head of family makes a testament of will in which he makes a distribution of his properties to his sons and daughters on his death the children shall get their shares as mentioned in the testament of will accordingly.

86. **Zi Nokik Tungtang**: If a husband, after his death leaves his wife alone without any offspring, the wife normally returns to her parents as she is 'Sisan Pallou'.

87. **Zinawn Tungtang**: After the demise of awife, her husband got married another woman to be the step mother of his children, she became the mother of his children. If she has no child, it doesn't mean 'Sisan pal or pallou'. If she refuses to live together with the children and go back or gets remarried,

she will leave the house on the day of marriage itself and will have no right to claim nay of her deceased husband's properties.

88. **Succession of Illegitimate Son**: If an illegitimate son is born between a man and a woman, and if the man takes custody of the son without the mother, the illegitimate son is called "Zawlta". If the father was unmarried at the time of having son, the illegitimate son will be regarded as the eldest son and he will be entitled to inherit the properties of his father.

89. **Adopted son as Inheritor**: If a husband and wife fail to produce a child to inherit them, and if they adopt a child in witness of the Household Council (Inndongta), it is called 'Ta Lak'. The adopted child will inherit all properties belonging to the husband and wife when they die, and he will have to adopt the house owner's cland and tribe.

Offences and Accidents:

90. **Accidents**: If any person, without having any intention, causes bodily harm, injury or death, to any person with, or without, using any materials, it is called Accident (Khutkhial).

91. **Death Caused by Accident**: If any person causes death to any other person, without having any intention, he will bring tea (zu lup) and approach the party of the victim in this manner:

    i.   The one who causes the injury will make agreement.

    ii. He will bear all the medical expenses of the injured person unless he is pardoned.

    iii. He will seek pardon with a pot of tea.

    iv. He will cover the dead body with 'Puandum' (Shawl) if he succumbs, he will kill a four-legged animal as 'Hiamkham' and pay a fine of not less than twenty standing mithun as well.

92. **Murderer**: If any person, causes intentional death to another person, it is called 'Murderer' (Tualthat).

93. **Fine for Murderer:** If a person commits murder of another person, he will pay the following fine to the family of the victim.

   i.   He will perform the 'Hiamkham' ceremony with a four-legged animal.

   ii. He will cover the dead body with Puandum (Shawl).

   iii. He will pay not less than fifty standing mithuns, or an equivalent amount in cash, as fine for the offence.

94. **Injury to the Trespass:** If one or more presons, enter by trespassing into the house of another person, thereby causing exchange of hot words between the parties resulting in physical fights amongst them as a result of which the house owner suffers injury and death, the trespasser (s) shall be deemedas Murderer and will be liable to pay a fine fixed for murder; but if the house-owner uses force in self-defense, causing injury, or death, to the trespasser, then it shall be treated as a case of Accident (Khutkhial).

95. **Goup Fight:** If two persons physically fight and another person intervenes to stop them, and while doing so, if one of them gets injured or killed, it will be treated as a case of Accident; but if one of them cause injury or death intentionally, it will be treated as murder.

96. **Stealing/Abduction:** If any person forcibly abducts, or take away another person, he will pay the following items:

   i.   He will bring 'Zubel', 'Singpi', 'Sasat', and pay a fine of not less than ten standing mithuns if the victim is recovered alive.

   ii. If the victim is not recovered alive, the abductor wil be fined for murderer.

97. **Death During   illegitimate Pregnancy:** If a woman conceives an illegitimate child and dies during pregnancy, the person who is responsible for the pregnancy shall be fined as follows:

   i.   He will perform 'innlut' by killing a four-legged animal.

   ii. He will cover the deadbody with 'Puandum' (Shawl).

iii. He will pay a fine of not less than ten standing mithuns.

98. **Embracing Chief's Pillar**: If a person commits an offence knowingly or unknowingly, and another person(s) chases or pursues him with the aim to cause harm to such person and if such person takes refuge, or shelter, in the house of the Chief, it is called 'Hausa Sutpi Kawi' (Embracing the Chief's Pillar). After taking shelter, no one is allowed to cause harm to such person and the case may be tried according to the offence subsequently.

99. **Stealing**: If any person is found stealing a domestic animal belonging to another person, he shall be fined one standing mithun for the offence.

   i.   He will bear the cost of the animal as much as fixed by the owner.

   ii. He will perform 'innlut' with tea (Zubel tung).

100. **Injuring Animals by Accident**: If any person causes injury to the domestic animal belonging to another person by accident:

   i.   He will perform 'innlut' with tea (Zubel tung).

   ii. He will pay for the entire cost of treatment of the injured animal.

   iii. If the animal dies, he will pay its equivalent value in cash to the owner and will get the animal killed.

101. **Animal Entering Garden**: If a domestic animal is found entering a garden/jhum causing damage to standing crops and vegetables, the owner of the animal shall pay compensation which is equal to the value of the crops damaged, in cash. If the animal is let loose by the owner due to negligence, the animal can also be caught by the owner of the garden/jhum. If the animal is caught, the owner of the animal will redeem the animal in cash as deemed suitable in the case.

102. **Causing Animals to Fight**: If any person causes animals fighting each other, resulting in the death of one animal in the fight, the person who causes them fighting shall

make 'Innlut' and the owner of the dead animal will get his animal.

103. **Causing Injurty to Tied Animals:** If any person causes injury or death, to an animal which is tied in a place, the person shall be laibel to bear all expenditures incurred upon the treatment of the injured animal. If the animal dies, he will perform 'inn lut' with tea and pay the value of the animal in cash, but the animal will go to the owner.

104. **Joint Owner of Animal:** If one persons's animal is kept or fed, by another person and if the animal is sold in cash, the price of the animal shall be divided equally between the owner and the keeper; and if the animal is killed, the flesh shall be equally divided between them, but the keeper shall take the head and heart of the animal.

105. **Keeping Other's Animal:** If one person keeps a female animal belonging to another person for the purpose of getting the young ones when the animal gives birth, they shall be equally divided between the owner and the keeper; but if there is only one, the keeper will get the young one and the owner the mother, or vice versa.

106. **Death of Hired Animals:** If a person hires an animal belonging to another person on payment of hiring charges, and the hired animals dies due to natural causes, and not due to negligence of the keeper, the keeper is not liable to pay anything for the death of the animal unless there is a written agreement between them otherwise.

107. **Injury/Death to Man Caused by Animal:** If an animal causes injury to any person, the owner of the animal shall bear all expenses incurred for the treatment of the injured. If the animal causes death to any person, the owner of the animal shall cover the dead body with Puandum (Shawl) pay a fine of not less than ten standing mithuns, or the value. The animal shall be killed for the owner.

108. **Unclaimed Animal:** If there is an animal whose owner is not known in a village, such animal is called Unclaimed Animal- 'Gan Val'. That animal can be claimed by the owner

within fifteen days with a definite proof of ownership. If there is no claimant within the stipulated period, the animal shall go to the village Chief or the Village Council automatically.

109. **Animal Giving Birth:** If any animal gives birth to young ones in a house other than that of the owner, the owner of the animal shall give one of the young ones to the owner of the house where the birth takes place.

Offences Relating to Property:

110. **Definition of Property:** Any substance belonging to a person, whether moveable or immoveable, is called Property (Van).

    1. **Immoveable:**
        i.   Land;
        ii. House;
        iii. Plants and Trees and the
        iv. Garden Crops.

    2. **Moveable:** All other properties not mentioned in sub-section (1) above are called moveable.

111. **Offences Relating to Immoveable Property:** If any person causing damage to immoveable property of another person by setting it on fire or otherwise, the offender shall be liable to pay the value of the property so destroyed, in cash, and he shall bring tea and make compromise for the offence.

112. **Theft:** If a person takes away any property of another person without the knowledge, or consent of the owner, it is called 'Theft'

113. **Penalty for Theft:** If a person steals any property belonging to another person, the property which are still available or recovered, shall be returned to the owner. If the property is not available, or could not be recovered, the offender shall pay the value in cash. He shall also be liable to pay a fine of one standing mithun for the offence.

114. **Causing Death While Committing Theft:** If any person, while committing theft, death to another person, it shall be treated as murder, and the offender shall be liable to suffer the penalty prescribed for murder.

115. **Destruction of Erected Structure:** If any person destroys, or damages an erected structure such as stone or wooden sign board belonging to another person, the offender shall construct a similar structure afresh at his own cost. He shall also be liable to pay a fineof one standing mithun.

116. **Buring of Jhum/Garden:** If any person causes the burning of jhuk or garden belonging to another person intentionally, the offender shall be liable to pay the value of the property damaged and also a fine which may extend to one standing mithun, 'Sasat and 'Zubel/Singpi'; but if the fire results from an accident, the case may be settled on mutual agreement.

117. **Burning of House/Barn:** If any person causes the burning of a house or a barn intentionally, the case shall be treated as murder and the offender shall suffer the penalty prescribed for murder.

118. **Jhumland Boundary Dispute:** If two or more persons have a dispute over the boundary of their jhumland, the Village Council shall settle the case as follows: One of the contending parties shall draw the boundary of the jhumland according to his own choice, and after that the other party shall make a choice of the two jhumlands. The remaining jhumland shall be given to the former.

119. **Burning of Property Belonging to a Stranger:** If a Stranger leaves his article or property in the house of another person, and such property get burnt along with the property of the house owner accidentally, the house owner shall not be liable for the loss of the stranger's property.

120. **Defamation:** If any person communicates, either verbally or in writing, to another person, stating that a third person, dead or alive, has done so and so in a destructive manner wrongly. For example, to state that "A" has conceived an illegitimate child from "B" while "A" is not actually

pregnant, such statements with malafide intention is called defamation.

121. **Fine for Defamation:** If any person defames another person, the case may be decided according to the gravity of the matter and the offender shall be liable to pay a fine of not less than one standing mithun with 'Zubel'/'Singpi'.

122. **Eave's Dropping:** If a person eave's drops the conversation of other persons without their knowledge, it is called 'Ki In Ngaih Guk' and is an offence punihsbale with fine which may extend to one standing mithun, 'Sasat'/'Zubel'/'Singpi'.

123. **Zehpphi/Village Defiled:** If a stranger is prohibited from entering a village on account of disease or a community sacrifice performed there, and if the stranger still enters even though he knows that it is prohibited and that there is an alternative route, it is called 'Zehphi'. Such a person is liable to pay all the expenses incurred for making arrangement and a fine which may extend to standing Mithun, 'Sasat' and 'Zubel'/'Singpi'.

124. **Inn A Zehphi/House Defiled:** If a stranger is prohibited from entering a house in a village in which a family sacrifice has been performed, and a sign has been shown at the gate or wall by hanging green leaves or branches, but if a stranger enters the house knowingly, the offence is called 'Inn a Zehphi' (House Defiled). The offender is liable to pay the cost of such sacrifices and a fine which may extend to one standing mithun.

125. **Sanctification of House (Inn Sian):**

    i.   If a person dies at the house of another person or a dead body is carried into the house of another person, it is considered that the house has been defiled. The bereaved family will come to the owner of the defiled house with 'Zu'/'Singpi' or Killing a four-legged animal to seek sanctification which is called 'Inn Sian'. But the owner felt it not necessary, it is not a must.

    ii. If a person among the tenant dies, it does not need to perform 'Inn Sian' for he pays the rent.

126. **Boarding with Maternal Uncle:** A 'Tupa'/ 'Tunu' staying and eating at the house of the maternal uncle even for years together is never counted as debt, no matter how much expenditure is being incurred for the stay.

Procedure for Case Settlement:

127. **Registration of Case:** If any person has a case or problem which requires settlement with another person, he shall depute one member of his Household Council (Thusa) to the opposite party and register his case with them.

128. **Settlement at Household Council Level:** As far as possible, a case or dispute involving two or more persons shall be discussed and settled by the Household Council for the parties concerned.

129. **Power of the Household Council:** The power and authority to hear and settle disputes and cases mentioned in Paite Customary Law & Practices rests with the Household Council (Inndongta).

130. **Zubel Tung:** If anybody has a case or dispute and if he/she is not satisfied with the settlement of the case at the Household Council level, or no agreement could be arrived at on the case, he/she may bring the case to the Chief's Village Council for adjudication with 'Zubel'/ 'Singpi'. This is called 'Zubel Tung' which is equivalent to Court Fee.

131. **Settlement of Disputes at the Village Court:** If any case or problem is brought ot the Village Court for settlement, the Chief and his Council shall –

    i.   Summon and hear the complainant, the defendant and their withesses.

    ii. Pass judgment of the case in accordance with the Customary Laws.

    iii. The convicted person is required to abide by any judgement passed on him/her by the court and will also perform 'Salam' at the Chief's Court.

132. **Power of the Chief's Court:** The Chief's Village Council has the power to hear and settle cases not mentioned in the Customary Laws and it is also empowered to make laws and award penalties on anyone within the jurisdiction of the village.

133. **Registration of the Cases at PTC Court:** If there is anybody who is not satisfied with the settlement of his/her case or problem at the Household Council level or Village Council level, or if the case is one of the utmost urgency, he/she can approach the Paite Tribe Council (PTC) General Headquarters' Court for adjudication by paying the requisite court fee.

134. **Petitions Admitted by the PTC Court Other than the Case:** The petitions for Court Marriage or Divorce being admitted, have not been treated as cases and which are not referred to the PTC Court Judge Team. In Court Marriage, when both the Household Councils (Inndongta pihte) have cleared 'thaman/manpi' which date is accepted as their marriage day; then President, PTC/GHQ becomes the Officiating Minister/Chairman and the Secretary (Customs & Culture), PTC/GHQ will be the PTC Court Secretary; where both parties should sign on the Marriage Certificate. Likewise in Divorce Certificate, President and the Secretary (Customs & Culture) should be the Certificate Issuing Authorities, and the date of divorce will be accepted as the date of refunding 'thaman/manpi'. Since the Couple has already separated each other, both parties need not sign on the Divorce Certificate. Any petition in this section needs submission of the Court fee in lieu of 'Zubel'.

135. **Settlement of Case at PTC Court:** If any case or problem is brought to the PTC Court for settlement, the Court shall-

    i.   Summon and hear the complainant, defendant and their witnesses.

    ii.   Carefully peruse and study all documents pertaining to the case.

   iii. Pass judgment on the case in accordance with the Customary Laws.

   iv. The convicted person shall perform 'Salam' or 'Sasat' at the PTC Court.

136. **Debarring of Council Members:** A member of the adjudicating Council/Court will be debarred from attending the Court proceedings, if he/she has a stake on the case or if either the complainant or defendant is his/her close relative.

137. **Vaihawmna Sutpi Kawi:** If any person approaches the PTC Court for settlement of any case or problem by paying the requisite fee, it is called 'Vaihawmna Innpi Kawi'. Once the Court takes up the case, no person is allowed to cause physical harm or nay other action relating to the case. Defaulters can be fined, depending on the gravity of the offence.

138. **Sasat:** When any case is heard and decided at the PTC Court or Village Council Court, the convicted person is liable to be fined with 'Sasat'. The 'Sasat' shall be bigger than a four-palm sized pig and it shall be eaten by the adjudicating Council.

139. **The Highest Court of the Paite Tribe:** The highest Court/ Adjudicating Council of the Paite Tribe is the Paite Tribe Council (PTC) General Headquarters Court.

These Paite Customary Laws are now being enforced among the Paites of Manipur. There is a Paite Tribe Council Court which decides cases of dispute between and among the Paite speaking community inconformity with the Customary Laws.

The highest Court of Appeal among the Paites now is The Paite Tribe Council Court which is endowed with the power to interpret and decides cases between and among the Paites speaking Community according to the provision of the Paite Customary Law. However, if either of the party to the dispute is not satisfied with the verdict of the PTC Court, it can appeal to the District Session Court/Munsif Court or Higher or even Supreme Court.

In 1956, the Manipur (Village Authority in the Hill Areas) Act was passed which provided for the creation of Village Authority in the hill areas of Manipur. Accordingly, the institution of Village Authority was created in all hill villages of Manipur including Paite villages. As per the provision of the said Act, the Village Authority shall also act as Village Authority Court in which all the members of the Authority shall be members of Village Authority Court. The jurisdiction of Village Authority Court as per the provision of the Act, within the limit of the village boundary shall also be the member of the Court. On the other hand, as far as the Paites are concerned, in addition to the Village Authority Court, Paite Tribe Council was established in 1986 to decide cases in both the disputing party are from Paite community. Therefore, there appears to be an overlapping of power and jurisdiction between the two courts of appeal i.e. The Village Authority Court and the PTC (Paite Tribe Council Court) because both the Courts have the same powers and the same jurisdiction over the same people. However, inspite of this seemingly overlapping of powers and jurisdiction, there seldom was a problem as the disputing parties are given the liberty to appeal in either of the two courts.

8.   THE MANIPUR STATE HILL PEOPLES (ADMINISTRATION) REGULATION, 1947:

However, in 1947 the Manipur State Hill Peoples (Administration) Regulation was passed for the administration of the hill areas of Manipur. According to the provision of the Regulation, the administration of the hill areas of Manipur was vested in the Maharaja –in – Council and exercised in accordance with the Constitution Act of the State, 1947, a Provision for nominated members of village authority, and the administration of justice in the hill areas of Manipur was managed by the court of the village authorities, the court of Circle, Authorities and the Hill Bench at Imphal and the Chief Court of Manipur.

Again, in 1956, the Manipur (Village Authority in the Hill Areas) Act was passed which provided for the elected members of Village Authority with the chief as its ex-officio Chairman. According to this Act, the Chief Commissioner may appoint any two or more members of Village Authority Court. But this provision of the Act is not implemented. Instead, all the members of the Village Authority are also the members of Village Authority Court and all the members of the Village Authority participated in deciding cases. Being the only court of appeal in the village it decides almost all cases except the serious ones, which are to be decided by the District Court. It has the power to decide even criminal cases. If a person files a case in the Village Authority Court which is of insignificant, the Village Authority Court can dismiss the case. But, if the Village Authority Court feels that the case filed was beyond its jurisdiction or it if feels that its power is limited to punish the guilty, it can refer the case to the higher court for final decision. The Village Authority Court has the power to punish the convicted person with a fine of not more than Rs. 200. But if the convicted person refused to pay the fine, the Court has the power to imprison him for a period of not more than one month. The Village Authority in the Hill Areas of Manipur has a limited power with regards to the administration of justice in the sense that its judgement can be declared null and void by the Deputy Commissioner or Sub-divisional Magistrate. Besides, if any one is not satisfied with the judgement of the Village Authority Court, he has the right to go to the District Court or other higher court, for seeking justice. Therefore, the judgement of Village Authority Court is not final and binding to the disputing parties.

Thus, with the passing of the Manipour State Hill People (Administration) Regulation in 1947 and the Manipur Village Authority in the Hill Areas Act in 1956 the power of the Paite chiefs has declined considerably. A person being aggrieved with decision of the household council or village Court may refer an appeal to the Civil Court of the State. The Village Authority Court is not the final Court of justice, and even in the Village Authority Court, there are elected members who have the backing of the people of the Village. The hereditary chief remains as the ex-officion Chairman of the Village Authority, but he can no more dictate his will on the duly elected members of Village Authority.

The Abolition of Chieftainship
in Lushai Hills (Mizoram):

When the British had finally put the entire Lushai Hills under their control in 1890 by subjugating all the chiefs, they administered it through a Superintendent stationed at Aizawl. The Superintendent of Lushai Hills worked under the direction of the Chief Commissioner of Assam. Soon after the administration of Lushai Hills was taken over by the British, the Superintendent of Lushai Hills increased the number of chiefs from 30 to 300. Since the British did not have sufficient knowledge of the situation, they did not want to directly interfere with the affairs of the people, and as such entrusted the overall administration of the village to the chiefs. Except severe cases, which were decided by the Government, the chiefs were entrusted to settle all disputes between individuals. The chief decided cases according to the customary laws of the land. He was directed to collect taxex on behalf of the Government, and was also supposed to act as a Police Officer, and had the right to arrest persons who commit crime like murder and kept him under custody till the arrival of Police. The Superintendent of the District tried his best not to weaken the chief by the administration of the District. The chiefs were informed that as long as they behave properly the Government wil not interfere with the affairs of the chiefs. The Superintendent did not want to decide petty cases as it diminish the power of the chiefs. However, in 1937, the Government directed the Superintendent to abolish smaller chiefs. But the bigger and stronger chiefs were still allowed to retain their chieftainship.

The chief and Mizo Union: Prior to 1946, there was no political party in Lushai Hills. There was Young Mizo Association (YMA) which was a non-political organization concerning itself with social services. Vanlawma and Dahrawka thought of forming a political party for the protection of the commoners and their interest. And on the 9th April 1946 the first political party in Lushai Hills known as Mizo Peoples Union came into existence. The aim of this new political party was to improve the social, economic and political condition of the people, and to establish a cordial relation between the common men and the chiefs.

Vanlawma made an appeal to the chiefs to join the new political party which was formed mainly for the promotion of the interest of the commoners, and the chief had no place in it. Then the name of the party was changed from the Mizo Peoples Union to Mizo Union to enable any one to join the Party. However, the party became popular only with the commoners. Therefore, the counteract the Mizo Union, chiefs set up their own council. Thus, the relation between the chiefs and the commoners deteriorated further. The Mizo Union launched a mass movement for the abolition of the chieftainship.

People were asked to disobey the order of the chief and not to pay taxes. In the month of October 1946, the Mizo Union proposed that the administration of the village should be vested not only in the chiefs, but it should be vested with the chief and his elders who were to be elected by the people. They wanted to abolish the right of the chief to appoint his elders. They also wanted the abolition of force labour. It also suggested that the District Council should consist of more members form the commoners than the chiefs. Therefore, the Superintendent of the District was asked to increase the representation of the commoners in the Advisory Council. In fact, the Mizo Union was not fighting for the total abolition of chieftainship, but was fighting for the delimitation of the powers of the chiefs.

However, with the growing misunderstanding between the chiefs and the Mizo Union, the latter decided to fight for the total abolition of the institution of chieftainship in Lushai Hills. The Mizo Union fought the general election to Assam Legislative Assembly and the election to the District Council, and was able to send its representatives to the Assam Legislative Assembly, and was also able to form a Government in the District Council. After forming the Government in the District Council it was finally able to abolish the institution of chieftainship in Lushai Hills in 1956.

9. VILLAGE COUNCIL:

Following the successful ablolition of chieftainship in Lushai Hills, the Paite chiefs in the Sialkal Range of Lushai Hills were also thrown out of their chieftainship. As a result, many Paite chiefs left Lushai Hills and migrated to Lamka, Churachandpur, in the late 50s. Some of those chiefs migrated to Manipur from Lushai Hills are still alive which includes Mr. Lalbuang, chief of Zotlang village and Mr. Galkap, chief of Mimbung village.

With the abolition of chieftainship in Lushai Hills the administration of village has been taken over by village council the members of which are duly elected by the people in most democratic manner. The V.C. in Lushai Hills is headed by a President selected from among the members of the V.C.

A V.C in Lushai Hills is responsible for the overall administration of the village and has to see the general wellbeing of the people. It appoints the managing committee of a village school which is responsible for the perfect and efficient working of village school. This school managing committee enforces strict discipline to the teachers while the teachers enforce strict discipline to the students. It also collects taxes from the people on behalf of the government. Regarding the administration of justice, the V.C decides petty cases according to the customary laws of the Mizos. If any one is satisfied with the judgement of the V.C Court, he can go to the District Court even in petty cases.

The V.C also acts a police force where there is no uniform police. To assist athe V.C. in the maintenance of peace in the village, there is a Village Defence Party (VDP). The VDP acts as the village police under the direction of V.C. The VCP is responsible for the protection of the village from anti-social elements. The VDP and the V.C work hand in hand for the welfare of the village.

10. THE IMPACT OF THE ENCATMENT OF THE MANIPUR HILL PEOPLE (ADMINISTRATION) REGULATION 1947 AND THE MANIPUR (VILLAGE AUTHORITIES IN THE HILL AREAS) ACT 1956 ON THE TRIBAL CHIEFS OF MANIPUR:

The entire Manipur, both hills and plain, came under the direct control of the British India Government. But the British did not want to interfere with the affairs of the tribal chiefs in

Manipur, as a result of which, most of the tribal chiefs enjoyed the same powers as they enjoyed before. The chief of Mizos/ Zomis continued to enjoy the same rights and privileges they enjoyed before the coming of the British. They were allowed to administer the village according to the customary laws of the land. Except the payment of house tax of Rs. 3 annually the hill people were practically free to administer themselves.

However, with the passing of Manipur State Hill people (Administration) Regulation Act 1947, there had been a slight decline in the powers of the chiefs. The Regulation provided for the nominated members of V.A. in Manipur Hill areas. As a result of this, the members of V.A. had little voice in the overall administration of the village. The Regulation also provided for the management of village Authority Court (VAC) which was responsible for the administration of justice in the village. But, the village authority court was not the final court of justice as there were highter courts like the Court of the Circle Authorities, the Hill Bench at Imphal and the chief's Court at Imphal.

If any one is not satisfied with the judgement of the Village Court, he is at liberty to go to the higher Court for seeking justice. Therefore, the passing of Manipur State Hilll People (Administration) Regulation Act of 1947 was defomote; a setback for the Village Chiefs, particularly in the sphere of the administration of justice. This Regulation was enforced from the 15th October 1949 to 1955.

Again, in 1956 the Parliament has passed the Manipur (Village Authority in the Hill Areas) Act 1956 which provided for the elected members of V.A. With the passing and enactment of this Act, the members of the V.A are elected by the people of the Village concerned. The chief remains as the ex-officio Chairman of the V.A the size of the V.A. as provided by the Act varies from village to village, depending upon the size of the population of the village. The Act provided that a village with twenty to sixty tax-paying houses shall have five members of V.A and a village with more than hundred but less than hundred and fifty tax paying houses shall have twelve members of V.A.

Earlier, the term of the office of the members of V.A. was three years but it has now been increased to five years by the Manipur (Village Authority in the Hill Areas Amendment (Act 1984. The Deputy Commissioner of the District concerned has the power to remove any member of the V.A who, had his opinion, is not suitable or otherwise, from the membership. Any member of the V.A can also resign voluntarily from his membership by tendering his resignation to the Chairman of V.A. The members of a V.A. can also be removed from his membership by a resolution supported by ½ of the majority of the members present and voting.

Every V.A under this Act performs its functions to the best of its ability for maintaining law and order within the local limit of its jurisdiction, and for that purpose, exercised and performed the powers and duties generally conferred and imposed on the police. Some of the cases which came withint he purview of the V.A were forcibley opposing the cattle or rescuing the same, damage caused to the land or crapers public roads by pigs, pond-keeper failing to perform duties, cruelty to animals, obstructing passengers, indescent a person or persons, throwing in the street, theft, assault, etc.

Since the V.A. concerned mainly with the general administration of the Village, it was felt necessary to constitute a Village Court (VC) consisting of two members of V.A to be appointed by the Chief Commissioner by declaring in the official gazette. But this provision of the Act was not implemented. Therefore, instead of having a V.C. consisting of two members appointed by the Chief Commissioner, ther is a VAC in each of the village in Manipur Hill areas, and all members of the V.A. are also the members of the VAC. As such, all the members of V.A participate in the judicial matter. But it should be remembered that no legal practioner is allowed to practice before the V.C., and also no woman can be compelled to appear in person before the V.C. against her will, as an accused, as a party or as a witness. At present there are as many as 364 V.A in Manipur Hill Areas.

With the passing of the Manipur (Village Authority in the Hill Area Act) 1956, the powers of the chief has considerably gone down. Though he remains as the ex-officion Chairman of the V.A., he can no more exercise his veto power on the duly elected members of the V.A. Though there is no specific provision in the Act for the discontinuation of the payment of the traditional chef's share like *Buhsun*, *Saliang* etc. people in most of the village have stopped such payment to the chief. Besides the Manipur (Village Authority in the Hill Areas) Act 1956, there are various Acts passed from time to time to dismantle the office of chieftainship in Manipur of which the following are worth mentioning:

a) The Manipur Land Revenue and Land Reform Act, 1960.

b) The Manipur (Hill Areas, Acquisition of Chiefs Right) Act, 1967.

c) The Arm Forces (Assam and Manipur) Special Power Act, 1978.

d) The Manipur Hill Areas District Council Act, 1971.

e) The Manipur Municipality Act, being extended to the Churachandpur District Headquarters in 1980.

Of the above Acts, the Manipur Hill Areas (Acquisition of Chief's Rights) Act, 1967 directly interferes with the powers of the chiefs in Manipur. However, this Act has not yet been enforced. This Act seeks to abolistht he institution of chieftainship with all its rights and privileges. But in the Act, it is not mentioned as to when this Act shall be enforced.

Thus, thought the chieftainship is still in existence, it has a very little work to do with the village administration in the presence of elected members of V.A. In fact, chieftainship is neither actually alive nor dead. The chief in Churachandpur District formed a Union under the presidentship of Paudoumant, chief of Behiang Village to fight either for the restoration of chief's rights or for the abolition of chieftainship by giving satisfactory compensation to the chiefs. The Chief's Union of Churachandpur District organised a Conference-cum-Seminar on the 28th to 30th May 1986 regarding the Hill Areas, the Hill Administration and the Hill Development at Lamka, Churachandpur. In the Conference –cum-Seminar, the Union passed the following resolutions:

1. The Chief's office status shall be properly maintained with the tribal customary laws.

2. A demand be made to Government to no longer enforce Manipur (Village Authority in the Hill Areas) Act, 1956 and repeal the said Act.

3. A demand be made to the Government to withdraw the order/notification under sub-section (3) Section (1) of Manipur Land Revenue and Land Reform Act, 1960 against some hill village chiefs and to declare the said villages of Section (2) of the said Act.

4. A demand be made to the Government to withdraw the Municipality and small town introduced in hill villages of the chiefs.

5. Keeping in view the importance of forest belonging to the chiefs for the livelihood of the hill people, the chief's are warranted by circumstances to properly protect and look after forest growing within their respective jurisdiction, and a demand be made to the Government to this effect to vacate the forest reserve areas by the Government in the Chief's village lands and hand over the same again to the chiefs concerned.

6. As circumstances invited the chiefs shall now on words look after the overall implementation of the Government program (Schemes for the welfare and upliftment of the backward hill areas and people to meet the actual purpose in the respective villages, and a demand be made to the government to this effect to give sufficient plant to the Chief.

In order to achieve their demand, the Chiefs Union of Churachandpur District submitted a memorandum to the Prime Minister and Chairman of the Hill Area Committee on the 26th and 14th July, 1986.

However, there has not yet been any solution to the problem of the chiefs as such. The chief in fact have softened their original stand for the restoration of chieftainship with all its rights and privileges. They are now demanding the abolition of the institution of chieftainship with adequate compensation. Therefore, it is our hope that a solution acceptable to both the chiefs and the Government is reached as early as possible.

The Manipur (Village Authority in the Hill Areas) Act, 1956 covered about 364 villages in the hill areas including all the Paite dominated villages in Manipur South District (Churachandpur). Taking advantage of the Act, people in most of the Paite dominated villages now refused to pay their traditional dues to the chiefs. As a result of this the chiefs can no more depend upon the people for their livelihood, and they have also to work for themselves. Therefore, in order to meet their own requirement they have to practice different kinds of professions, and to do this, they have to migrate from rural areas to urab areas. This is because of the fact that gainful employment cannot be expected in rural areas. This resulted in the migration of people from rural to urban areas of Churachandpur. Each year hundreds of Paites migrated from rural areas to urban areas among whom chiefs of some villages are included. This led to the rapid increase of the urban population which on the other hand led to a steady decline in the population of rural areas.

CHAPTER VII

Pressure Group And Administrative Development in Hill Areas Since 1891

(A) PRESSURE GROUP

PRESSURE GROUP in India represents a vital element in the process of political modernization, in so far as it represents a response to increasing functional differentiation and to the break down of traditional type of authority. While apolitical party is a collection of individuals clustering around on interest and possesses a political programme, a pressure group is a collection of individuals who do not appeal to the electorates on the basis of any programme, but who are concerned with the protection of specific interests. They are not political organizations who put up candidate for election but are, the channel through which people with common interest may endeavour to affect the course of public affairs. Thus, any social group which seeks to influence the behaviour of political officers, both administrative and legislative, without attempting to gain firm control of government, can be designated as a pressure group. It seeks to obtain certain political decision without actively seeking power through per quasive powers.

In India, in view of widening activities of the government, a large number of pressure groups have made their appearance. The Indian National Congress itself began as a pressure group with the object of influencing the British government on behalf of certain special interest. It was only in 1930s that the Indian National Congress became a fullfledged political party and took a leading role in the National Movement with a view to get independence for the country, and assume political control in its own hand.

FORMATION OF THE PAITE NATIONAL COUNCIL (PNC NOW PTC):

As discussed above as to what is a pressure group, the PNC which was changed to PTC on 27th June, 2003 at the 48th General Assembly held at Hiangtam Lamka, was formed on the 27th June 1949 at Tangnuam Village, near Lamka, Churachandpur is one of the many pressure group based on community in Manipur. Except the Naga Tribes, all the other recognised and non-recognised tribe groups of Manipur have such national organization. For instance, the Kukis have the Kuki National Assembly (KNA) which is a recognised political party in Manipur; the Vaipheis have the Vaiphei National Organization (VNO now Vaiphei People's Council); the Hmars have the Hmar National Union (HNU); the Gangtes the Gangte Tribal Union (GTU), etc. The random use of the term 'Nation' by these tribal communities of Manipur gives us the impression that they are either ignorant of the meaning and connotation of the word 'Nation' as interpreted by political scientists or aware though, it was a manifestation of their longing for the time when they were politically, socially and economically independent. They continues to have the desire and aspiration to become, once again, politically independent people as before.

The PTC is an urban concept formulated by the neo-literate or the intelligentsia Paites for driving home the cause of Paite Community. It is a political organization as it aims at the upliftment of the Paite Community in the political field.

POLITICAL DEMANDS OF THE PAITE NATIONAL COUNCIL:

Prior to 1956, the Paites were not recognised as Scheduled Tribe in Manipur; and therefore, the first and foremost task of the PTC was to fight for the constitutional recognition of the Paites as one of the Scheduled Tribes in Manipur.

Memorandum for Recognition: Taking advantage of the visit of the then Prime Minister, Jawaharlal Nehru to Imphal, the PTC submitted a memorandum to him demanding the recognition of the Paite tribe as one of the Scheduled Tribes of Manipur.

The Government of India sent a ten member team of Backward Commission to look into the problems of the tribals in Manipur in 1952. Following the report of the Backward Commission, the Government of India, under the Modification to Constitution (Scheduled Tribe Part 'C', State order, No. 52, Part II) finally gave formal recognition not only to the Paites but also to other 28 tribal communities of Manipur in 1956.

These tribal communities are:

1. Paite	2. Angami	3. Aimol
4. Anal	5. Chiru	6. Chothe
7. Gangte	8. Hmar	9. Kabui
10. Kacha Naga	11. Keirao	12. Koireng
13. Kom	14. Lamgang	15. Lushai
16. Mao	17. Maram	18. Maring
19. Mayon	20. Monsang	21. Purum
22. Ralte	23. Sema	24. Simte
25. Sukte	26. Tangkhul	27. Thadou
28. Vaiphei	29. Zou	

DEMAND FOR CHIN PEOPLE RE-UNIFICATION:

The PTC has always been for the re-unification of the divided Chin people of India, Myanmar and East Pakistan (now Bangladesh) under one administrative umbrella, preferably India. This led to the submission of a memorandum to the Government of India on May 30, 1960 under the signature of T.Goukhenpau, as President and S.Vungkhom, as Chief Secretary of the PTC. The following are the tribes which it claimed to have belonged to Chin racial group:

1. Allam	2. Aimol	3. Anal
4. Bangjogi	5. Bete	6. Chiru
7. Cho	8. Chinma	9. Chimbok
10. Chibon	11. Hmar	12. Jiroi-Lamgang
13. Kolen	14. Kom	15. Kyang or Sho

16. Khami	17. Lai	18. Lakher
19. Lushai	20. Langrong	21. Paite
22. Pankhu	23. Purum	24. Ralte
25. Rangkhol	26. Sokte	27. Siyin
28. Thadou	29. Tashon	30. Welaung
31. Yindu		

In pursuance of the resolution adopted in the General Assembly held at Hansip Village, Churachandpur, in Manipur from the 10th to 13th October 1957, the Council submitted a lengthy memorandum to the then Prime Minister, Jawaharlal Nehru to pressurise the Government of India for the reunification of the above mentioned 31 different tribes of Chin ethnic group living in India. Myanmar and East Pakistan. The memorandum reads –

... the territory inhabited by the Chin tribes extends from the Naga Hills in the North down into the Sandoway District of Myanmar in the South, from the Myntha river of Myanmar in the East, almost to the Bay of Bengal in the West. Hence, the territory of Chin had been demarcated so as to include some parts of India and Myanmar and their existence of geographical bounds also had been circumscribed by their consolidated ethnological habitat of these areas. ...

The Chins lived in a complete independence before the British Regime without any outside interference whatsoever from any quarter, and no part of her territory was ever subjugated under Burmese or Indian administration. They even raised into the plains of Myanmar. The contiguous area inhabited by the Chin as already mentioned was a compact and homogeneous one. But as far as in the nineteenth century, the Britishers came and eventually conquered the Chins (in all nearly 7, 000 guns were taken from the tribes between 1893 and 1896 and the area was arbitrarily divided under them for administrative convenience by disintegrating it into Chin Hills, Manipur, Tripura, Arakan, Chittagong Hill Tracts and North Cachar Hills. The land so conquered was annexed to their administration. Even then the Chins in various regions were knitted together by common tradition, custom, culture, mode of living, language and social life. During the British regime, the Chins of Myanmar and India freely mixed together and lived harmoniously. As there was no restriction of movement as imposed today there was free intermarriage and social and commercial trading intercourse amongst them.

They administered themselves in accordance with their own customary laws and ways. It was rather a sovereign land where the people enjoyed a perfect harmony of their own, and their recognition attributed by the Government was the leveying of nominal house tax by the Britishers. When Myanmar was partitioned from India in 1937, we were not consulted nor was a chance given to us to explain what we were and are.

When India was in the threshold of Independence from the shackles of foreign domination, the terms were agreed upon that Myanmar and Pakistan would also be given self-domination status. Thus, the Chins have undisputable right of regaining their former political status. But unfortunately, no such provisions were guaranteed to the Chins nor were they given a chance to claim perhaps, due to their ignorance and unconsciousness of their political fate. In spite, the artificial Indo-Myanmar boundary demarcated by the Britishers was secretly confirmed between the contracting parties themselves without considering the culture, custom, history, tradition, relating, economic condition, political rights, etc. of the Chin people in this regions. This division not only leads to the detriment of the people's weal but deprives of their political, economic and social rights and is quite unfair, unconditional, undetermined and unadaptable because no strong voice as to preserve their fundamental rights can be raised from either side.

Since no part of the Chin territory was ever subjugated under the Burmese or Indian Government and the Chins enjoyed their self-administration before the British annexation, they after the British left the country, have legitimate right to be free again. But when India achieved her Independence in 1947, the Chins in this region were too ignorant and illiterate as to determine what future form of political status would be most desirable and conducive for them and for the Indian Independence. They in the true sense were far from being realised, and subsequently some part of the Chin areas were annexed to Myanmar and some to India without their knowledge. The consequence is that while the other brethren of India, for more than ten years of keen exercising their right to enjoy self-determination to solve their political destiny, the Chins have neglected too much and given no chance other than the step-motherly treatment as a second rate citizens, to enjoy such status irrespective of their legitimate right and of provision incorporated in Indian Constitution for minorities and tribes. Hence, something could be done for their preservation and checking all there shortcomings and maladjustment by re-uniting all the Chin tribes, for they will surely succumb sooner or late to extinction and extermination and may even cause costly and irrepairable loss. Thus, for a stable and a sound administration of the country and as our legitimate rights, we for and on behalf of all the Chin people, out forth this demand for the re-unification of the Chin within one country where every community can have District or Division or Region for the preservation of their fundamental rights.

Therefore, for all the facts and reasons enumerated rights, we approach the Government of India with good will and understanding to take initiative step immediately as to re-unite all the Chin tribes into one territory by rectifying the artificial demarcation of the boundary between India and Myanmar as specified thereof".

However, before the Re-Unification of Chin people under the administrative umbrella of India could be materialised, the Chin Liberation Army (CLA) was formed under the leadership of Mr. Tunkhopum Baite, which advocated for not only the re-unification of Chin people, but also for the sovereign and unified Chinland. Therefore, the CLA opted for armed rebellion to liberate the Chin people. It sets up several camps in Manipur, Myanmar and Lushai Hills, and of them the following are worth mentioning:

1.   Mualngat in Tengnoupal District (Manipur).

2.   Khaukual in Churachandpur District (Manipur) and

3.   Teikhang in Lushai Hills.

On the 22nd July 1963, Mr. Tunkhopum Baite was sent to Rangoon to have a talk with the Chinese and Pakistan delegations. As the outcome of the talk, Pakistan President, Ayub Khan was willing to supply arms and ammunition to the CLA. The CLA received arms and ammunition from Pakistan and intensified its activities in Manipur and Lushai Hills. However, before it could carry out its purpose, it met its untimely death when its leader Mr. Baite and some of its followers were captured and killed by the Mizo National Fronts' volunteers some where in Mizoram.

POLITICAL ASPIRATIONS OF THE PAITES IN MIZORAM (LUSHAI HILLS):

In the meantime, the Paites of Lushai Hills were demanding for a separate Regional Council for the Paites within Lushai Hills. In February 1966, the Pataskar Commission visited Lushai Hills to study the various demands of Mizos. The Mizo Union demanded a separate Mizo state while the Mizo National Front (MNF) demanded a sovereign state of Mizoram. Taking advantage of the visit of the Pataskar Commission, the Paites of Mizoram also submitted a memorandum to the Commission, demanding the creation of a Regional Council for the Paites of Mizoram. They have earlier declared the boycott of the Mizo District Council in 1965. The declaration of the boycott reads,

"Hitherto we, the cultured Paite people of Mizo District have incessantly appealed to the Government of Assam to constitute a separate Autonomous Regional Council in our favour in the Range where we live in compact area, in furtherance of provisions sub-paragraph (2) of paragraph (1), and sub-paragraph (2) and (6) of paragraph 2 of the Sixth Schedule to the Constitution of India. Many words spoken and written as memoranda to the State Government seem not to have been given due attention to. Full seven months have gone by since, Saigal, Deputy Commissioner of Mizo District toured the Paite region aproposaccelerating favourable condition of our constitutional demand. No tangible result could be seen therefrom so far and so long. Yet, there can be no point of return nor repose in the voyage of our ship to bring us Home cargo of Regional Council, since it has crossed the Rubicond".

"Let facts be submitted to men in power and to a candid word. Neither Government of Assam nor the Mizo District Administration can make the Paite people a scapegoat for their age long denial of the constitutional rights entitled to us, as free citizens of free India. While other tribes in the District had been enjoying privileges of Regional Council, noble Paite people are, it is a fact, still tortation. In the course of events, Government of India has earmarked certain privileges for us. The Government of Assam plays the part of a steward.

"A steward has nothing to do but deliver properties to the real owner on demand. This is true of our case. This is a basic justification of our demand. Number of our population in Mizo District is over 20, 000. But of this, 15, 000 live in a solidly compact region of Sialkal and neighbouring ranges. But to a great shame, 1961 census figures in Mizo District showed that not a single Paite was found living in the District – a big lie. We are distinct tribe, have been recognised by the President of India as one of the Scheduled Tribes of our Republic, India. Fear Comples in our minds can never be redressed under the present Administrative set up. Such has been the patient sufferance of our noble Paite tribe, and such is now the exigency which constrains us to have a separate autonomous Regional Council within Mizo District. Our demand is nothing less and nothing more than our political rights enshrined in the Constitution of India.

"We, therefore, the people of Paite in Mizo District, in special session, assembled at Salem village from August 2 to 3, 1965 appealing to the Government of Assam for the rectitude of our demand for immediate creation of the Regional Council in our favour, in the name and by authority of the good people of our tribe solemnly released

DECLARATION OF THE BOYCOTT
OF THE MIZO DISTRICT COUNCIL:

"Commencing from 1, 1965 and that all allegiance to the District Council, such as payment of house tax and District Council fund, is totally dissolved from that date. Members of District Council in our Region have unanimously resigned with promptness.

Our loyalty to the Union and State Government, however, remains ever as before".

"Dated: Selam   Sd/- Vungthang
The 5th August 1965   Chairman

         PNC Special Assembly, Selam North Mizo District"

THE PAITES AND THE MNF (MIZO NATIONAL FRONT):

Mautam, the flowering of bamboos, in 1958 was followed by a deadly famine caused by an alarming multiplication of rats in millions. A relief measure from the Government of Assam was far from adequate. Some persons who went to receive relief fainted and died on the way in the Pawi-Lakher region. A group of young men came together to render relief and organised themselves and formed Mizo National Famine Front (MNFF), headed by Mr. Laldenga. After famine was over, this social service organization converted into a political party, known as the 'Mizo National Front (MNF)'.

This MNF demanded sovereign Mizoram, and in March 1, 1966 declared independence. Except Aizawl, the entire Mizoram was under complete control of the MNF. Having intensified its activities in every knook and corner of Mizoram, the Paite people were equally effected. Some leaders of the Paite were killed in 1966 which included Mr.Suakdam, the Block President of PNC, Mr Lianhnun, Mr Vungzakhai, Mr Pachhung, Mr Thangsum, MDC, Mr Damsong and Mr. Thanglian. Hence the dream of the Paites for separate Regional Council in Mizoram could not be punished forward.

The killing of the leaders of Paite community in Mizoram by the MNF, a sense of hatred in the minds of Paites, non tribes in Mizoram, but also in Manipur, causing stranged relationship between the two (Paites and MNF) there existed a strained relationship between the MNF and the Paite Community. Therefore, instead of supporting the MNF policy of sovereign Mizoram, the Paite people developed a sense of hatred towards not only the MNF, but also towards the whole Lushai speaking community. This has become a hindrance to the unification of Paites under the 'Mizo' till today.

The MNF in the meantime, intensified its activities in Manipur South District; and to counter the activities of the MNF in Manipur, the PNC under the leadership of its President, Mr.Vanlalau, took initiative to form the Village Volunteer Force (VVF) popularly known as 'Home Guard'. Mr. Thuamkhanthang, Nengzakham, T.Kaigou and Vanlalau were sent to Gwaldam in Uttar Pradesh for leadership training. When these people returned back to Manipur, rigorous recruitment for VVF was done and a large number of young Paites joined the VVF. The VVF was given a free hand to deal with the MNF and their activities in Manipur South District. As a result, the MNF could not make large scale law and order problem in Manipur, baring a few encounters with the Security Forces and the VVF.

DEMAND FOR PAITE TRIBE RECOGNITION:

After the demad for a Paite Regional Council remained dormant for over 15 years, the political aspiration of the Paites in Mizoram, once again resurfaced in 1980. The Mizoram Paite Organisation (MPO) was formed on the 10th April, 1980 at Teikhang Village, located in Sialkal Tlang (Sialkal Ranges/Hills) of Champhai District. With the formation of MPO, the following persons were nominated as members of the organisation:

1. President   :   Thangzakap of Teikhang Village

2. Vice President   :   Phungkhai of Kawlbem Village

3. General Secretary :   Dalkam of Hiangmun Village

4. Secretary   :   Hnunlian of Teikhang Village

5. Treasurer   :   Thangzalian of Hnahlan Village

The Organisatioin, immediately after its formation constituted Action Committee and nominated H.Thansanga (the then Speaker of Mizoram State Assembly) as Chairman, K.Vungzamuan as Secretary and Chalthianga as Treasurer.

Initially, the MPO was formed as a pressure group to pressurise the governments, both state and central, to include the Paite tribe in the Scheduled Tribe lists of Mizoram, Assam and Meghalaya. Memorandums were submitted to the Governor of Mizoram and Prime Minister of India demanding the inclusion of Paite in the

Scheduled Tribe lists of Mizoram, The MPO in its Memorandums maintained that the Paites are the original inhabitants of Mizoram and they lived there right from the pre-British period. The memorandum reads

"We, the Paites are the original inhabitants of Mizoram (formerly Lushai Hills under the greater Assam state since 1300 AD (Mizoram Encyclopedia published and Edited by Dr. Subhas Chatterjee in 1990) we are now one of the prominent and major tribes in Mizoram. We are living in 32 compact villages in the North-Eastern part of Mizorams with a population of 35, 000 approximately besides living together with other tribes in almost all villages and towns in Mizoram......"

The MPO and its Action Committee pursued the matter with the active support of the Paites living in Delhi, and (L) N.Gouzagin (the then MP from Outer Parliamentary Constituency of Manipur). After persistent peressure at every level, the Government of India, under the Ministry of Law and Justice, and after obtaining the approval of the Parliament, issued an order for the inclusion of Paite as one of the Scheduled Tribes of Mizoram on 8th January, 2003. The Act is called, the Scheduled Castes and Scheduled Tribes orders (Amendment) Act 2002, and the Paite tribe was included or the name Paite was inserted in PART XVII- Mizoram, after entry 14 i.e. Paite was inserted in entry 15.

Text of the Order/Act, 2002 Scheduled Castes and Scheduled Tribes Order (Amendment) Act, 2002 reads

"Ministry of Law and Justice

(Legislative Department)

New Delhi, the 8th January, 2003/Pausa 8, 1924 (Saka)

The following Act of Parliament received the assent of the President on the 7th January, 2003 and is hereby published for general information:-

THE SCHEDULED CASTES AND SCHEDULED TRIBES ORDERS (AMENDMENT) ACT, 2002

No. 10 of 2003

An Act to provide for the inclusion in the lists of Scheduled Tribes, of certain tribes or tribal communities or parts of or groups within tribes or tribal communities, equivalent names or synonyms of such tribes or communities, removal of area restrictions and bifurcation and clubbing of entries; imposition of area restriction in respect of certain castes in the lists of Scheduled Castes, and the exclusion of certain castes and tribes from the lists of Scheduled Castes and Scheduled Tribes, in relation to the States of Andhra Pradesh, Arunachal Pradesh, Assam, Bihar, Goa, Gujarat, Himachal Pradesh, Jharkhand, Karnataka, Kerala, Madhya Pradesh, Maharashtra, Manipur, Mizoram, Orissa, Sikkim, Tamil Nadu, Tripura, Uttar Pradesh and West Bengal.

Be it enacted by Parliament in the Fifty-third Year of the Republic of India as follows:-

This Act may be called the Scheduled Castes and Scheduled Tribes Orders (Amendment) Act, 2002.

In PART XVII-Mizoram, after entry 14, insert "15 Paite".

N. Chaturvedi

Additional Secretary to the Government of India

DEMAND FOR PAITE AUTONOMOUS DISTRICT COUNCIL:

In the meantime, with the initiative of Paite National Council, Manipur, the Paite Nam Khawmpi (Conference of the Paite People) of North-East was held at Mimbung Village, Mizoram from March 6-9. 1991 which was attended by almost all prominent leaders of the Paites all over North-East India. The Conferenc, among others, resolved that the Mizoram Paite National Council, would be formed and a demand for Paite Autonomous District Council under the provision of Sixth Scheduled to the Constitution of India would be made by the newly formed Paite National Council, Mizoram.

In pursuance of the resolution adopted at the Conference, the PNC (PTC) submitted a memorandum to the Governor of Mizoram on the 18th August, 1991 demanding the creation of Paite Autonomous District Council in the Paite dominated part of North-East Mizoram bordering Manipur in the North and Myanmar in the East. The proposed Autonomous District Council covers a geographical areas of roughly 2000 sq kms with a population of approximately 35, 000 living in 32 villages. The PNC (PTC) maintains that unless a separate District Council is created for the Paites of Mizoram, they would sooner than later extinct from Mizoram. The Paites are socially, culturally, linguistically distinct from other tribes of Mizoram. They have in the past, their own chiefs and were ruled-over by them. Major J.Shakespear, the first Superintendent of Mizoram (Lushai Hills) described in his 1901 Census Report, "Paites are having distinct culture, custom, tradition and language as different from the Lushais, the Paite language is unintelligible to Lushai".

The PNC (PTC), therefore, put-forwards its own argument that 'to protect, preserve and promote the identity, culture, custom, language etc. as a distinct tribe, distinct from the dominant Lushai Mizo community, a separate Autonomous District Council under the provision of Sixth Scheduled to the Constitution of India should be created at the earlilest. Another argument put-forward by PNC is that the Paites are comparatively far more backward in all areas-social, economic, political, education, etc. and that the creation of a a separate Autonomous District will help them to develop themselves so that they are in par with other Mizo tribes who are comparatively more advanced.

However, the Government of Mizoram was not receptive to any demand for the creation of a new administrative unit based on tribe. It even wanted to abolish the existing Lai, Mara and Chakma Autonomous District Council. At the sametime, the most influencial NGO, the Young Mizo Association was consistently opposed to the creation of a new tribe based Autonomous District Council or Regional Council or even Development Council in Mizoram. They maintained that Mizoram was for the Mizos which includes all the Mizo tribes like the Hmars, the Paites, the Pangs, the Lushais, etc. and that the need for a separate administrative unit does not simply arise. The YMA, and for that matter, the dominant Lushai speaking Mizos, are apprehensive that the creation of such new administrative setup based on community or tribe will only further encourage other Mizo tribes to demand their own separate administrative units which will ultimately result in the fragmentation Mizoram. They maintain that the term, 'Mizo' is an inclusive term which include all the Zo ethnic communities living in Mizoram, and the land, 'Mizoram' is the land of the Mizos, which also includes the Paites, the Hmars, the Lushais, etc. and, therefore, the need for creation of a separate Autonomous District Council or Regional Council or Development Council etc. does not arise.

It is, therefore, so clear that the Government of Mizoram has no intention to create any new administratiave unit in the name of a particular tribe or community.

Like any other minority tribe in the North-East, the Paites have a long history of political aspiration for the creation of a separate administrative unit. They have submitted a number of memorandums to that effect to successive governments, both State and Centre. But till date, there is no positive response from the governments, except recognition of the tribe as Scheduled Tribes in Mizoram in 2003.

The following is the sequence of memorandums so far submitted to the concerned authority of the government both at the State and Centre by the Paites:

1. Memorandum submitted to Shri S.Bartaki, the first Deputy Commissioner of Lushai Hills District in Independent India in 1952 for the creation of Paite Regional Council.

2. Memorandum submitted to the first Prime Minister of India, Pandit Jawaharlal Nehru for the creation of the same Regional Council in 1953, and again in 1963.

3. Representation submitted to the Pataskar Commission for Hill Areas of Assam Re-organisation in 1965 for the creation of Paite Regional Council in Mizoram.

4. Memorandum submitted to the Governor of Mizoram for the creation of Paite Autonomous District Council under the provision of Sixth Scheduled of the Constitution of India in 1991, and in 1992.

5. Memorandum submitted to the then Prime Minister of India, Shri Deva Gowda on his visit to Aizawl in 1996.

6. Memorandum submitted to the Home Minister on his visit to Mizoram in 1996.

7. Memorandum submitted to the President of India, her Excellency Pratiba Devi Singh Patil on her visit to Aizawl, Mizoram on 13th September, 2010.

As seen above, the Paites are having long history of political aspiration for the creation of a separate administrative unit in Mizoram. In the early 50s and 60s, they were demanding the creation of Regional Council as was given to the Pawis and Lakhers. As mentioned earlier in this Chapter, the demand could not be pursuied further because of the disturbed condition of Mizoram. The MNF was demanding sovereign independent state of Mizoram which over-shadowed all other political movements and activities including that of the Paites for a Regional Council. The MNF after 20 years of bloody battle for sovereign state of Mizoram, signed a memorandum of understanding with the Government of India in 1986. Taking advantage of the peaceful atmosphere of Mizoram, the political aspiration of the Paite surfaced once again in the 90s in the form of a demand for inclusion of Paite in the Scheduled Tribes Lists in Mizoram, and the demand for the creation of an Autonomous District Council for the Paites by Mizoram Paite Organisation (MPO) and Mizoram Paite National Council respectively.

While the Paites are demanding the creation of Autonomous District Council under the provision of Sixth Scheduled to the Constitution, the Government of Mizoram, instead of recommending their demand for creation of Autonomous District Council, took Cabinet decision for the formation of Sialkal Development Board on 1st December,2011. It is to be noted here that the State Government has no constitutional power to create or abolish a Regional Council or Autonomous

District Council setup under the provision of Sixth Scheduled. It is only a recommending authority to recommend to the concerned authority of the Central Government. In pursuance of this Cabinet decision, the Governor of Mizoram formally constituted the said Development Board to be effective from the date on which the Act. is published in the official Gazette of the Government of Mizoram.

The official Notification as published in the Gazette of the Government of Mizoram on 24th February, 2012 reads:-

The Mizoram Gazette

EXTRA ORDINARY

Published by Authority

RNI No. 27009/1973 Postal Regn. No. NE-313(MZ) 2006-2008 Re.1 /- per page

VOL-XLI Aizawl, Thursday 28.2.2012 Phalguna 9, S.E. 1933, Issue No. 94

NOTIFICATION

No. B.12012/1/2010-GAD, the 24th February, 2012. Subsequent upon the decision of the Council of Ministers on the 1st December, 2011, the Government of Mizoram is pleased to constitute **"Sialkal Tlangdung Development Board"** with effect from the date of publication in the Gazette of Mizoram as follows:-

1. **Composition :-**

    1. Chairman   : Sitting Local MLA

    2. Vice Chairman   : VCP of the area on rotation

    3. Members   : All VCPs of the area (To be `selected by the Board in its meeting).

    4. Secretary   : SDO (Civil) Ngopa will function as an interim Secretary until the board appoints a regular Secretary.

    5. Jt. Secretary   : BDO, Ngopa will function as an interim Jt. Secretary Until the Board appoints a Regular Jt. Secretary.

2.	**Term of Office**	: 2 years
3.	**Headquarters**	: Mimbung
4.	**Aims & Objectives**	: Development of Sialkal area.
5.	**Powers & Functions**	: Preparation of Development Programmes for the area Coordination of the implementation of development Works as approved by the Govt. from time to time.The Board will submit draft Manual/Amendment of Sialkal Tlangdung Development Board for Govt.Approval and Notification.
6.	**Frequency of Meeting**	: The Board shall meet at least,once in six months.
7.	**Jurisdiction**	: Sialkal Range.
8.	**Subsequent Constitution**	: Dissolution and Reconstitution of the Board is subject to Approval and official Notification of them Government of Mizoram.

Renu Sharma,
Commissioner & Secretary to the Govt. of Mizoram,
General Administration Department.

Published and Issued by the Controller, Printing & Stationery, Mizoram
Printed at the Mizoram Govt. Press, Aizawl, C-500.

Proposed Draft Map of Sialkal Development Council by PTC, Mizoram

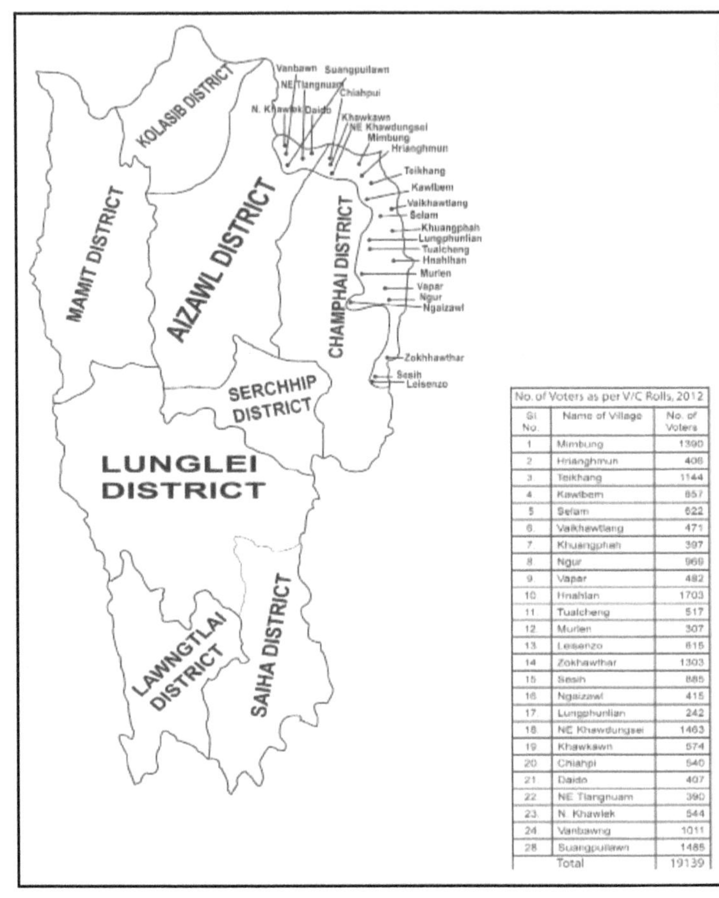

No. of Voters as per V/C Rolls, 2012		
Sl. No.	Name of Village	No. of Voters
1	Mimbung	1390
2	Hrianghmun	406
3	Teikhang	1144
4	Kawlbem	857
5	Selam	622
6	Vaikhawtlang	471
7	Khuangphah	397
8	Ngur	969
9	Vapar	482
10	Hnahlan	1703
11	Tualcheng	517
12	Murlen	307
13	Leisenzo	615
14	Zokhawthar	1303
15	Sesih	885
16	Ngaizawl	415
17	Lungphunlian	242
18	NE Khawdungsei	1463
19	Khawkawn	574
20	Chiahpi	540
21	Daido	407
22	NE Tiangnuam	390
23	N. Khawlek	544
24	Vanbawng	1011
28	Suangpuilawn	1485
	Total	19139

The Government of Mizoram, in pursuance of and in continuation of the said notification issued an order relating to the administrative jurisdiction of the Sialkal Development Board which reads:-

R-30/2012

No. B.12012/1/2010-GAD, the 25th July, 2012. Consequent upon the constitution of the Sialkal Tlangdung Development Board vide Notification of even No. dt.24.2.12 which has become effective from the date of publication in the Gazette of Mizoram i.e. 28.2.2012, the Government of Mizoram is pleased to include the following villages under the administrative jurisdiction of the Board with immediate effect and until further orders:-

1. Mimbung   2. Hrianghmun
3. Teikhang   4. Kawlbem
5. Selam   6. Vaikhawtlang

Renu Sharma,

Commissioner & Secretary to the Govt. of Mizoram,
General Administration Department.

As a response to the issue of notification for the creation of Sialkal Development Board, the Paite Tribe Council (PTC/PNC) Mizoram Paite Union and the Siamsin pawlpi (Paite Students' welfare Association) Mizoram, convened a joint meeting on 5th May, 2012 at Aizawl and had a threadbare discussion on the newly constituted Sialkal Development Board as took the following resolution on the Sialkal Development Board:-

1. Since the Paites of Sialkal Tlangdung (Sialkal Range) are the likely beneficiaries, the meeting resolved to caustiously welcome the step taken by the Government for the creation of the Development Board.

2. The Paites are consistently demanding the creation of a separate Political Autonomy in the form of first, Regional Council and later, Autonomous District Council, both under the provision to Sixth Scheduled to the Constitution; and never before in its history Paites in Mizoram ever demanded anything less than the two.

3. The Meeting, unanimously resolved that, even if the Government could no concede to the demand for an Autonomous District Council and instead, created a Development Board, the territorial and the administrative jurisdiction of the Board should be demarcated so as to include all contagious Paite dominated villages.

Sd/-
(H CHINZAPAU)
Chairman

Sd/-
(THANGLIANZOU)
Recording Secretary

As per the Government Notification effecting demarcration of the administrative jurisdiction of the Sialkal Development Board, on 25th July, 2012, it is found that, out of the Paite dominated Villages, only 6 are included within the territorial jurisdiction of the Board.

The PTC (Paite Tribe Council) Mizoram, not satisfied with provision of the Act under which the Sialkal Tlangdung (Sialkal Range) Development Board was constituted, has submitted its own draft constitution with certain modification including the nomenclature.

Summary of the Draft Sialkal Range Development Council Act, 12013.

A BILL/AN ACT

"to provide for the establishment of a Council for the Accelerated Development and Advancement of Sialkal Range and its adjoining areas in Mizoram and for matters Incidental thereto or connected therwith.

Whereas it is expedient to provide for the establishment of a Council giving it powers for the social, economic, educational and cultural advancement and development of the people residing in Sialkal Range and its adjoining areas in Mizoram.

It is hereby enacted in the Sixty-Third Year of the Republic of India, by the Legislature of Mizoram, as follows:-

1. SHORT TITLE, EXTENT AND COMMENCEMENT:

(a) This Act may be called the Sialkal Range Development Council Act, 2013.

(b) It extends to the Villages mentioned in sub-section (1) of Section 3.

(c) It shall come into force on such date as the Government may, by notification, appoint.

2. DEFINITIONS:

In this Act, unless the context otherwise requires

(a) "Council" means the Sialkal Range Development Council established Under this Act;

(b) "General Council" means the General Council constituted under Section 4;

(c) "Executive Council" means the Executive Council constituted under Section5;

(d) "Chief Executive Officer" means the Chief Executive Officer of the Council;

(e) "Constituency" means a constituency for the purposes of election to the Council as delimited from time to time.

(f) "Village Council" has the same meaning as defined in the Lushai Hills District (Village Councils) Act, 1953 as amended;

(g) "Council area" means the area of the Council as mentioned in sub section (1) of Section 3;

(h) "Government" means the State Government of Mizoram;

(i) "Prescribed" means prescribed by rules;

(j) "Council Fund" means the Council Fund established under Section15;

(k) "Rules" means rules made under this Act.

3. ESTABLISHMENT AND INCORPORATION OF COUNCIL:

1. There shall be established and constituted by the State Government, a Council to be known as the Sialkal Range Development Council (SRDC) for the accelerated development and advancement of area of the Council which

shall comprise the Villages of **Mimbung, Hrianghmun, Teikhang, Kawlbem, Selam, Vaikhawtlang, Khuangphah, Ngur, Vapar, Hnahlan, Tualcheng, Murlen, Leisenzo, Zokhawthar, Sesih, Ngaizawl, Lungphunlian, NE Khawdungsei, Khawkawn, Chiahpui, Daido, NE Tlangnuam, Vanbawng, Suangpuilawn and N.Khawlek** in Aizawl and Champhai District and may include any other as may be prescribed by the Government from time to time.

2. The Council shall be a body corporate with the name aforesaid having perpetual succession and a common seal with power, subject to the provisions of this Act, to acquire, hold and dispose property, both moveable and immovable, and to contract with approval of the Government, and shall, by the said name, sue and be sued.

3. The Council shall be deemed to have been incorporated for the purposes, among others, of preparing plans and programmes for the all round development in the Council area promoting original research of advancement of education, of educational and financial condition of the people, of inspecting the different institutions, organisations, local authorities and suspervision all matters relating to the general standard of the people of the area and of promoting their physical, mental and moral welfare.

4. The headquarters of the Council shall be at Mimbung.

4. CONSTITUTION AND COMPOSITION OF GENERAL COUNCIL:

The Composition of the General Council shall be as under:-

(a) Chairman   :   To be elected by the elected members;

(b) Vice Chairman :   To be elected by the elected members;

(c) Members   :

  i.   All members chosen by direct electionfrom territorial constituencies in the Council area.

  ii. Chief Executive Officer, who shall be the Member Secretary of the Council;

iii. Five persons to be nominated by the Government from amongst persons who have-special knowledge of law, planning, rural development, social service, finance and accounts of Government, education, agriculture, industries, irrigation, public health, forestry, mining, pubic works, employment and management of problems faced by the general public.

(d) Ex-officio Members:

i. All sitting members of the Mizoram Legislative Assembly elected from any constituency, either wholly or partly within the Council area;

ii. Deputy Commissioner of the District concerned under which the Council area is situated.

5. Executive Council:

There shall be an Executive Council consisting of the Chairman, the Vice Chairman and three Executive members. The Chairman and Vice Chairman shall be elected by the elected members of the General Council from amongst themselves in accordance with such procedure as may be prescribed. The other Executive Members shall be nominated by the Chairman from amongst the Members of the Council as soon as possible after the Chairman enters into office.

6. Terms of office and conditions of service of Chairman, Vice Chairman, Executive Members etc.:

1. All the General Council members, including the Chairman and Vice Chairman, shall hold office for a period of three years from the date appointed by the Government for the first meeting of the General Council after the election for constitution of the Council, unless it is superseded earlier under section 17.

2. The Chairman, Vice Chairman, Executive Members or any member other than the Deputy Commissioner and the Chief Executive Officer may, by writing under his hand addressed to the Government; resign from his office/membership and shall be deemed to have vacated

his office with effect from the date his resignation is accepted by Government.

3. The Government may by notification, remove the Chairman and the Vice Chairman of the Council, if he-

    (a) is found, in performance of his functions under this Act, to have exceeded or abused his powers; or

    (b) refuses to act or is incapable of acting or acts in a manner which the Government consider to be prejudicial to the"

Thus, the PNC (PTC) both in Mizoram and Manipur is one of the various pressure groups in the two States. It seeks to obtain certain political decision in its own favour while it does not directly seek to obtain political powers. Though its demand like the creation of U.T. for the Chins/Zomi/Mizo tribes of Manipur, etc. could not be materialised, its demand for the creation of District Council, its demand for recognition of Paite tribe as one of the Scheduled Tribes of Manipur and Mizoram, its demad for the extension of Paite program in AIR, Imphal station etc. are met by the Government.

Besides, the District Autonomy Demand Committee was formed at the initiative of the PNC in 1969 for the creation of Autonomous District Councils for the Hill Areas of Manipur. The Committee headed by Mr. N.Gouzagain met the Prime Minister, Mrs. Indira Gandhi and submitted a memorandum to her. As the outcome of the demand, Six Autonomous District Councils were created in 1973 under the Manipur Hills Autonomous District Act, 1971.

The other political demand of the PNC worth mentioning was the demand for the creation of the U.T. for the Zomis (Chin-Kukis) of Manipur in 1980. This demand was adopted by the Hill people's Conference at its fourth meeting held on the 24th September 1978 at Churachandpur. In 1980 this Conference submitted a memorandum to the Government of India for the creation of U.T. for the Zomis of Manipur comprising the Autonomous District of Tengnoupal, Sadar Hills, Manipur South District, the Jiribam Sub-division Nungba Block of West District and the Sialkal Range of Mizoram. This demand, however, was not conceded to by the Government of India till today.

Besides the above discussed political demands, the PNC made various social, economic and political demands for the upliftment of the Paite people in particular and the hill tribes of Manipur in general. Some of the various activities of the PNC can be seen as follows:

1. A Paite Cultural Society was formed which is entrusted to preserve and protect the traditional culture of the Society.

2. A Paite Literature Society was formed to see the development of the Paite in the field of literature.

3. A Famine Relief Committee was formed which is entrusted to look after the afamine effected Paite people.

4. A memorandum was submitted to the Ministry of Home Affairs, New Delhi for the recognition of Paite as one of the Scheduled Tribes of Assam.

5. The Council also submitted a memorandum to the Prime Minister of India in 1985 demanding the creation of Autonomous District Council in the Paite inhabited Sialkal Range of Mizoram.

(B) Administration of Manipur Hills Since 1891:

THE KUKI REBELLION OF 1918:

Until 1919, the administration of the hill areas of Manipur was much neglected by the Government; and no proper provision was made in the state budget for the administration of the hill people. The administration was managed by the Political Agent through petty Manipuri Officers called **Lamboos.**

Even after 1891, there was no proper administration for the hill tribes and no proper provision for them in the budget. The expenditure on them was only the quarter of the amount they paid in taxes. Neglect and lack of touch between the administration and the hill people led to the outbreak of Kuki rebellion in 1918, which cost nearly 20 lakhs of rupees.

It is thus clear that though the immediate cause of the Kuki rebellion in 1918 was the recruitment of the Kukis for the labour corps in France, the lack of touch with the hill tribes and the neglilgence of their welfare were the remote causes of the rebellion.

There is no doubt the administration had been seriously out of touch with their hill subjects, that the latter were not always well treated, and that there were genuine abuses behind the immediate cause, i.e. the question of recruitment for the Labour Corps which turned discontentment into open rebellion. Such was the position in the beginning of 1917 when recruitment commenced for labourers for employment in France. The chiefs were against this recruitment, while the lamboos used it **unscrop** as an opportunity to make money for themselves. In spite of all these difficulties, however, by May 1917 the first Manipur Labour Corps consisting of 2, 000 Nagas and Kukis from the hills was completed and went away. The chiefs of the hill tribes were against the sending of second corps. Therefore, in November 1917, the recruitment was suspended owing to the opposition. In December the same year, the Thadou Kuki Chiefs who responded poorly to the calls for Labour Corps sent to France early in the year broke into open rebellion and raided into Manipur Valley. Sir Nicholas Beatson Bell described the rebellion as "the most formidable with which Assam has been faced for atleast a generation".

As mentioned earlier, though the immediate cause of the rebellion was the recruitment of labour Corps, the Government of India accounted the lack of adequate provision for the administration of the hill areas to be partly responsible for the outbreak of a rebellion of such large scale. It was impossible for a single officer to tour satisfactorily the huge areas under his control. Secondly, between the hillmen and the British Officers, there intervened a most unsatisfactory intermediary in the shape of a petty Manipur Officers termed '**Lambus**'. These men were responsible in no small measure for the rebellion. Thirdly, changes in the rules made in 1916, resulted in the President of the Durbar being very much lied to Imphal and so prevented from making long tours in the hills. Again, the war and other local troubles made it more difficult than ever for the President to devote the proper amount of time for the hill tribes.

THE MANIPUR STATE DURBAR:

Since the President of the Manipur State Durbar was responsible for the administration of the hill areas of Manipur since 1919, it would be important to know something about the formation of the Manipur State Durbar and the position of the President of the Durbar.

The Manipur State Durbar was established on the 15th May 1907 for the administration of Manipur. The Durbar consisted of one member of Indian Civil Service lent form Estern Bengal and Assam and six Manipuris. The administration was then made over to His Highness assisted by the members of the Durbar. As the system of administration in Manipur underwent changes from time to time, and the systems of administration after the outbreak of Kuki rebellion was framed in 1919, and was approved by the Government on the 1st October 1919. Some of the features of the rules are as follows:

(a) The Maharaja will be responsible for the administration of the state. He is assisted by a Durbar, the President of which is selected by the Governor of Assam and is usually a member of the Assam cadre of the Indian Civil Service. There are at least three Manipuri members of the Durbar. His Highness can veto any resolution of the Durbar, but copies of his orders have to be submitted to the Political Agent. The latter can refer any matter to the Governor.

(b) As regard to justice the Durbar is the highest original and Appellate Court both Civil and Criminal, and may in its latter is capacity, pass sentence upto and including death, subject to confirmation by His Highness in the case of imprisonment of 5 years and upwards, and by the Governor in the case of death.

This was the system of administration of Manipur before the passing of the Manipur State Constitution Act, 1947.

After the Kuki rebellion was quelled, the Government of India felt the need to administer and control the hill tribes of Manipur more effectively. Knowing the tribal way of life and their interest through the rebellion, the Government of India decided to make a better and adequate provision for the administration of the hill areas. William Shaw writes, "The operation against the rebellious Thadous of Manipur State in 1918 and 1919 led to a very much better acquaintance with him; from then onwards the more I like him". Since 1919, Government of India entrusted the administration of the hill tribes to the Political Agent and the President, Manipur State Durbar. The President, through the Political Agent administered the hill tribes on behalf of His Highness. The Political Agent in consultation with the Durbar gave effect to His Highness. The Political Agent in consultation with the Durbar, gave effect to His Highness wishes so far as was consistent with the order of the Governor.

The President of the Durbar administered the hill areas of Manipur through the Political Agent since 1919. He administered the hills under the supervision of the Government of British India, without the interference of the Maharaja of Manipur. The most important sphere in which the Political Agent and President of the Manipur State Durbar exercise control is that of over the hill tribes.

The Chief Commissioner of Manipur, Sir Nicholas Beatson Bel held an open Durbar on the 16th October 1919 at the palace in which a proposal for the geographical division of the hill areas was made. Accordingly, the hills were divided into four sub-divisions with a headquarters each at Churachandpur, Imphal, Ukhrul and Tamenglong. The President of Manipur State Durbar was normally a member of India Civil Service loaned from the Government of East Bengal and Assam. He was assisted by four Sub-divisional Officers each stationed at Imphal, Churachandpur, Tamenglong and Ukhrul respectively.

However, the administrative arrangement made in1919 was once again reviewed in 1930; and the geographical division of the hills into four Sub-divisions was reduced to only two Sub-divisions. With this the outlaying Sub-divisional headquarters were done away with, and the entire hill areas was placed under the control of the President of the Manipur State Durbar with two Sub-divisional Officers, one being the incharge of the South and one of the North.

THE UPRISING OF KABUI NAGAS UNDER THE LEADERSHIP OF JADONANG:

Once again trouble started in the hill areas of Manipur in 1930 when Jadonang of Kabui Naga started a new religion, and induced the superstitious Kabuis to believe that, he would overthrow the existing administrations, and enable them to make revenge on the Kukis. The Political Agent then proceeded to the temple of Jadonang with a column of Assam Rifles at Kambiron, and destroyed the idols and the temple. Jadonang himself was arrested in Cachar and was sent to Manipur authorities. He was then hanged on the 29th August 1931 for a murder of four Manipuris as his sacrifice to his new gods.

Even after the hanging of Jadonang, the movement was continued under the leadership of a girl called Gaidiliu. She was arrested, but escaped, and after her escape the movement became more serious and revolutionary. It was semi-religious, semi-martial movement, affecting both Kabui and Kacha Nagas; and a movement spread even beyond the borders of Manipur into the North-Cachar Hills, the plain of Cachar and Naga Hills and gave anxiety to the Government of Assam. However, Gaidiliu was arrested In October 1932 at Kenoma in Naga Hills, and was given life sentence in the Political Agent's Court for abetment of murder.

When the uprising of Kabui Nagas was quelled, the Government felt the need to control the hills more effectively; it was felt that the uprising of Kabui Nagas was the result of the abolition of Tamenglong Sub-division in 1930. Therefore, the Tamenglong Sub-division which was abolished in 1930 was once again reopened in October 1932, and from 1st May 1933 a new administrative arrangement was made according to which the hills were divided into three Sub-divisions Sadar, Ukhrul and Tamenglong. This remained enforced till the passing of the Manipur State Constitution Act, 1947.

THE MANIPUR CONSTITUTION ACT, 1947 AND MANIPUR STATE HILL ADMINISTRATION REGULATION, 1947:

Because of the Kuki rebellion of 1917 and the uprising of the Kabui Nagas in 1930, the authority of the State of Manipur felt the need to pay special attention to the aspiration of the hill men. In 1947, one court called 'Hill Bench' consisting of two members- one Kuki and one Naga, and another judge of the Chief Court as its Chairman, was established. Under the Hill Bench, some lower courts were also established to try minor cases. The primary duty of the Hill Bench was to see that the hill people have a hand in the administration of justice without the interference of the State authority. The main duty of the Hill Bench, therefore, was to try cases in which one of the parties is a hill man, and to hear appeals and revision petitions from the decrees and order passed by the Hill Courts below. Appeal and the revision petition could be filed to the Chief's Court against the decree and orders of the Hill Bench. These powers were subject to the limitation provided by the law for the time being enforced. The importance of the Hill Bench could be assessed, not only from the point of view of their having a share in the judicial administration, but also from the fact that the cases concerning hill people could reach the Chief's Court. Thus, the administration of justice in the hill areas was left to the tribals themselves. During the colonial period, the British did not want to interfere in the affairs of the tribals as long as the tribals did not confront the authority of the State.

It was only on the 10th August 1947 that the administration of the tribal areas of Manipur was formally handed over to the Maharaja of Manipur by the Government of British India.

Manipur was merged with the Indian Union from the 15th August 1949. Even before it merged with the India Union, there was much demand for the establishment of a responsible Government in Manipur. Therefore, on the 29th March 1947 the constitution drafting sub-committee consisting of the following members was formed:

1. Shri L.M. Iboongohal Singh, B.A., B.L.
2. Shri A.Ibotombi Singh, B.A.
3. Shri Duijamani Sharma, M.A.
4. Shri S. Krishna Mohan Singh, M.A., B.L.
5. Shri A.Daiho, B.A.
6. Shri Thangkhopao Kipgen, B.A. (Hons.)

Regarding the hills, the Hill Local Self Government Regulation Sub-committee consisting of the following members was set up:

1. F.F. Pearson, M.A.
2. Shri A.Tombi Singh, B.A.
3. Shri Daiho, B.A.
4. Shri Suisa
5. Shri T.C. Tiankham, B.A.
6. Shri Teba Kilong
7. Shri Dr. Leiren Singh

These two Sub-committees drafted the Manipur State Constitution Act, 1947, and the draft constitution was finally passed by the constitution making committee. This Act was extended to the whole of Manipur including the Hill Areas. However, the Act did not apply in any matter, where specific reservation of powers was made to any authority in the hills, under the provision of Manipur State Hill (Administration) Regulation 1947. Regarding the administration of the hills, the Manipur State Constitution Act, 1947 made a provision for the Manipur State Hill People (Administration) Regulation, 1947. The administration of the hill areas of the Regulation, as per the provision of the Regulation can be broad be seen as under:

Out of the total 51 Assembly seats 18 seats were reserved for the hill tribes of Manipur; and out of the total 6 ministers two were from the hill areas of which one was the in-charge of Manipur tribal Officers Promotion of the welfare of the hill tribes was the primary responsibility of the Council of Ministers; and $17^{1/2}$ of the total annual revenue of the State was reserved for planning and development of the hill tribal areas. The administration of justice in the hill areas was managed by the Court of Village Authorities, the Court of the Circle Authorities. Hill Bench at Imphal and the Chief Court of Manipur.

There is a provision in a Regulation for a tier system of local self-governing bodies for the hill areas of Manipur. At the village level, it has provided for the establishment of Village Authority, and Circle Authority was given the power to administer the hill area above the Village Authority. The establishment of Circle Authority necessitated the appointment of Circle Officers.

It was Circle Authority which was responsible for the encouragement of better method of cultivation and introduction of improved seeds and spread of wed rice and terrace cultivation with gradual reduction of jhum cultivation in the hill areas. It was also responsible for the promotion of lower and upper primary schools, maintenance of paths and bridges (other than iron bridges). Besides, it was also entrusted to look after the personal hygiene, cleanliness and water supply; and ensure preservation of timber in the open reserved forest areas.

The above mentioned administrative arrangement of the local self government in the hill areas continued even afte the merger of Manipur with the Union of India on the 15th October 1949 till 1955.

THE TERRITORIAL COUNCIL ACT, 1956:

When in 1949, Manipur merged with the Indian Union the administration of Manipur came under the direct control of the Government of India. As a result of the merger of Manipur with India, there have been some changes in the management of the local self governing institutions in the Manipur hill areas. The Territorial Council was established in 1957 under the Territorial Council Act, 1956 and the Territorial Legislative Council was again established in 1963 under the Union Territories Act 1963. These two Acts were a new arrangement made for the administration of Manipur which operated till 1971 when North Eastern Reorganization Act was passed. Tribal members of the Assembly functioned as the Hill Standing Committee of Assembly incharge of some hill affairs; and also some tribal members of the Assembly were appointed as members of the Council of Ministers constituted under the said Act.

DISTRICT COUNCIL IN THE HILL AREAS OF MANIPUR:

The latest arrangement of local self-government for Manipur hill areas in the Manipur (Hill Areas) District Council Act, 1971. When the Indian Parliament decided to give fullfledged Statehood to Manipur in 1971, the tribal people also felt the need to have more autonomy under the State of Manipur. The District Autonomy Demand Committee was formed to spearhead the demand for Autonomous District Council. The Committee accordingly submitted a *memorandum* to the then Prime Minister, Mrs. Indira Gandhi, on the 14th October 1970, as follows:

Honourable Madam,

….. We the non-Naga Hill tribes of Manipur, … in the surrounding areas of Manipur belonging to different tribes, sub-tribes and clans, viz., Kuki, Hmar, Vaiphei, Zo, Mizo, Paite, Thadou, Lushai, Simte, Gangte, Kom, Chiru, etc. are homogenous people.

Our Culture, customs, tradition, society, physical appearance and languages are so identical that we form one distinct ethnical unit together. Perhaps, among the tribals of India we have the strongest tribal kinship. Our having one and the same folklore, mythology and legend are proofs enough, to confirm our same origin.

Our Culture and custom and our mode of living keep us distinct from any other tribes of our great country. Before the advent of 'Divide and Rule' policy of the Britishers, we live in sovereign land where we enjoyed perfect freedom of administering ourselves with our own varied customary laws. Till today these customary laws administer swiftly on our village. We hardly need any outsider to decide our disputes and cases of any variety. This peculiarity itself needs a great safeguard and we doubt its security unless otherwise our demand is granted.

The richness of our culture and custom is to be founding our songs and poety.

One more distinctive beautiful feature is that we can converse freely in our respective tribal languages without any hitch. ...

As to the area we occupy, it spreads far and wide, within and without Manipur. But at present, we want to concentrate on the area we occupy in Manipur. The main population is to be found in the south and then it spreads into two wings surrounding the valley of Manipur over theeastern and western ranges, i.e.... the whole Manipur South District, part of Manipur North District (Sadar hill area) now known as Mao East and Mao West Sub-divisions; part of Manipur Chakpikarong areas of Central District. ... We demand a fair dealing by the Government at this critical juncture. We demand that when the whole North Eastern Region is reshuffled to meet the demand of Manipur, Tripura and Nagaland (Unification)l, we also be not neglected but he put under one political roof and the area inhabited by our people all over Manipur be brought under one compact administration unit without leaving anyone and a single piece of land inhabited by us.

In order to effect concrete and immediate safeguards to the hill tribes of Manipur as a whole, the following important points, inter alia be incorporated in the impending legislation in Parliament for granting Statehood to Manipur:

1. That, to maintain the administration at the District levels, each hill district to be granted full autonomy, with Autonomous District Councils with the following subjects, inter alia:

   (a) Education upto Higher Secondary Stage.

   (b) Land settlements within the districts.

   (c) Health and Sanitation.

   (d) Forest (open and reserved) within the district.

   (e) Agriculture and allied subjects within the district.

   (f) Jhum Cultivation.

(g) Village administration within the districts including matters relating to chiefship, succession of chief of headman.

(h) Codification of customary laws and usages (both Criminal and Civil).

(i) Administration of justice-District and Session Court.

(j) Regional Councils within the districts.

(k) Property rights.

(l) Marriage and divorce.

(m) Social customs.

(n) Assessment and imposition of land revenue, taxes, and duties on profession, trade, callings, animals, vehicles, boat, ferries.

(o) Employments.

(p) Maintenance of schools, hospitals and dispensaries.

(q) Public works-originals and maintenance within the districts including State Highways.

2. That, in the State Legislature, a regional committee consisting of members of Legislative Assembly from the Hill Districts be formed with full legislative powers in respect of Hill Areas.

3. That, in the State Legislature, a separate Hill Ministry be formed with tribal members as the Hill Minister advice by the regional committee.

4. That, a quota of half the seats of the State Legislature be reserved for tribals.

5. That, a separate Hill Secretariat maintained with full facilities be established.

6. That, a separate budget be passed in the Assembly for the Hill Areas, which will be introduced by the Hill Minister as recommended by the Regional Committee.

7. That, physical demarcation of tribal/hill areas be made.

8. That, 60% of employment and services be reserved for bonafide tribals' residents of the Hill District.

We, therefore, demand that those safeguards for Manipur tribals be provided for in the constitution when full fledged Statehood is granted to Manipur. Anything short of this demand is nog acceptable to us.

Yours faithfully,

Sd/-Thangkhanlal   Sd/- N.Gouzagin

    Secretary   Chairman

THE DISTRICT AUTONOMY DEMAND COMMITTEE:

The District Council consequently came into being following the granting of Statehood to Manipur in 1971 under the Manipur (Hill Area) District Council Act, 1971. Under this Act the hill areas of Manipur were divided into six autonomous districts and for each autonomous district, a district council was set up. However, the district councils are not given powers and functions as demanded by the District Autonomy Demand Committee.

Each of the six district council consists of elected representatives selected by adult franchise. The total members of the elected representatives in each of the District Council are 18, but the total number of members is 20 including two nominated members who usually are from a minority community of the District. The term of the office of the members of District Council is 5 years starting from the date of the declaration of the election or nomination in the Official Gazette. However, the Governor of the State is empowered to extend the term of the office of the members by one year if circumstances so demand. A member elected to fill a casual vacancy shall hold office for the rest of the term of office of the member whom he replaced.

In order to contest election to the member of District Council, one must fulfil the following qualifications:

(a) He/She must be the citizen of India.

(b) He/She must not be less than 25 years of age.

(c) He/She must be a resident of the autonomous district.

(d) He/She must not hold any office of profit under any District Council.

Any and every person whose name is, for the time being entered in the electoral roll of a constituency is entitled to vote in the election of member of the District Council from that constituency. The election of the members of District Council is held according to the rules made by the Governor, by notification in the Official Gazette. It is provided that no person shall be member bothe of Legislative Assembly of the State of Manipur and of the District Council. If a person is elected as the member both of the State Legislative Assembly and of the District Council, then at the expiration of the fourteen days from the date of publication in the Official Gazatte that he has been so less he has previously resigned from his membership in the Legislative Assembly. If any member of District Council is absent for six months without the permission of the District Council, the Council may declare his seat vacant. If any question arises as to whether a member is disqualified because of holding any Office of profit under any District Judge having jurisdictions in the area in which constituency concerned is situated and his decision shall be final.

POWERS AND FUNCTIONS:

The powers and functions of District Council in the hill areas of Manipur are limited as compared to the powers and functios of Autonomous District Councils in Assam which are created under the provision of the six schedule of the Constitution. Though the District Councils in Manipur are given the power to undertake developmental works, maintenance of law and order, public health, education, communication, etc. the Governor empowered to limit such powers and functions as he may deem necessary. The District Councils in Manipur hill areas are empowered to control and administer on the following subjects.

1. The maintenance and management of such property, movable and immovable institutions as may be

transferred to the Council by the Administrator, i.e., the Governor.

2. The construction, repair and maintenance of such of the roads, bridges, channels and buildings as may be transferred to the Council by the Adminstrator.

3. The establishment, maintenance of primary schools and the construction and repair of all buildings connected with these institutions and institution of scholarship.

4. The establishment, maintenance and management of dispensaries.

5. The establishment and maintenance of cattle ponds including such functions under the cattle trespass Act, 1871 as may be transferred to that Council by the Administrator.

6. The establishment, maintenance and management of markets fairs and the construction, repair and maintenance of all buildings constructed therewith.

7. Storage, supply and prevention from pollution of water for drinking, cooking and bathing purposes.

8. The construction, repair and maintenance of embankments and the supply, storage and control of water for agricultural purposes.

9. The preservation and relaimation of soil.

10. The preservation, protection and improvements of live-stock and prevention of animal diseases.

11. Public health and sanitation.

12. The management of such ferries as may be entrusted to the charge of that Council by the Administrator.

13. The institution, inspection and control of relief works.

14. The allotment, occupation or use, or the setting apart of land, other than land acquired for any public purposes of agriculture or grazing or for residential or other non-agricultural purposes or for any other non-agricultural purposes or any other purposes likely to promote the

interest of the inhibitants of any village or town situated within autonomous district for which the Council is situated.

15. The Management of any forest not being a reserved forest.

16. The regulation of the practice of jhum.

17. Any other matter which the Administrator may in consultation with the Hill Areas Committee, entrusted to the District Council in the field of agriculture, animal husbandary, community development, social and tribal welfare, village farming or any other matter referred to in Section 52 of the Government of Union Territories Act, 1963.

Besides, the District Councils in Manipur Hill areas are empowered to recommend to the State Government regarding legislation to the –

(a) Appointment of succession of chiefs.

(b) Inheritance of property.

(c) Marriage and divorce, and

(d) Social customs provided that such matter concerned members of Scheduled Tribes.

Besides, with the removal of municipality from Churachandpur town, its administration has been taken by the District Council.

Since the largest concentration of the Paite-speaking community is in Churachandpur District, the Paites are able to send the largest number of members to the District Council of Churachandpur. The following table shows the number of members representing the Paite community from the inception of the Council.

Table 7:1

Year of Election	Name of Representatives	Name of District Council Constituency
1973	1.T.Goukhenpau	Tuivai Constituency
	2. T.Phungzathang	Ngazam Constituency
	3. H.Khatkhojam	Lungthul Constituency
	4.Thangkhum Valte	Lamka Constituency
	5. Dougin (PNC Support)	Thanlon Constituency
1978	Sumkhanjam	Ngazam Constituency
1984	1. G.Kaigin	Ngazam Constituency
	2. T.Haukholian	Tuivai Constituency
	3. Genthanlian	Lungthul Constituency
	4. L.B. Sona	Lanva Constituency
	5. Ginzamang (PNC Support)	Thanlon Constituency
2010	1. Langkhanpau Guite, MDC - Chairman	Tuivai
	2. H.Mangchinkhup, MDC – Executive Member	New Lamka West
	3.M.Gouzamang, MDC – Executive Member	New Lamka East
	4. S.Kamsuanlun, MDC – Executive Member	Hiangtam Lamka
	5. V.Khaikhanmung, MDC	Zenhang Lamka
	6. G.Suanchinpau, MDC	Lungthul
	7. T.Sumlianthang, MDC	Lanva
	8. M.Ginzapau Guite, MDC	Ngazam

Source: PTC Office, Hiangtam Lamka, Churachandpur.

There are 18 elected members in Churachandpur District Council representing 29 different tribes. The Paites being the most populous tribe in the District have the largest number of members to the District Council in 1973 and 1984 to the District Council. However, they failed to send largest member of in 1978 election as more Paites are contesting among themselves in each constituency. In 1978, the Paites have only one member to the Council.

THE HILL AREA COMMITTEE:

The Constitution of India under Article 371-C provided for the Constitution of Hill Area Committee within the Manipur State Legislative Assembly. Out of 60 seats in the Manipur State Legislature, 19 seats are exclusively reserved for the Scheduled Tribes of Manipur. This in other words means that there are 20 Scheduled Tribes members in the Manipur Legislative Assembly; and this 20 Scheduled Tribe members constitutes the Hill Area Committee within the Manipur Legislative Assembly. It is constituted to see the overall administration of the Hill Areas of Manipur and that any legislation effecting the Hill Areas required the approval of the Hill Area Committee.

At present the Hill Area Committee is the highest and the apex of the administration which is constituted at the State level, for the administration of the Hill Areas of Manipur. The District Council at the District level is the highest administrative machinery and the Village Authority constituted in 1956 is entrusted with the overall administration of the village.

CHAPTER VIII

POLITICAL PARTICIPATION OF THE PAITES

A. POLITICAL PARTICIPATION

Meaning: Political participation is a process by which citizens participate in the decision making process of the government. The social and material needs of men necessitated that men must live in a society. So, was society created, and when society comes into existence, there is a need for an authority for making rules and regulations for the proper functioning of the society. Therefore, state and government were created to govern and regulate individuals and their activities. Political participation is, therefore, a process by which individuals participate, directly or indirectly in the decision making process from the government. Political participation in a broad sense can be defined as, 'the involvement for participations of members of the society in the decision making process of the system' Mc Clasky has defined political participation as, 'those voluntary activities by which members of society share in the selection of rulers, and directly or indirectly in the formation of public policy' while there are morethan one forms of political participation, democracy is the form of government in which maximum number of citizens participate or have the chance to participate in the decision making process of the government. The participation of citizens in such process may be by contesting in the election, by supporting or sponsoring a candidate or by joining political party. The participation may also be in the form of exercising their franchise or even by exposing ideas about the government and its activities through mass media, both print and electronic etc.

POLITICAL PARTICIPATION AMONG THE PAITES:

Based on the above definition and explanation of the meaning of political participation, the level of political participation among the Paites can broadly be discussed as follows:

i. Political participation during the era of chieftainship ie upto 1956.

ii. Political participation from 1956 to 1971.

iii. Political participation from 1971 to 2011.

i. Political participation during the era of chieftainship ie upto 1956 :

Prior to the enactment of Manipur Village Authority (in the Hill Areas) Act 1956, the Paite people have a very little opportunity to participate in the political process of the political system. They lived in a traditional village which was ruled over by an authoritarian chief. Though the chief was not necccessarily a despotic chief, the people had no poltical and administrative role to play. The chief, since his power were not derived from the people, was not answerable nor responsible to the people for his act of commission and omission. The traditional village chief was the sole owner of the village and village land, and that he naturally was the final authority in every aspect of village life. He appoints a group of elders to assist him in the performance of his functions, both administrative and judicial. Even in the appointment of his elders, he does not consult or seek advice from anyone, but appoints, who in his opinion is most loyal to him and to his Chieftainship.

Therefore, the political system that exist during a period preceding to the passing of Manipur Village Authority(In the Hill Areas) Act, 1956 did not favour the participation of the people in the decision making process of the system. With the exception of Hausa Upa (Chief's Elders) who had a little say in the administration of the system, yet they do not have the right or power to go against the will of the Chief.

Therefore, the question of political participation, whether directly or indirectly, during the era of traditional chieftainship simply does not arise. In other words, there was a near zero political participation during this period.

ii. Political participation from 1956 to 1971:

With India's attainment of political independence in 1947 and with its adoption of democratic political system the Paites masses, along with the rest of the country men began to enjoy their democratic right to participate in politics by voting, contesting in the election, campaigning for a particular candidate and for a particular political party; and aligning themselves with one or the other political party or group. Even before the merger of Manipur with India Union in 1949, the Paite people exercised their democratic right to send their representatives to the then Manipur State Assembly. Mr. T.Tualchin represented the Paites of Tipaimukh Constituency while Mr. T.C. Tiankham represented the Paite people of Thanlon Constituency, and became the first speaker of Manipur. Before the merger of Manipur with the Indian Union in 1949, though the Paite did exercised their voting right, the level of political consciousness was very low. They had no political platform own to develop their political consciousness. People had no interest in politics as they were too much preoccupied with earning their livelihood, which was primitive, unproductive and wasteful jhum cultivation. As a matter of fact, they did not have the time as they work day in and day out to earn their livelihood. Therefore, the level of political participation among the Paites before the merger of Manipur with the Indian Union was very low.

On the 15th October 1949, Manipur was merged with Indian Union and became a part and parcel of the Indian Dominion; it was, then administered by Chief Commissioner and was given the status of Territorial Council.

The other new development in the post independent and post merger of Manipur is, the enactment of the Manipur Village Authority (in the Hill Areas) Act, 1956. As per the provision of the Act, members of Village Authority shall be directly elected by the people, while the hereditary chief shall be its Ex-officio Chairman. This new development has opened a new avenue for the people to have a say in the administration of the village, also it has given the people to participate in grass root level democracy. Though the chief remains the undisputed owner of the village and village land, the people, through their elected representatives to the Authority participate in the administration of the village. Therefore, the enactment of the Manipur Village Authority (in the Hill Areas) Act, 1956, is an important contributing factor for the development of political consciousness and political participation among the hill tribes of Manipur, including the Paites.

In the meantime, there were as yet, a few educated intelligentsias among the Paite, who felt the need for having a political platform to develop the political consciousness of the Paites. The PTC was, then formed in 1949 with the aim to serve as a political platform for the Paites. The PTC (PNC), therefore was instrumental in the growth of political consciousness among the Paites, which ultimately led to the increased in the level of political participation among them.

Prior to 1947, the Paite had no political system in which the masses could participate in the decision making process. The only political institution existed was the institution of chieftainship. Each village was an independent political entity which was ruled over by a hereditary chief who was usually the founder of the village. He was the only source of authority and his power was absolute. The village chief was assisted in the performance of his various functions by a group of elders called *Hausa upas* or chief's council who were selected and appointed by the chief according to his own will and liking. The chief has the power to dismiss any member of his council who goes against his will; as such each member of his council was bound to act according to the advice of the chief. This was the nature of political system existed among the Paites before the Independence; and that the masses did not participate in politics nor did they have the chance to participate.

In the meantime, the Paite people realised the necessity of having a political platform own to develop their political consciousness, to promote the spirit of mutual understanding with other tribes of Zo ethnic racial group of the state, and to press the Government of India for the recognition of Paite tribe as one of the Scheduled Tribes of Manipur. With these ends in view, the PNC was formed in 1949. Each and every member of Paite speaker in and outside Manipur is the member of the newly formed organization. The Paite National Council developed political consciousness among the Paite masses steadily, and each Paite voter developed the feeling that the defeat a candidate from Paite community in an election is the defeat of Paite community. Therefore, every Paite voter casts his vote in favour of a candidate belonging to Paite community. In case, there are more than one candidates from Paite community in one constituency, the majority of voters cast their votes for the candidate put up by the PNC. Usually, the leaders of the PNC are put up by the Council as its candidates for election.

Though the PNC is not a recognised political party, it does influenced the voting behaviour of Paite voters since its inception in 1949; and it is the Paite National Council which decides as to who, should be selected for contesting in the election from among the Paite-speaking community. It also decides as to which political party the Paite people should support. Right from the participation of the Paites in the electoral politics of the country, they have always been voting in favour of Indian National Congress (INC) which had been the ruling and the only dominant political party at the National level. They feel that to achieve their political aspiration and demands, aligning themselves with the ruling political party at the Centre are necessary. Therefore, the leadership of PNC are, at one time or the other the active members of the INC at the District and State level. Usually, the PNC sends its own candidate to contest in the election in Congress ticket, and all the voters from Paite community are expected to cast their votes for the candidate put up by it.

In each election to the Manipur State Legislative Assembly the Paites had been represented by one or more members in the Assembly. The Paite representatives to the Manipur State Legislative Assembly from 1947 to 2012 can be seen as below:

Table 8:1

Year of Election	Name of Representatives	Name of Constituency
1947	1. T.Tualchin	Tipaimukh
	2. T.C. Tiankham	Thanlon
1951	1. S.Vungkham	Thanlon (ST)
1961	1. T.Goukhenpau	Thanlon (ST)
1966	1. N.Goukhenpau	Thanlon (ST)
1971	1. N.Gouzagin	Thanlon (ST)
	2. T.Goukhenpau	Churachandpur (ST)
1974	1. N.Gouzagin	Thanlon (ST)
1980	1. Phungzathang Tonsing	Thanlon (ST)
	2. K.Vungzalian	Churachandpur (ST)
1984	1. Phungzathang Tonsing	Thanlon (ST)
	2.T.Goudou (PNC Support)	Singngat (ST)
1990	1. Phungzathang Tonsing	Thanlon (ST)
	2. V.Hangkhanlian	Churachandpur (ST)
1995	1. V.Hangkhanlian	Churachandpur (ST)
	2. N.Songchinkhup	Thanlon (ST)
2000	1. V.Hangkhanlian	Churachandpur (ST)
	2. N.Songchinkhup	Thanlon (ST)
	3. N.Zatawn	Singngat (ST)
2002	1. Phunzathang	Churachandpur (ST)
	2. N.Songchinkhup	Thanlon (ST)
2007	1. V.Hangkhanlian	Thanlon (ST)
	2. Phungzathang	Churachandpur (ST)
2012	1. Phungzathang Tonsing	Churachandpur (ST)
	2. Vungzagin Valte	Thanlon (ST)

Source: PTC Office, Hiangtam Lamka, Churachandpur.

Not satisfied with the provision under which the existing Autonomous District Council was created, the the Sixth Demand Committee was formed to put pressure on both the

State and Central Governments for the creation of Autonomous District Council under the provision of Sixth Scheduled to the Constitution of India. Elections to the Autonomous District Council created under State Act, were boycotted and election had not been held since then.ie 1984 After making some amendments to the provision of the Act under which the existing Autonomous District Council was created, the State Government elections to the Council in 2010 in which, 8 candidates from the Paite community were elected. The following table shows the representation of the Paite people in the District Council election since its inception in 1972.

Table 8:2

Year of Election	Name of Representatives	Name of District Council Constituency
1973	1.T.Goukhenpau	Tuivai Constituency
	2. T.Phungzathang	Ngazam Constituency
	3. H.Khatkhojam	Lungthul Constituency
	4.Thangkhum Valte	Lamka Constituency
	5. Dougin (PNC Support)	Thanlon Constituency
1978	Sumkhanjam	Ngazam Constituency
1984	1. G.Kaigin	Ngazam Constituency
	2. T.Haukholian	Tuivai Constituency
	3. Genthanlian	Lungthul Constituency
	4. L.B. Sona	Lanva Constituency
	5. Ginzamang (PNC Support)	Thanlon Constituency
2010	1. Langkhanpau Guite, MDC - Chairman	Tuivai
	2. H.Mangchinkhup, MDC – Executive Member	New Lamka West
	3. M.Gouzamang, MDC – Executive Member	New Lamka East

4. S.Kamsuanlun, MDC – Executive Member	Hiangtam Lamka
5. V.Khaikhanmung, MDC	Zenhang Lamka
6. G.Suanchinpau, MDC	Lungthul
7. T.Sumlianthang, MDC	Lanva
8. M.Ginzapau Guite, MDC	Ngazam

Source: PTC Office, Hiangtam Lamka, Churachandpur.

Most of these elected members of Assembly were elected in Congress ticket.

Political Participation between 1972 and 2012:

With the attainment of full fledget statehood by Manipur, Autonomous District Councils were introduced for the administration of the hill areas of Manipur under Manipur (Hill Areas) Autonomous District Council ACT, 1971, which gave a wider chance of participation in politics for the Paite and other hill tribes of Manipur. Besides the Assembly election, elections to the members of District Council were held at an interval of five years in which more Paites could contest and more Paites got the chance of being elected. When more Paites were directly involved in politics, more people are interested in politics which in other words means that political consciousness among the Paite masses developed. As political consciousness developed, the level of political socialization and political participation also increases.

The first election to members of the District Council for Churachandpur District was held in 1973, and the Paite community was represented in the District Council by four members. However, in 1978 District Council election, only one candidate from Paite community was elected. This was because of the fact that the Paites were contesting among themselves. In 1984 District Council election, the Paites were able to capture four seats. Most of these elected councillors contested in Congress ticket. Thus, it has been seen that out of the total 18 elected members, the Paite community has been represented by four members in 1983, one member in 1978, and four members in 1984.

In 1974 Manipur Assembly election, Mr. N.Gouzagin was elected and became Cabinet Minister. In 1980 Assembly election Messrs T.Phungzathang and K.Vungzalian became Ministers of State. In 1984 Assembly election, T.Phungzathang became Cabinet Minister.

Thus, we have seen the participation of Paites in the electoral politics of Manipur. Besides the Assembly and District Council elections, Mr. N.Gouzagin who had been a prominent member of PNC got elected in 1980 Parliamentary election from Outer Manipur Parliamentary Constituency in Congress ticket.

The above discussed political involvement of the Paite speaking community since 1982 signifies that, with the attainment of fullfledged Statehood by Manipur with 60 Assembly constituencies and the introduction of District Council in the hill areas of Manipur, the Paite community got more chance to participate in the electoral politics of the State and the Country as well. Churachandpur District was divided into 6 Assembly constituencies; out of which the Paites have the prospect of getting elected in 3 constituencies, viz., Thanlon constituency, Singngat constituency, and Churachandpur constituency. The Paite tribe is a single dominant tribe in these constituencies, and therefore, they have the largest number of voters.

Besides the Assembly election, the District Council elections were held after every 5 years. The Paites are represented by one to eight members in each election to the Members of the District Council. This in other owrds means more Paites are directly and indirectly involved in the electoral politics which further implies that the Paites are more conscious politically. More consciousness in politics means more participation in it.

Thus, till 1947 when India was given political Independence by the British, the Paite masses did not participate in politics actively as they were ruled over by absolute hereditary chiefs. From 1947 to 1972, when Manipur was given the status of Stathood with 60 members Assembly constituencies, and when Autonomous District Council was introduced for the administration of the tribes of Manipur, the Paite people have greater chance of participation in politics.

Besides the PNC, the *Siamsin Pawlpi* (The Paite Students Welfare Association) and the Young Paite Association (YPA) are also responsible for the growth of political consciousness of the Paite masses. Again, the level of educational attainment is also responsible upto certain extend for the growth of political consciousness among the Paites.

B. Voting Behaviour of the Paite Voters:

Voting, a collective event in the total political process, is considered, since time immemorial, a symbol of willingness to participate in the political process of the country and to accept the decision arrived at by majority simple, extraordinary, or unanimous by participants. The term voting behaviour is quite old but the old concept of voting behaviour has been replaced by a new one in contemporary period. Voting behaviour connotes today more than examination of voting records, compilation of voting satistics and computation of electoral shifts.

Though the election law has clearly forbidden the appeal to the voters on the basis of religion, race, caste/clan, language etc. the voting behaviour of the voters in India is much influenced by these factors. This is true with the case of Paites and other hill tribes of Manipur. Though caste system does not exist in the tribal society of Manipur, clanist feeling dominated the society including that of the Paite community. We have mentioned in the early chapter that the Paite community is divided into many clans like Thomte, Guite, Hangzo, etc. A person belonging to a particular clan is likely to vote for the candidate from his own clan. Clanist feeling among them dominates the voting behaviour of the Paite voters.

We have already discussed how the Paites are converted into Christianity from their animistic beliefs. The Paites are divided into various Christian denominations like the Evangelical Baptist Convention, Evangelical Lutheran Church, Church of Christ, and the Presbyterian Church of India, etc. These denominations also play a vital role in determining the voting behaviour. Of these denominations, the Evangelical Baptist Convention is most numerous as nearly 90% of the Paite population belong to it.

In any election a candidate belonging to the EBC has a greater chance of being elected than those belonging to other denominations. This in other words means that Church denomination also plays an important role in determining the voting behaviour of the Paite voters.

The purchase of vote is also an important tool of election campaign not only among the Paites, but among all the voters of India. The workers of political parties try to contact each household individually, and try to secure support for their candidate through all possible means. Usually, normally such attractions are offered not to individual voters, but to a particular group leader who promises to get the entire lot of voters of a particular group within the community. Of late even payments to individuals are being resorted to. Therefore, since the votes are purchasable with money, money becomes an important factor determining the voting behaviour of the Paite voters.

The prospect of getting job in the government also sometimes, determines the voting behaviour of some voters. Sometimes, some candidate during election campaign make promises to certain educated voters that, they would be given a good and well paid government jobs if they are elected. Such promises, sometimes conditioned the voting behaviour of certain educated people in their favour. Therefore, the prospect of getting government job does play an important role in conditioning the voting behaviour of educated Paite voters.

The moral character of individual candidate also determines the voting behaviour of Paite voters. Since most of the Paite voters are Christians, they are naturally inclined to vote for a candidate, who has a good moral character. No person can be called a good Christian unless he or she has a good moral character. Though the EBC often time asserts its natrality in the elections, most of its active members like deacons, Pastors, Church elders etc. judge the candidates on their moral personal character. Thus, the personal moral character of individual candidate becomes an important determining factor of voting behaviour among the Paite in particular.

Above all, the various political and social organizations within Paite community conditioned the voting behaviour of the Paite voters. The role of Paite National Council in influencing the voting behaviour of the Paites is already discussed. Besides the PNC, the Siamsin Pawlpi, the YPA and various local youth clubs also influence the Paite voters to vote in a particular way and in support of a particular candidate.

Unlike other parts of the country, the role of political party in conditioning the voting behaviour of Paite voters is negligible. No political party other than the Congress ever got the chance to win in the election in Paite dominated constituencies. Usually, people cast their vote for the Congress not because they like its policies and programs, but because it is the only political party contesting in the election.

Besides the Congress, many independent candidates contested in the elections to Assembly and District Council and many independent candidates also got elected. But after election most of the successful independent candidates joined hand with the Congress because Congress was the ruling party in the State as well as the Centre.

CHAPTER IX

CONCLUSION

THE POPULATION of the tribals of Manipur constitutes about 34% of the total population of State whereas the area occupied by tribals constitutes nearly 10/11 of the total area of the State. In other words 34% of the total population occupied 10/11 of the total area of the State. There are as many as 29 distinct tribal groups in Manipur, but they can broadly be classified into two ethnic groups: the Zo ethnic group and the Naga. The Paites belong to the Zo ethnic group although many a time they tend to identify themselves as totally a distinct tribe. While the Zo tribes of Manipur occupied Churachandpur District, Chandel District, Sadar Hills, Jiribam Sub-division of Central District and some area of Ukhrul and Tamenglong Districts, the Paites, are found predominantly in Churachandpur District and Jiribam Sub-division. Unlike other Zo ethnic tribes of Manipur, the Paites occupied nearly a compact area and are consolidated in Churachandpur Sub-division, Thanlon Sub-division and Singngat Sub-division of Churachandpur District. They also occupied Sialkal Range of Mizoram which is contiguous to Thanlon Sub-division of Manipur South.

The well known anthropologist, Dr. B.S.Guha who was against the policy of segregation of tribes of India stated that complete isolation has never led to progress and advancement, but always to stagnation and death In every part of the world, such has been the case; on the other hand, civilization, everywhere, has been built up by the contact and intercourse of peoples which has been built up by the contact and intercourse of peoples, which has been the chief motivating power behind progress. The Paites of Manipur, who began a settlement in small groups and away from the mainstream of life, become part and parcel of socio-economic as well as political life of the State. No society whether primitive or modern, remains static and is dynamic. It changes either slowly or rapidly under pressure of internal or external forces or both. Such internal or external forces are the products of biological technological and cultural factors. The Paite society is no exception. It has undergone changes through the decades.

It has been pointed out that the bulk of the Paite population in Manipur migrated from Myanmar and Lushai Hills at different periods of time, but mostly during the late 19th century and early 20th Century.

Most of the Zo ethnic tribes of Manipur were nomadic in the past. The Paites, like any one of them seldom stayed at a particular village site forever. This was so because of the method of cultivation as well as security situation. They practiced jhum or shifting cultivation which required a fresh and new land each year. When the land within the reach of the village exhausted after 10 to 30 years of cultivation, they were bound to leave the village for a new fertile land. As discussed earlier, there was perpetual war between villages and when a village was destroyed by an other Chief, they have to move to other location for fear of enemy.

Since the early period of British rule, the British administrator restored better law and order situation and inter tribal feud became less frequent. Head-hunting was no more encouraged by the British administrators and slavery was also discouraged. When peace was restored, the settlement of Zo ethnic villages including that of the Paite became more stable than before, and in the early part of this century many Paites gave up their nomadic habit of changing village site after every 10 or 15 years. Today, most of the Paite villages in Manipur and other neighbouring state of Mizoram are in permanent nature. This is evident from the settlement pattern as well as from the costlier materials like stones, bricks, and C.I. Sheets used in the construction of house. Other facilities like electricity, water supply etc. are also made available in some villages in the vicinity of Lamka town of Churachandpur District; and the provision of such facilities have made the Paite villages more stable today.

The transformation of the people from nomadic habit to a settledlife has brought tremendous changes in different aspects of life of the Paites; and one of the most conspicuous changes in the Paite society is found in their material culture. The traditional homes of the Paites were built on stilts, and the houses of the chiefs were exceptionally large. Today, the chief of a Paite village had no such exceptionally big size house. What can be seen today in a Piate village is house built with better material, as well as modern shape and designs which stand side by side with houses of moderate means, mostly katcha houses having thatched roofs. It is interesting to note that though stilt houses are still found in almost all the Paite villages, there are also houses built on earthen plinths. Since plinths houses are not the house type of Paites, the existence of such type of houses is due to cultural contact, particularly with the plain people. With regards to the internal changes of a Paite house, mention can be made of partitioned rooms. Many houses, particularly in the urban areas have a number of partitioned room for in the urban areas have a number of partitioned room, for different purposes, e.g., drawing room, bed room, kitchen, etc. More windows are provided for better ventilation and lighting of interior of the house. A change is also noticeable in household equipments like furniture and utensils. Today most of the houses, both in urban and rural areas, have wooden furniture. Almost everything made of cane and bamboo, is now replaced with a more rich and the poor families in rural and urban areas use aluminium pots.

Another aspect of change in the lifestyle of the Paites is the change in their dress. The change in the style of dress may be attributed to a number of factors like education, transport and communication, Christianity and modernization. Though traditional clothes are still found particularly in rural and remote villages, most of the young boys and girls prefer western style of dressing. In fact, western style of dress and makeup were unknown in the past. The use of western style of dress spread only after the World War II. It is seen that men are more susceptible than the women to the use of modern dresses. Though the use of blouse is common among both the yound and old women of today, other western dresses like stitched skirts and longpant are also randomly used by urban Paite girls. The use of skirts, longpants, brassier etc. is more or less confined to women of the younger generation. The adoption of western style of dress can largely be attributed to the conversion of the people into Christianity, which brought western education among the Paites.

The major change in the Paite society can be seen in the field of occupation. The spread of educational facility and increase of contact with other people as a result of the expansion of road communication have made the Paites more mobile, informative and intelligent. Though agriculture is the main occupation of a large majority of Paites population, many of them have also taken up other type of occupations like different kind of business, teaching, office work and similar such non-agricultural occupations. The change in occupation is partly responsible for the change in the style of habitation or settlement and life style. The workers in the office have naturally to leave their villages and stay in government quarters or rented buildings in places like Imphal Delhi and other metropolitan cities in other parts of India. Under such circumstances, they are away from homes, friends and relatives. They made new friends, learn new customs and traditions of the new localities, and adopt new lifestyle, usually associated with urban life.

We have discussed in the earlier chapter that Christianity has a far reaching impact on the lifestyle, and general outlook of the Paites. Christianity was brought in among the tribals of Manipur by the Western missionaries in the early part of this century, and today almost all the tribes of Manipur have become Christian. In the Paite society, as in other society, Christian missionaries have rendered invaluable services by establishing schools, and by providing medical facilities. Christianity has changed their beliefs, general outlook, practices, social concept and values and partly their economic life. The Christian missionaries and evangelists taught them to be neat and clean in their person as well as their homes. The moment a person becomes a Chirstian, he or she learn personal cleanliness and that sanitation and cleanliness have become a way of life. When a person becomes a Christian he cuts his hair short. The practice burying the dead in front of the house is replaced now by the practice of burying in a common cemetery for which every village sets apart a portion of land outside the village. They no longer observed the traditional festival or taboos associated with devils worship. These festivals are replaced by Christian festivals like Christmas, Good Friday, Easter Sunday, Missionary Day, etc. The system of dormitory is no longer practiced. Inter-village and intertribal rivalry is replaced by Christian love brotherhood.

The age-old practice of a young man marrying the daughter of his maternal uncle is no more considered meritable. Since the coming of Christianity, this custom is no longer enforced among the Paites. Today, marriage arrangements are purely made on the principle of mutual love between the two marrying couple. The custom of fixing price of bride is slowly dying down, and is replaced by the practice of gifts and presentation. Therefore, Christianity brought a spectacular transformation of the Paite society.

The spread of education among the Paite has also brought changes in the Paite society. The Christian missionaries at first set up schools in the hill areas of Manipur with the aim to enable the tribals to read the Bible. They introduced Roman script among them. The traditional social institution called *sawm* was replaced by school which enables them to contact with the advanced people, and the spread Christianity paved the way for gradual disusage of the dormitory system. They realised that education provided in schools gave them far better prospects than their own traditional types of education under dormitory systems. After India attained political independence the number of modern educational institutions has increased and facilities like exemption from tuition fee, stipends for maintenance and special facilities for employment etc. have been increased. Now a number of Paite students study in and outside Manipur. Many Paite students can be seen in different cities and towns of India like Shillong, Gwahati, Delhi, Bombay, Calcutta, Bangalore, etc. even in foreign countries. Those students studying in other parts of the country made contact with the people of other parts of the country. This changes their lifestyle and outlook. They developed a new ideas, new beliefs, new practices, new customs and new social value which widen their horizons. Now, many

Paite youth are also able to compete in all India and state services examinations and so are many in such services.

The introduction of democratic political institution in the administration of village has brought about socio-political change in the Paite society. Before the introduction of democratic political system, each Paite village was administered by hereditary chief who was assisted by *hausa upas* selected by him. They were the final authority in all matters concerning the village. The chief enjoyed a sovereign power over his village. After the British annexed Chin Hills, Manipur and Lushai Hills, the British ruled over the Paite village through officials like political agents and political officers who inturn entrusted *lamboos* to collect taxes. Since the Paite chiefs were tributary to the British government, they were no more enjoying sovereign powers. That is to say that with the coming of the British, the Paites lost their sovereignty. However, the chiefs still enjoyed a vast administrative power so far as the village is concerned. But, after India got political Independence, the Paite dominated areas in Manipur and Lushai Hills were brought under Indian Union; and with the adoption of democratic political system in India the administration of the village was entrusted with elected village authority. The Manipur Hill Areas Village Authority Act was passed in 1956. Though the institution of chieftainship still exists, the chiefs no longer enjoy the powers which they enjoyed earlier. He remains as the titular head of the village. Thus, the introduction of political institution in the administration of the village enables the Paites to enjoy their political and democratic right to participate in the election to members of Village Authority.

Again, newspaper and magazines serve as the agency of social and political change. Newspapers and Magazines widen the mental horizon of the Paites as they contain political and social life of other parts of the world. By learning through newspapers and magazines about the political change, political development, etc. in other parts of the world the Paites become politically conscious.

Therefore, it can be concluded that the Paite society has undergone changes in the field of social, economic, religious and political life. The factors responsible for these changes can be attributed to their contact with other people of the world. Their contact with the British administrators and Christian missionaries brought changes in their social, political and religious life.

BIBLIOGRAPHY
A.Primary Sources
1. Interview

GUITE,   Hawlkhai (b.1933) of Zawllian Village, Assam.

Interview.   July 25, 1987.

GUITE,   Liansiam (b. 1923) of Zawllian Village, Assam.

Interview.   August 20, 1987.

GUITE,   Piangzathang (b. 1933), chief of Takvom Village, Churachandpur,District, Manipur.

Interview.   March 10, 1987.

NGULTHUAM, V. (b.1933) of Lamka, Churachandpur.

Interview.   June 29, 1987.

JAMGIN,   G. (b. 1927) of Lower Lamka, Churachandpur.

Interview.   June 20, 1987.

KHAIZALIAN, D. (b. 1913) of Lamka, Churachandpur, Manipur.

Interview.   September 26, 1988.

LALBUANG   (b. 1917) of Lamka, Churachandpur, Manipur.

Interview.   March 20, 1987.

NENGKHOHAU, T. (b. 1925) of Lamka, Churachandpur, Manipur.

Interview.   September 26, 1988.

SANGTHANG (b. 1953) of Khawdungsei, Mizoram.

Interview.   June 16, 1987.

TUALCHIN, T. (b. 1914) of Paite Veng, Imphal.

Interview.   September 25, 1988.

Other Informants:

1. Dalkhenkhup, President Paite Tribe Council, Mizoram.
2. Thangkhanlal, General Secretary, Paite Tribe Council, Mizoram.
3. Ruata Tonson, Aizawl, Mizoram.
4. Chinkhansuan, General Secretary, Paite Tribe Council, General Headquarters, Manipur.

PUBLICATIONS OF THE GOVERNMENT, LEARNED SOCIETIES, AND OTHER ORGANIZATIONS:

The Manipur State Constitution Act, 1947, Section 2.

The Evangelical Convention Church Census 1986.

The Young Paite Association at a Glance 1984.

The Constitution of Young Paite Association 1978.

A Seminar on Tribal Poverty; Its causes and Remedies, August 8, 1987, Imphal.

In Search of Identity. Imphal: Kuki-Chin-Baptist Union, 1986.

Tribal Bench Mark Survey of Manipur South District 1982.

Manipur State Hill People (Administration) Regulation, 1947.

Chiefs Union of Churachandpur, *Resolutions in the Conference-cum-Seminar,* Churachandpur, May 30, 1986.

District Council Manual, Vol. I, n.d.

Souvenir of The Third Annual Conference of Northeastern Historical Association, Manipur University, December 6-8, 1982.

PERIODICALS AND JOURNALS:

The Young Paite Association Annual Magazine 1979.

The Young Paite Association Annual Magazine 1982, Vol.2.

The Young Paite Association Annual Magazine 1987.

The National Times of Paite 1984.

Thinglhang Post 7th Anniversary Magazine 1988.

Siamsin Pawlpi Annual Magazine 1974.

Siamsin Pawlpi Annual Magazine 1975.

Siamsin Pawlpi Annual Magazine 1979.

Siamsin Pawlpi Annual Magazine 1982.

Siamsin Pawlpi Annual Magazine 1984.

NEWSPAPERS:

Aizawl Daily News, 8 February 1966.

Manipur Express, 30 September 1987.

Manipur Express, 6 October 1987.

UNPUBLISHED DOCUMENTS:

Politico-Economic Development of The Zomis of Manipur Since Statehood by Dr.Chinkholian Guite.

Declaratioin of Boycott of the Mizo District Council, 1965. LIANKHOHAU, T.,

MEMORANDA:

Paite National Council, Re-Unification of Chin People. A Memorandum to the Prime Minister of India, 1960.

THE DISTRICT AUTONOMY DEMAND COMMITTEE, A Memorandum to the Prime Minister of India, October 14, 1970.

HILL PEOPLES' CONFERENCE, A Memorandum to the Prime Minister of India, 1980.

THE ALL PAITE STUDENTS UNION, A Memorandum to the Chief Minister of Manipur, October 27, 1987.

Proposed Draft of Sialkal Development Council by the Paite Tribe Council, Mizoram.

B. SECONDARY SOURCES
BOOKS:

The Paite, a Transformed Community and the Evangelical Convention Church
(M.A.R. Thesis, South Asia Institute of Advanced Christian Studies, 1986, Bangalore).

AGARWAL, A.K., North East India: An Economic Perspect' New Delhi, 1985.

ALAM, K., Planning in North East India. New Delhi, 1985.

ALAN, R. Ball, Modern Politics and Government. London, 1974.

ALLEN, B.C., Assam District Gazetteer, Vol. IX – Naga Hills and Manipur, 1905.

ASOSO Yono, The Rising Nagas. New Delhi, reprinted 1984.

BOWER, V.G., Naga Path. London, 1950.

CAREY, B.C. and TUCK, H.N., The Chin Hills. Calcutta: Reprinted 1976.

CASTLES, F.G., Pressure Groups and Political Change. London, 1967.

CHADURVEDI and UPPAL, B.N., A Study in Shifting Cultivation in Assam (Indian Council of Agriculture Research Series No. 2). New Delhi, 1953.

CHAKRAVORTY, Birendra Chandra, British Relations with the Hill Tribes of Assam since 1958. Firma KLM Private Ltd. 1981.

CHAMBER, Capt., Handbook of Lushai Country, 1889.

CHHABRA, Harindar K. & Wit Jones, State Politics in India. New Delhi, 1980.

DALTON, E.T., Descriptive Ethnology of Bengal. Calcutta, 1872.

ELDERSVELD, S.J., Theory and Methods in Voting Behaviour Research. Political Behaviour, ed. Heinz Enlay & Others. Illinois, U.S.A.: The Free Press Glenco, 1956.

ELLY, Col. E.B., Military Report on the Chin-Lushai Country. Aizawl: Reprinted 1978.

EVANS, G & Brett-James, A., Imphal, A Flower on Lofty Height. New York, 1965.

FOX, Robin, Kinship and Marriage. Baltimore, 1967.

GHURYE, G.S., The Scheduled Tribes. Bombay, 1959.

GIN ZA TUANG, Zomi Inkuan Laibu. Tedim, 1986.

GOUGIN, T., Discovery of Zoland. Lamka, 1980.

History of Zomi. Lamka, 1983.

GIERSON, Sir G.A., Linguistic Survey of India, Vol. III, Part-3. Calcutta, 1904.

GUHA, B.S., Adivasis of India and Their Place in India Life – Tribes of India, Part II, n.d.

HANSON & JANET DOUGLAS, India Democracy.

HARVEY, G.E., History of Burma, London, 1925.

HODSON, T.C., The Meiteis of Manipur. London. 1908.

HUTTON, J.B., The Angami Naga. London, 1921.

IBOONGOHAL SINGH, L.M., Introduction of Manipur.

JACK DENNIS, Socialization to Politics, New York, 1973.

JOHNSTONE, J., My Experience in Manipur and the Nagas Hills. London, 1896.

KAROTEMPREL, S., The Tribes of North East India. Shillong, 1984.

KHAIZALIAN, D., Tangthu Pha Tunma leh Tunnung Thu. Lamka, 1986.

KHUP ZA GO, Christianity in Chinland. Guwahati, 1985.

KROBER, A.L., Anthropology. New York, 1948.

LALCHAWNZO, Upa, Manipur Rama Chanchin Tha Luhdan. Lamka, 1982.

LEACH, E.R., Political System of Highland Burma. Cambridge, 1954.

LEHMAN, F.C., The Structure of Chin Society. Illinois, 1963.

LIANKHOHAU, T., Paite Kalcha r. Lamka: Directorate for Welfare of Tribals and Backward Classes, Manipur, 1988.

LIANGKHAIA, Rev., Mizo Chanchin. Aizawl, 1938.

LIEN, Z.Z., The U-Now People, Lamka, 1981.

LORRAIN, J.H., Dictionary of the Lushai Language. Calcutta: Royal Asiatic Society of Bengal, 1949.

LOUISE, Paw, Spriritual and Material Progress in Chin Hills (Burma Newsletter, Vol.2, NO.3, Aug.1969) Valley Forge, U.S.A.

MACKVAR, R.M. & Charles, H., Society. London, 1955.

MACKENZIE, A., History of the Relation of Government with the Hill Tribes of Northeast Frontier of Bengal. Calcutta, 1884.

MAJUMDAR, D.N., Races and Culture of India. Bombay. 1961.

MCCALL, Major A.G., Lushai Chrvsalis. Calcutta, reprinted 1977.

PEMBERTON, R.B., The Eastern Frontier of India. Delhi, 1979.

PRIMS S., The Vaiphei Tribe. Imphal, 1975.

PUDAITE, Rochunga, The Education of the Hmar People. Calcutta, 1963.

RAO, V.V., A Century of Tribal Politics. New Delhi, 1976.

ROBERT Reid, History of Frontier Areas Bordering on Assam. Delhi, Reprint 1983.

RUSTOMJI, Nari, Enchanted Frontiers. Bombay, 1971.

————————, Imperilled Frontiers, India's North-Eastern Border Lands. New Delhi, 1984.

SCOTT, A. Reid, Chin-Lushai Land. Calcutta, 1893.

SHAKESPEAR, L.W., History of Assam Rifles. London, 1929.

SHAKESPEAR, J. Lt. Col., The Lushai-Kuki Clans. Aizawl, Reprint 1975.

SHAKESPEARE's Census of India 1901, Vol. II, Part I.

SHAW, William, Notes on Thado-Kukis. London, 1929.

SINGH, K.B., Seven Tribes: An Introduction to Tribal Language and Culture of Manipur. Imphal, 1979.

SINGH, W.J. Bohal, The Vaipheis: A Sociological Studies. Imphal.

SOPPITT, Short Account of the Kuki-Lushai Tribes of North-East India Frontier Districts, Cachar, Syhlet, etc. 1887.

THANGCHINLIAN & JAMKHANTHANG, T., The Paite Customary Laws, Lamka, 1986.

VALTE, Doutluang, Khantawn Hinna. Lamka, 1987.

ZAWLA, K., Mizo Pipute leh An Thlahte Chanchin. Aizawl, 1966.

The Paite Customary Laws and Practices (Amended) 2013, by the Paite Tribe Council, Churachandpur, Manipur.

Bird's eye view of Lamka (Churachandpur) Township the only urban settlement of the Paites

Map of India and Myanmar showing the location of Paite inhabited Areas.

Map of Paite Inhabited Areas in Manipur

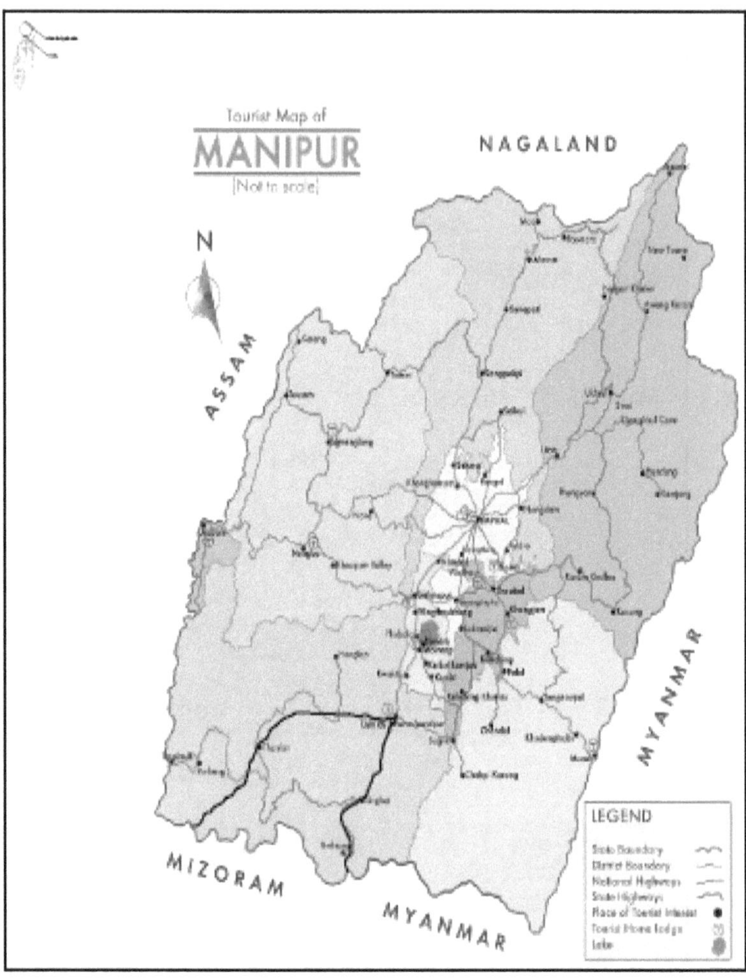

Map of Paite Inhabited Areas in Mizoram

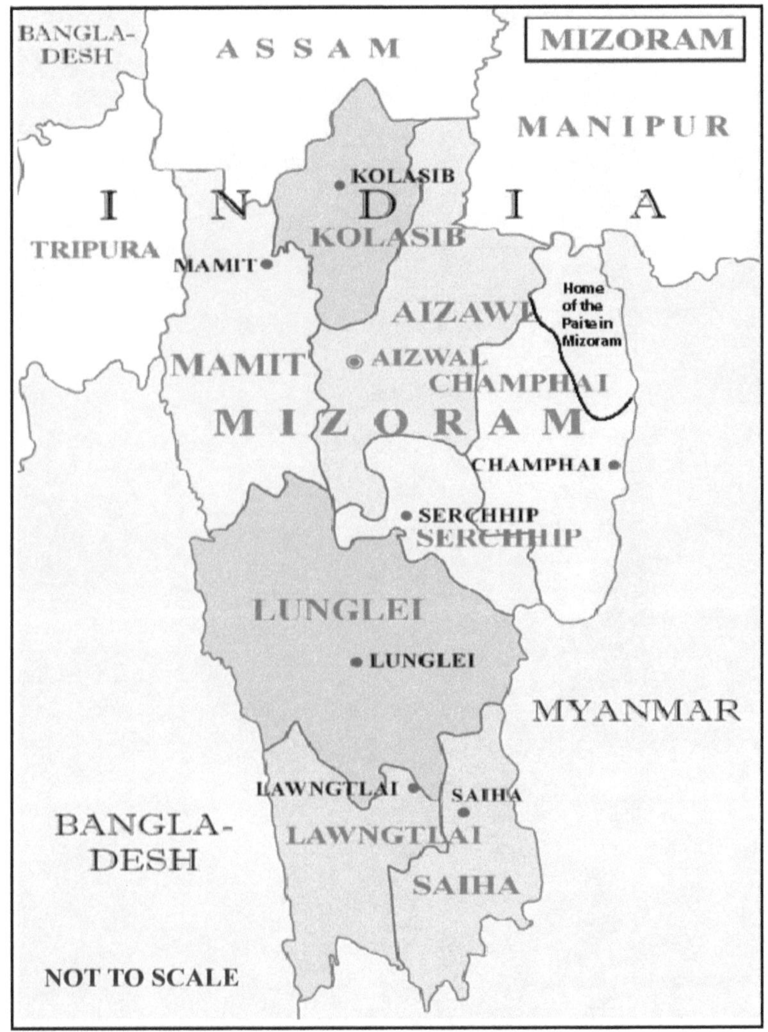

About the Author

Born on 1st January, 1965 from a humble parentage at Mimbung, a small remote border village of Mizoram, bordering Chin Hills of Myanmar in the east and the state of Manipur in the north, Dr Th. Siamkhum is the eldest son of (L) Thangsiam. When he was yet young, his family migrated from his birth place of Mimbung Village to Zawllian Village in Karbi-Anglong District (Mikir Hills) of Assam owing to disturbed situation there, and spent most of his youthful days there. After living in Karbi-Anglong for over 20 years, he, along with members of his family again migrated to Churachandpur, Manipur in 1986 where he lives till today.

EDUCATIONAL CAREER:

Regarding his educational carrier, he completed class III Standard from Govt. L.P.School in Mizoram and matriculation from Union Christian English School at Diphu, Karbi-Anglong in 1978. He got his Graduation in Pol.Sc (Hons) Post Graduation from St. Anthony's College, Shillong in 1982 and North-Eastern Hill University in 1984 respectively. In 1987 he got himself registered with Manipur University for the Degree of Doctor of Philosophy, and was awarded the Degree in 1989 becoming the youngest Ph.D. degree awardee by the university.

PROFESSIONAL CAREER:

He joint Churachandpur Govt. College as Lecturer in 1990 and was given placement as Sr. Lecturer in 1996, Selection Grade in 2001 and Associate Professor in 2006. He is still serving in the same College as Associate Professor in Pol.Sc.